SAVING *Beauty* FROM THE BEAST

SAVING *Beauty* FROM THE BEAST

How to Protect Your Daughter
from an Unhealthy Relationship

by
VICKI CROMPTON
AND
ELLEN ZELDA KESSNER

LITTLE, BROWN AND COMPANY
Boston New York London

AUTHORS' NOTE: Featured in this book are true stories of individuals, not composites. Many of the persons interviewed have kindly permitted us to use their real names. Others have requested that we change their names. We have indicated aliases with asterisks. (First names beneath the italicized quotes throughout the book have also been changed to protect privacy.) We thank all the interviewees for sharing their stories.

First Edition

Library of Congress Cataloging-in-Publication Data
Crompton, Vicki.
    Saving beauty from the beast : how to protect your daughter from an unhealthy relationship / by Vicki Crompton and Ellen Zelda Kessner. — 1st ed.
        p. cm.
    Includes bibliographical references and index.
    ISBN 0-316-09058-1
    1. Dating violence — Prevention. 2. Teenage girls — Abuse of — Prevention. 3. Interpersonal relations in adolescence. 4. Parent and teenager.   I. Kessner, Ellen Zelda. II. Title.
HQ801.83 .C76 2003
362.88 — dc21   2002019153

10   9   8   7   6   5   4   3   2   1

Q-FF

Book design by Oksana Kushnir
Printed in the United States of America

This book is dedicated to the
memory of our beloved daughters,

Jennifer Crompton
and
Sheryl Kessner-Shalom,

and
to the memory
of all the young women
who did not survive
their boyfriends' "love"

CONTENTS

ACKNOWLEDGMENTS

We are most grateful to the young people and to the moms and dads who agreed to tell their stories for this book. They generously gave us hours of their time and courageously relived their experiences, sharing with us in great depth their anguish, fears, frustrations, and eventual triumphs. We would like to name them all, but some, wishing to protect their privacy, have asked us to disguise their identities. And so, we broadcast our appreciation to those who have allowed us to use their real names:

Meredith Blake   Jennifer Coleman   Emiliano de Leon
Maria Fedele   Kate Landis   Helen Tarnares
Vasso Tarnares   Rosalind Wiseman

We would also like to give our sincere thanks to the mom-and-daughter team of Lorre and Nikki Taylor and the dad-and-daughter team of Brien and Zeina Kinkel, who so articulately described the ways in which they communicate the *possibility* of abuse before the situation can develop.

Without the insights and practical advice of experts in many fields — psychologists, school principals and counselors, family therapists, law enforcement officers, and threat-assessment professionals — this book would not have been possible. For their unending patience in answering every new question that came up and for

sending us a wealth of helpful materials, we are especially grateful
to

Leah Aldridge	Janet Berger	Jacey Buel
Sarah Buel	Carol Eagle	Eva Feindler
Karen Harker	Eugene Hyman	Antoine Jeter
Pamela Linker	Barrie Levy	Shanterra McBride
Lori McIntyre	Stephanie Meyer	Shelley Neiderbach
Noelle Nelson	Jeanine Pirro	Edna Rawlings
Barri Rosenbluth	Diane Scricca	Suzanne Stephens

We give special thanks to our agent, Rita Rosenkranz, for her
belief in us, for nurturing our project from the beginning, for her
brilliant editorial suggestions during the proposal stage, and for
continuing to give us her skilled advice and unfailing moral support throughout the journey.

We wish to thank Deborah Baker, our editor, for her encouragement and for her commitment to bringing the issue of dating
violence to the attention of parents of teenagers and preteens. We
appreciate her insightful editing; it was Deborah who, in many stories throughout the book, detected and articulated the recurring
theme of "Beauty" trying to save the "Beast" with her love. We
also send our thanks to her always gracious and helpful assistant, Al-
lison Powell, and to the other members of the Little, Brown and
Company staff involved in this project.

Vicki Crompton

I thank Bonnie Campbell, director of the Violence Against Women
Office under the Clinton administration. Bonnie reached out to
me with compassion and understanding when my grief was raw.
Most important, she listened to crime victims nationwide, turning
our words into action.

I'm grateful to my coauthor, Ellen Zelda Kessner, for writing
the first national magazine piece about dating violence, with
Jenny's story as the main focus, and for her continued dedication to
the issue. I cherish the friendship we have developed and the shared
experiences we have had as two mothers who lost daughters.

Finally, I want to recognize the love and support of my family:

my parents, Joan and Mac McAdams; my children, Kate Crompton and Steven Tetter; and my husband, Greg Tetter. They are the people who sacrificed their time with me over the years as I traveled to one high school after another, who supported my wish to return to school for my master's degree so that I could more effectively counsel crime victims, and who took a backseat to my many victim advocacy activities. Most especially, I send my love and thanks to Greg. From the moment he found Jenny dying on the floor, he has devoted himself to protecting me and supporting my efforts to survive the tragedy. He willingly picked up the pieces and ran the household when I was unable to; he stayed behind and parented the children when I was speaking. He is content to be "the wind beneath my wings." He is my hero.

Ellen Zelda Kessner

I want to thank my coauthor, Vicki Crompton, for her constant inspiration and friendship. Vicki and I became linked by a confluence of events. After writing the story of my twenty-eight-year-old daughter Sheryl's murder for *Woman's Day,* I was assigned by *Redbook* to write an article about teenage girls who were murdered by their boyfriends. As both bereaved mother and writer, I attended a national conference of Parents of Murdered Children, where I met Vicki — in deep mourning for her daughter Jenny, whose sixteenth birthday celebration would never be. During our long telephone conversations, we became a mini support group, emotionally drawn into each other's life, and I found myself sharing Vicki's mission to educate the public about teen dating violence. It has been an enriching experience.

I want to give thanks to my family — my daughter Deborah Indursky and her husband, Jerry, and my son, Neil Kessner, and his wife, Sandi, for their encouragement. Special kudos go to my husband, Fred, for all his love and support throughout the years, for keeping me supplied with reams of paper and ink cartridges, for driving me to mid-Manhattan in rush-hour traffic to arrange interviews for this book, and for giving up our weekends together when I was in "lockdown" at my computer, meeting deadlines. And our grandson David gets special mention for keeping his "gramps" company at restaurants and movies during those week-ends. I am also grateful for the encouragement of our other grand-children — Sam, SarahBeth, Alyson, Leah, and Evan — who I hope will someday use the information in this book to develop healthy relationships of their own.

SAVING *Beauty* FROM THE BEAST

JENNY'S STORY

TIME RUSHES HEADLONG, and our daughters are on the cusp of their teen years — or already there, thinking of boys, perhaps beginning to date. We try to prepare them for the problems they will encounter in a complex world. But the tempo has quickened and intensified since the decades when we were in our teens. We discuss premature sex and its perils, disease and pregnancy, ways to say no to drugs and drinking, the risks of eating disorders and of dangerous drivers. But what about the overlooked, understated danger, which most of us have never experienced in our own dating days — dating abuse?

In 1985, when my daughter Jennifer entered high school, we were totally ignorant of the existence of teen dating violence. At fourteen, Jenny had never dated, and I had strict rules: she was not to see any boy older than sixteen — and only in school and in my house — and she was never to ride in cars with teenagers. My deepest fear was that I would lose Jennifer in a car crash.

One evening in October 1985, Mark Smith appeared on our doorstep — tall, handsome, polite, with a charming smile. Jenny's first boyfriend. Although he was a senior, she told me he was sixteen — a pretense he would keep up for three months — and, indeed, he seemed shy and much younger than his eighteen years.

He also seemed perfectly willing to abide by my strict rules —

4 SAVING BEAUTY FROM THE BEAST

visiting Jenny at our house no more than three times a week and leaving by nine o'clock. She had only two real "dates" with him — one to a school dance and one to the movies — and I drove them both times. Jenny's friends at school considered them "the ideal couple," sharing a locker, eating lunch together, and walking each other to class.

By the time I found out Mark's real age, although I was furious with Jenny, I had grown surprisingly comfortable with Mark. He was obeying my rules, he came from an intact middle-class family, and Jenny was so much in love with him that I didn't have the heart to stop her from seeing him. I reasoned that my strict edicts would soon send him looking for another girlfriend, someone closer to his own age. I also believed that Jenny, who loved books, dance, and family, would soon grow bored with Mark, a poor student with no plans for college.

But after several months, Jenny asked me to take her to a doctor for birth control pills. Horrified, yet grateful that she was discussing the issue with me, I put her in touch with an older teenager who had spoken of her regrets of having had sex at an early age. Jenny then made the decision herself that she was too young to have sex — or even to have a steady boyfriend — and that Mark was too possessive. "I just want to be free, Mom, but I don't want to hurt him," she said. I replied with words I will always regret: "Then let him down easy. Tell him you can still be friends."

Mark ignored Jenny's first attempts to break up. He would not move out of her locker, he still walked her to class, he still called. As she became firmer, he became more possessive, and his phone calls and unannounced visits increased. Jenny simply gave up and agreed to get back together. She admitted to me that sometimes she thought she still cared for him and wasn't sure she wanted to break up. And so, their relationship seesawed.

What Jenny never told me about was Mark's abuse, how he would slap and shove her and call her a slut. Her friends thought that was the way guys were, no big deal. It obviously wasn't a "big deal" to the adults in the community either — a teacher, my neighbor, and a lifeguard at my condominium who had witnessed Mark's violence and never took the responsibility of informing me.

In August 1986, eleven months after her relationship with Mark began, Jenny called me at work, triumphant that she had finally "cut the tie." Mark was no longer in her life. Having already graduated, he would not be in school with her. His phone calls stopped. There were no more visits. Mark Smith had finally gone away — or so I thought.

But Jenny and her friends knew he had not gone away. He was burgling her school locker, breaking into our house, warning other boys to stay away from her, stalking her. He was also threatening her life with notes like "You'll never make it to homecoming." She never told me. On the morning of the homecoming game, she even said laughingly to a friend: "Well, I'm still here." That day — September 26, 1986 — would mark my free fall into the world of teenage dating violence.

At four o'clock that afternoon, as I drove onto my street, I saw groups of neighbors standing in their yards looking toward my house. Then I saw the ambulance, the police cars, the fire truck with the red lights flashing, and the police officers running out of my house. I started shaking so violently that I could barely park my car. I jumped out, shouting, "What is happening here?" A policeman stopped me from entering my home. He told me that my daughter had been stabbed and said, "The paramedics are working on her." I watched as they carried her out on a stretcher and took her away in an ambulance. I hung on to my ashen-faced, shaken husband as he described walking into the house and finding Jenny "lying in a pool of blood." I sat in the hospital emergency room and heard them tell me that my daughter was deceased. *Dead? Not Jenny. I just talked to her this morning — she is only fifteen. How can she be dead?*

Three days later, Mark was arrested. He was tried and convicted of first-degree murder and sentenced to life without parole.

During his trial, I learned the truth of my daughter's last months. I heard Jenny's fifteen-year-old friends describe their attempts to handle the situation themselves. And their feelings of guilt, that they could have saved her *if only they had told someone.*

I listened to a re-creation of the last moments of my daughter's life: how she got off the school bus and entered our home alone to find Mark waiting for her, and how he stabbed her more than sixty times with a seven-inch butcher knife, leaving her on the living room floor to be found by my husband, who came in from work carrying our one-year-old son.

I heard the account of Mark's evening: how he had attended the homecoming football game with a date, and how he laughed and ate and appeared unconcerned that Jenny was dead.

I became obsessed with learning why Jenny herself, who talked openly with me — even about having sex — kept Mark's violence a secret. She must have been ashamed; she had never seen physical abuse at home. Her friends said that Mark made Jenny feel that she provoked his anger and jealousy and deserved to be hit. Then Mark would apologize and bring roses.

I realize now that there was at least one warning sign I could have picked up on. One night, when we stepped out to get ice cream, Jenny's stepdad discovered Mark crouching behind the cars, watching our house. He seemed embarrassed, so we invited him to join us. But at the time, I had no idea that this was a form of stalking and could end in violence.

When Mark began threatening her life, Jenny didn't want to upset her parents, her best friend told me through tears. She was afraid we would overreact and confront Mark. Jenny thought that she could handle the situation herself. "Mark won't do anything; he's all talk," Jenny and her friends agreed, but she had begun carrying our spare house key in her bookbag instead of leaving it in its usual hiding place — to keep Mark from breaking into our home with it. On the day of the murder, she confided in a friend in gym class that Mark had called her before school, cursing her. "Does he really hate me? I'm getting scared," Jenny said. "If he keeps bothering you, maybe you should tell your mom," her friend suggested. "Maybe tonight, when she comes home, I'll tell her," Jenny said.

For a long time after Jenny's murder, I did not believe I could survive my grief — even though I had a husband and two younger children who needed me, and parents, siblings, and friends who loved me. The middle-management job I had once enjoyed became increasingly difficult to focus on.

I haunted the library looking for information on violence against women. The focus in the literature was primarily on grown women, mothers, who were being battered by their husbands. Teen dating violence seemed to be a new phenomenon in our society, yet a reality, I learned, in many girls' lives. Why hadn't other mothers spoken out, tried to warn me or warn Jenny of the danger?

Eighteen months after Jenny's death, although I was still working full time and had never before done public speaking, I felt compelled to tell Jenny's story to as many teens and parents as possible. My first speech was to a local church youth group, a small gathering of teens, who were laughing and kidding and poking one another. As I stood at the back of the room before I was introduced, I was terrified, thinking I would never hold their attention. I began by playing a part of a song, "The Greatest Love of All." As the song had recently been popular, the kids started swaying to the music and mouthing the words. Then I turned off the player and said, "I chose that song for you today because it's about finding self-respect, learning how to love yourself. I also chose that song for the funeral of my daughter Jenny." Total silence. For the duration of my talk, not a soul moved.

At first, I was speaking out primarily to heal myself. I had to make people aware that Jenny Crompton had lived, that she had talent and friends and dreams. But little by little, as my involvement grew, I saw that my speeches about Jenny's life and death might be saving other girls. As I would look out at the audience, I could identify which girls were being abused by their boyfriends. I saw the looks that passed between friends. I saw the downcast eyes as I described Mark's behavior. I could pick the ones whose lives I was describing. A thousand speeches and seminars later, I still see these things, along with the more intense emotional reactions, the sobbing, the hugging. Occasionally, a girl will run out weeping followed by her friends.

Jenny's murder led me to a new career as both a lecturer and victim advocate, advising girls and their parents, and to a master's degree in counseling.

*   *   *

Since my journey began, the issue of teen dating violence has at times been covered by the media on television programs and in magazine articles. Yet, ironically, I have learned that dating abuse has escalated.

"When the issue is covered, many often treat it as an out-of-the-ordinary spectacle rather than an all-too-common social crisis," says Eva Feindler, a psychology professor at Long Island University, who treats anger disorders in adolescents. "There is a rising level of teenage dating violence today because this is a much more aggressive society than in the past. Everything's very glitzy, fast-paced, done on impulse, with no time for taking care. Violence in dating has become increasingly common, particularly among teens in the suburbs."

In April 2001, Kate Landis, whose story about her abusive teen relationship is in this book, spoke to a New Jersey high school audience, in which one of the kids said: "Hey, if he hits you, you just get out."

Getting out of an abusive relationship is a core element in the dynamics of violence against women, and getting out is surprisingly often more difficult for a teen girl than for an adult woman.

Because of the very complexity of the issue, my coauthor, Ellen Kessner — the mother of a murdered daughter herself — and I have decided to explore the gamut of expertise on the subject and have asked researchers in the fields of education, adolescent psychology, criminal justice, forensic psychiatry, sociology, and violence against women, along with psychiatrists, psychologists, sociologists, social workers, threat-assessment experts, and therapists working with teenagers, to give their insights and advice. The voices of teenagers themselves, as well as their parents, whom we have interviewed, are also featured.

This book will show you how to recognize the potential for dating abuse, be it emotional, sexual, or physical — or all three (one form often escalates into another). It will outline specific ways to protect your daughter's mental and physical health. The book will focus on daughters, since in 95 percent of violent relationships, girls are the victims, but we know that girls too can perpetrate abuse — it is estimated that 5 percent of abusers are female — and you will meet two of them in this book. (Boys who are the victims in unhealthy relationships usually do not feel that they are in physical danger; they may not consider manipulation to be abuse.)

The first section describes what dating violence is and the ways in which it manifests itself. It traces the unhealthy teen relationship from its ultraromantic beginnings, when the boy's attentions seem flattering and consume the inexperienced young girl, to its ultimate deterioration, when the boy drags her into a quagmire in which he is exerting complete power and control. The path of abuse generally spirals upward, from emotional to sexual and physical. Frequently, all the forms merge. But even when emotional battering, the more prevalent form, exists alone, it can severely damage a teen's self-esteem.

Many girls relate their experiences, expressing how trapped they felt in abusive relationships. Experts explain the special vulnerabilities of adolescents. Often, young girls, filled with idealist notions, find themselves living a twisted tale of "Beauty and the Beast."

At first, Beauty sees the Beast as the handsome prince he once was. But then the evil spell, which may have been cast by the "sorcery" of his abusive parents, rises up within him, changing him from a caring lover to a controlling monster, who keeps her locked away from family and friends. Only by staying with him forever — he says he will die without her — can she undo the spell. Only she, if her love is pure and strong enough, can change her monster back into her prince.

This is the myth that muddles girls' thinking and blinds them to the fact that only the boy himself, by gaining insight and making a lifelong commitment to changing his behavior, can transform himself — not into a prince (we don't marry princes) but into a responsible, loving man.

An array of experts explain the dynamics of abuse and discuss the dangers of breaking away from an abusive boyfriend. The girl may fear his threats, or she may ignore them, as Jenny did. Or, like Jenny, she may prefer to handle them herself. The girl often has a problem confiding in her parents: she is afraid they will no longer trust her judgment or may "overreact" against her boyfriend, whom she still wants to protect.

The book goes on to explore the question of why some people hurt and batter the person they love. Experts delve into the psyche of the abusers. They examine the complex reasons for their behavior — among them their own insecurities and their need to be, as professor of sociology Murray Strauss puts it, "compulsively masculine."

Most girls do not usually realize they are in an abusive relationship until it has gone too far. But parents can recognize one if they are aware of the patterns and early warning signs we discuss in part 2 of the book.

Experts give suggestions about what you can do if you suspect your daughter is in an unhealthy relationship, as well as specific pointers on how to help her break off safely from an obsessive/ abusive boyfriend — with effective intervention techniques and plans for her safety, including the use of the legal system. Parents reveal their conflicts and fears about their teens' unhealthy relationships and how they handled them.

In a chapter for parents who suspect their teen — boy or girl — may be the abuser, the experts give ways for them to confront the issue and seek help.

While your child may not be in an abusive relationship, he or she may be a close friend of someone who is. There is a chapter of advice for parents whose children are in that situation.

The latter part of the book discusses how we can prevent our daughters and sons from engaging in violent relationships long before their first date — by bringing them up to have relationships of trust and respect. As psychologist Noelle Nelson points out, dating violence, like AIDS, is 90 percent preventable.

The appendix includes a full list of resources that parents and teens can use, including prevention and education programs from around the country.

PART ONE

LOVE THAT HURTS

ONE

THE ROOTS OF ABUSE IN
AMERICAN SOCIETY

IN THE EARLY 1980s, as a prevention specialist in the movement to end violence against women and children, Barrie Levy spent a great deal of time in California classrooms defining rape, sexual abuse, and battering as crimes against women — as experiences that girls might encounter when they grew up. To her astonishment, Levy learned that many girls as young as twelve and thirteen were *already* encountering those crimes with their teenage boyfriends.

Yet two decades later, there is still some of the same lack of awareness in the general public. Reviewing twenty contemporaneous studies, Lynn Phillips, professor of psychology at the New School for Social Research in New York City, authored *The Girls Report: What We Know and Need to Know About Growing Up Female.* The findings show that violence against women is still considered an adult problem, although many young girls have been experiencing sexual violence, battering, and harassment earlier and earlier in teen relationships.

As psychologist Karen Harker of the Nebraska Domestic Violence Sexual Assault Coalition points out: "Our society does not show healthy relationships. One in three adult relationships are violent. These are the models that the teenagers are viewing — as well as those in the media." How did American relationships become so violent?

HOW DID IT ALL BEGIN?

Violence toward women dates back centuries. "Throughout Euro-American history, wife beating enjoyed legal status as an accepted institution in western society," writes psychotherapist Susan Weitzman in *"Not to People Like Us": Hidden Abuse in Upscale Marriages.*

When John Adams was attending the Continental Congress in 1776, his wife, Abigail, wrote to her husband, whom she addressed as "Dearest Friend," a letter that would become famous: "In the new code of laws, I desire you would remember the ladies and be more favorable than your ancestors. Do not put such unlimited power into the hands of husbands."

But John Adams and other well-meaning men were no more able to free the women than they were the slaves. When the founders of our country signed the Declaration of Independence, their own wives were still, in every legal sense, *their* property. Upon marriage, a woman forfeited the few rights she had, and her husband owned her just as he owned his horse.

Laws have changed since colonial times, but marriage has continued to trigger territorial notions, a sense of immediate ownership and entitlement. To some men, the marriage license is a "hitting license," in the words of Murray Strauss of the Family Research Laboratory at the University of New Hampshire.

"Any sense of spousal abuse as a criminal and immoral act only came into awareness in the late-nineteenth century, spurred primarily by the advent of the women's movement," writes Dr. Weitzman. The first wave of the women's movement, however, was focused more on a woman's right to vote than on her right to live her life free from violence.

American culture continued to reinforce the notion of male authority; men were *supposed* to be dominating and controlling. Even in nonmarital relationships, men within Western culture were socialized to conceive of their partners as their property. A man's home was his castle, and he was master of his wife — or his "woman." It was only recently that the criminal justice system stopped supporting that notion.

Why doesn't she just leave? was the question asked in the 1920s, when women did get the vote and the subject of battered wives arose once more. Back then, experts believed that a battered woman stayed in an abusive relationship because she didn't know any better; her intelligence was too low; she was always kept "barefoot and pregnant." And besides, *she must be doing something to make him so upset.*

At midcentury, psychologists theorized that women stayed with violent men because they were masochistic and enjoyed being beaten. In addition, the "makeup sex" afterward had to be great! The name that became famously associated with this type of neurotic, but earthy, female was "Stella-a-a-ah," brayed out every night as a mating call by the hunky abusive husband, Stanley Kowalski, in Tennessee Williams's *A Streetcar Named Desire.*

The second wave of the feminist movement came in the early 1970s. This time, women identified domestic violence for what it was: a significant social and health problem in America and a crime that they had to fight — with education and lobbying. In the 1990s, Congress passed the Violence Against Women Act, and many states have gradually started enforcing strict legal sanctions against the perpetrators.

Swept away in the cultural backlash against feminism that gathered momentum in the 1980s was the ideal of the sensitive male, in touch with his feminine side, and the strong, independent woman dressed for success. These ideals were replaced by the ultramacho guy, "in touch with his inner swine," as one magazine editor put it, and the supersexy girly-girl in her tiny skirts and stiletto heels. These retro images have been revived and dressed up in new, ever-tighter clothing and are gaining wider and wider acceptance, with many teen girls and boys eager to try them on.

Barrie Levy finds that the teen gender roles are often defined in extreme and stereotypical ways, the male totally dominant, the woman unnaturally passive. "Young men and women — afraid of being labeled 'different' — may not have the flexibility to be themselves. For example, fearing the stigma of homosexuality, adolescents may behave in ways that seem exaggerated to prove their heterosexuality."

"The message to boys in high school is: 'You're so strong, she's hot. . . . Why haven't you had sex with her yet?'" says Emiliano de

Leon, a children's advocate. "When boys are sexually active with their girlfriends . . . they have more control and a sense of ownership."

"Not only are boys learning that they *must* be in control, but *girls* are learning that boys are *supposed* to be in control. So girls are looking for controlling boys," observes therapist Barri Rosenbluth.

To add to the confusion, evolutionary biologists are popularizing the "scientific basis" for male aggression.

WHERE ARE WE NOW?

During the past decade, teen dating abuse has become even more of an equal opportunity evil — almost. It cuts across race, class, age, ethnic roots, educational background, and income. The only area of discrimination is sex. Ninety-five percent of victims of violence are girls.

On August 1, 2001, the *New York Times* noted on its front page a report that 20 percent of high school girls have been physically or sexually assaulted by someone they were dating. This survey, cited as the "most comprehensive to examine dating violence among adolescents, ages 14 to 18," was done by the Harvard School of Public Health and published in the *Journal of the American Medical Association.*

What was completely left out of the "most comprehensive survey" was the most pervasive — and what some girls find the most devastating — aspect of violence: emotional abuse. Most experts define dating violence or battering as a "repeated pattern of actual or threatened acts that emotionally, verbally, physically, or sexually hurt another person."

As the Centers for Disease Control and Prevention point out, when threats and emotional or verbal aggression are included in the definition of dating abuse, the figures rise to 65 percent — a number confirmed by the most recent National Teen Relationship Violence Survey conducted by the National Coalition Against Domestic Violence. For a majority of teens, abuse has become a "dating fact of life."

Other researchers working in the field of domestic violence estimate that one girl in three, of junior high, high school, and college age, has had a *physically* violent dating or relationship experience — being pushed, kicked, stalked, thrown from a car, or even choked — an experience she is less likely to reveal to her parents than sex.

It is difficult for many of us who have never experienced violence in our marriages or when we were dating to realize the power of today's "junk culture," as psychologist Mary Pipher calls it, a culture that stresses supermacho, aggressive role models for young men and weak, submissive ones for young women. In our postfeminist society, many of us, strong women ourselves, are often astonished to discover that once our accomplished daughters reach their teens, they can find their self-esteem only through the eyes of a boyfriend empowered to destroy it. And they never know it's happening until it's too late.

T W O

THE BLACK-AND-BLUE SOUL
Emotional Abuse

"EMOTIONAL ABUSE ABSOLUTELY predominates in unhealthy teen dating relationships," says Karen Harker, who has worked with abused
women and teens for almost twenty years.

Like Karen Harker, I meet girls after each school presentation I
give who come forward to describe the various kinds of emotional
assaults they have suffered at the hands of their boyfriends. Until
the signs are pointed out, they are usually not even aware that they
have been abused.

Verbal cruelty frequently exists alone, but it is always a component in sexual and physical violence. Experts agree that even if a
girl has not experienced the other forms of battering, she will be
deeply damaged by emotional abuse. Her family and many of her
close friends will notice marked changes in a girl's bearing, changes
that will have a ripple effect on everyone around her. In this chapter, we will explore the dynamic of emotional battering and its
many facets.

"IT'S ONLY BECAUSE I LOVE YOU — YOU KNOW THAT"

How does love turn to abuse? "The relationship with an abusive
boyfriend usually begins on a heady romantic note, with high
emotional intensity. He is Prince Charming, immediately smitten,"

says Dr. Edna Rawlings, professor of psychology at the University of Cincinnati, who specializes in abusive relationships in her private practice. "There's an almost-too-good-to-be-true, too-loving quality about him. He starts out by being seductive and charming — completely involved in everything wonderful about *her.* The girl is flattered. She finds him exciting and interesting."

Maria Fedele was sixteen years old and a sophomore in high school in an upper-middle-class rural area in New Jersey when she fell in love with another sophomore, who was two months younger than she was. "Mr. Popularity," she describes him, "handsome, athletic, a member of the wrestling team. He spoiled me with roses, jewelry, and dining out. Everyone in school thought we were the ideal couple. But little by little he started controlling me."

He began with clothes: "Do you know that if you wear that skimpy skirt, guys will look at you?" He would insist she wear a pair of baggy jeans. "These look good on you, right?"

Maria, whose Italian-French ancestry shows in her exotic looks — dark eyes, olive skin, and brown hair flowing down to her waist — always preferred clothes that outlined her tall, slender figure, but she did not want to anger him. She would nod and put on the baggy jeans. He was always "right." And he would invariably say: "I love you, you know that."

But Maria's clothing compliance would not stop her boyfriend's mounting accusations that she was trying to attract other boys.

"He'd be ranting and raving if I wasn't home from school as soon as he thought I should be. He couldn't believe I missed the bus." Her simple *hello* to a male friend, his best friend, would bring on his "how can I trust you" speech. Her tears would follow, then his apology with a red rose and a quiet dinner in a restaurant, where he chose her "favorites" for her from the menu. With dessert came his "sparkling look — the perfect gaze for getting his Friday night way, the way to my bedroom."

"Everything was always my fault," Maria says. "The issue was trust." The cycle of her apologies and tears, his apologies, roses, and jewelry would repeat. So would his passionate declaration: "It's only because I love you — you know that."

"Under the guise of love, the abuser is a 'master of manipulation,'" says Dr. Rawlings. "If a girl has no experience with love, ultrapossessiveness feels like love."

As Maria tells her story, certain words and phrases resonate with me from Jenny's relationship with Mark Smith: *handsome, popular, considered the ideal couple in school.* And of course there are the roses. They appear and reappear in many of the girls' stories. They have come to represent a potent symbol of apology for abuse. I refer to them as "deadly roses," because Mark had sent roses on several occasions. In my ignorance at the time, I thought: *How exciting, how romantic!* I had no idea that those roses were an attempt on his part to get back into Jenny's good graces. Whenever I hear "He sent roses," I sense a chill up my spine.

"HE NEVER LAID A HAND ON ME"

Although Ryan Lawrence* was her second boyfriend, never once during the thirteen months they were dating did eighteen-year-old Deirdre Weigert* realize she was in an abusive relationship. Handsome and charming, twenty-three-year-old Ryan was a welder at a Long Island aircraft company who played basketball on weekends. Deirdre, a sparkly-eyed girl with a Julia Roberts smile, was proud to have him escort her to her senior prom; they were deeply in love, and Ryan told her that he wanted to marry her.

But after three months of what seemed a "perfect relationship," Ryan became possessive and obsessive. He began his pattern of abuse by giving Deirdre a "makeover," insisting she wear different clothes and less makeup. More troubling was his constant calling and grilling her on her whereabouts. "If my beeper went off in my purse and I didn't hear it, when I checked the messages later I was afraid to call him back because ten minutes had gone by," says Deirdre. "He'd say I was lying about where I was, that I was with another guy, not my girlfriends, that I was a 'whore,' a 'slut.'

"He was jealous of all my male friends — even of my ex-boyfriend, who had died in an automobile accident. He took down all the pictures of the guys in my house."

But despite his excessive jealousy, controlling behavior, and humiliating name-calling, Deirdre did not realize that she was being abused. After all, Ryan had never *hit* her. Dr. Rawlings points out: "If the batterer can control a person through emotional, that is, psychological violence, then there's no need to hit."

"I wanted to believe we were happy," says Deirdre, "though we were fighting four out of seven days of the week. But he loved me."

Dr. Noelle Nelson, author of *Dangerous Relationships,* explains: "Ryan did not show Deirdre that he loved her just because he *said* the words. Not when he was removing pictures of her friends; that wasn't love, that was control, possession. He wanted her all for himself. Either her or death."

EMOTIONAL ABUSE IN THE POWER
AND CONTROL SPIRAL

At the core of an abusive relationship is the need for one person to have complete power and control over the other. The use of power and control begins with what often does not *seem* like abuse but morphs into more and more abusive behaviors. I visualize the dynamic of dating abuse as an ever-expanding spiral with power and control at its center. The Power and Control Spiral — with some of the major emotional elements highlighted for this chapter — is illustrated on the accompanying page (page 22).

Emotional battery takes many forms:

Remaking Her: He plays Pygmalion; he instructs her on how to think, dress, and act, what to read, what movies and TV programs to see, what music to listen to — all for "her own good."

> *Everything I wore I had to check with him, making sure it was okay. For my senior prom, I desperately wanted this black strapless gown, and it looked great on me. Instead, I got this silvery sheath that I really didn't pick out. He did. "I want you to wear it," he said, and I did.*
>
> Noelle, age 17

Asserting Male Privilege: He exhibits traditional supermacho behavior by "showing her who's boss"; he treats her like a baby, his

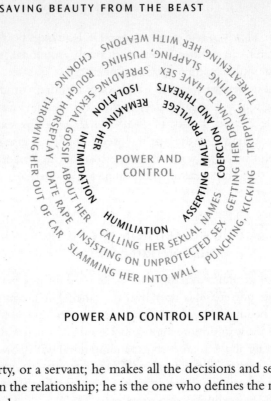

POWER AND CONTROL SPIRAL

property, or a servant; he makes all the decisions and sets all of the rules in the relationship; he is the one who defines the male and female roles.

> He had . . . chauvinistic friends. They thought, The worse you treat a girl, the better they like it. *"If they won't submit, force them into submission."*
>
> Natalya, age 16

Humiliation: He uses put-downs, verbal attacks, mind games (he makes her think she is going crazy), and manipulation; he makes her feel worthless — as if no one else would want her; he embarrasses her in front of people, makes her feel guilty, and stands her up.

> *He was always playing head games with me — saying we'd go to the mall one night, then not showing up and blaming it on me, calling*

me a "crazy bitch" because, he said, he told me he was seeing friends that night.

Marci, age 17

Denying, Minimizing, Blaming: He makes light of his put-downs, tossing them off as a joke; he maintains abuse never happened; he shifts the responsibility for his abusive behavior to her, saying that she provoked it or she was abusive too; he tells her everything wrong is her fault.

I had one guy friend who saw how my boyfriend was insulting me at a party and took him aside and told him to stop it. He said he was only kidding — it was all in fun. But my friend mentioned other things I had told him that he did to me. My boyfriend said: "She's making it up, she's crazy," but my friend saw how embarrassed I was at the party — he saw the abuse for himself.

Rosa, age 16

Intimidation (More subtle than outright threats): He keeps checking up on her or stalking her, yelling at her; he has his friends check up on her; he drives in a reckless way; he destroys her possessions; he induces fear by using looks, actions, or gestures; he smashes things, abuses pets, and displays weapons.

Sometimes he showed me his guns. Once he even pointed one at me. "Just playing," he said. "It's not loaded." But I kinda got worried.

Amber, age 15

Isolation: He uses jealousy and possessiveness as signs of love or to justify actions; he accuses her of cheating on him; he isolates her from her friends, family, and favorite activities; he controls what she does, whom she sees, where she goes; he limits her outside involvement, monitoring her with constant phone calls, beepers; he interrogates her about whom she's talking to.

He was jealous of my friends. He was jealous of anything that interested me. He was even jealous of my aunt. He was jealous of my music, thought I was practicing too much.

Kimberly, age 16

He would come to my high school. One day, when he saw a guy — not a boyfriend, just a guy — walking next to me, he got so jealous, he ripped up my bookbag.

Tadyce, age 15

If I had plans and he was not aware of it, there was always a fight. He had to control me down to the point where I was only spending Christmas morning . . . with my family. The rest of the time, I was with his family.

Ilona, age 15

He followed me after school; he wouldn't let me go to a friend's birthday party. He called all my friends sluts.

Cheryce, age 17

When a girl refuses from the beginning to be isolated, as Jenny did, her abusive boyfriend may try another approach, integrating himself into all aspects of her life, as well as her friends' and family's lives. Mark "adopted" Jenny's friends as his own and would join her and other girls in group activities, such as roller-skating and water sports, and would "show up" at the malls and the pizza parlor. He even turned up, uninvited, at our family reunion!

At first, Joe was very clever. He befriended Marci's three younger brothers, helping them with their basketball game, constantly doing "the right thing." But when it came time for graduation, Marci said she didn't want a party, because Joe wanted her just to be with him. We ended up having one anyway, but it was a struggle. She spent a lot of time worrying about talking to her friends and not being with Joe.

Pat, mother of Marci, age 17

Coercion and Threats: He says he cannot live without her; he constantly threatens to find someone else; he warns her that he will commit suicide if she breaks up with him; he induces her to do illegal things, blackmails her, threatens to expose embarrassing secrets, forces her to give him money, and takes her money.

All the money I made while working in high school was spent on him. Speakers for his car, gas money. I paid for dates. I had to. He was always broke. When he wanted something, he talked me into putting what he wanted above my own desires.

Nanci, age 16

HER FIRST REAL BOYFRIEND

Sixteen-year-old Vassiliki Tarnares — Vasso, as her friends and family call her — was a gifted artist who studied tap dancing and ballet, and coached cheerleaders at her Long Island high school when she began seeing twenty-year-old Raymond Purvis. "Ray was her first real boyfriend once she grew past the chunky stage to her full height — five foot nine — and became slender," says her mother, Helen.

At age twelve, Vasso had seen Ray at a local skating rink and "couldn't stand him." But when she met him at a mall a few years later, she found his personality, along with his wavy brown hair and big brown eyes, newly attractive. Her girlfriends seconded her opinion, but her mother did not. "He was too polite, schmoozed too much with me," says Helen, who distrusted his charm from the start. That he was a high school dropout, who took odd jobs, did not raise her comfort level.

Like Helen, I too had been uncomfortable with the low achievement level of my daughter Jenny's boyfriend. Although he hadn't dropped out of school, Mark was a poor student. He talked vaguely about joining the army, but he had no plans for his life. An honor student, Jenny was already talking about college and career at age fifteen. The difference between them was striking. I told her: "Jenny, you're not going to bring him up to your level; I'm afraid he's going to bring you down to his." She just shrugged it off.

Helen recounts how other things about Ray began to bother her. She realized how much Ray was controlling her daughter when she saw how he kept Vasso on the phone throughout dinner. "I just want to go to the mall with Michelle," she would hear Vasso plead as she was trying to get off the phone. "I have to eat now, you're gonna get me in trouble." His reply: "You'll hang up when I tell you to."

Sometimes Vasso would ask Helen to tell Ray that she was sleeping when he called, so that she could go out with her friends. "He would make such a fuss about seeing Vasso when *he* wanted, yet at times, *he* would stand *her* up," Helen says.

When Helen voiced her opinion about Ray, Vasso would become confrontational — unusual for her — and make excuses for his behavior: "You don't know him. His mother had a brain tumor and moved away, and his father is mean to him and makes him live in the garage." Helen realized Ray was playing on her daughter's sympathies. (They would later learn that Ray's father and sister had an order of protection against him.)

Dr. Carol Eagle, head of child and adolescent psychology at Montefiore Medical Center/Einstein College of Medicine in New York City, has observed that it gives a girl "a false sense of power to believe she can 'rescue' the boy from his unhappy past." Or his turbulent present.

Dr. Rawlings agrees: "The manipulator will tell his girlfriend that she's the only person who understands him. Ray Purvis was a master of manipulation."

The realization that Ray Purvis was exerting unhealthy power and control over her daughter galvanized Helen Tarnares into action.

"I knew I couldn't break away *for* Vasso," Helen admits pragmatically, but she decided to *do something*. "I can't forbid you to see him," she told Vasso, "but he is forbidden in my home."

When Ray nevertheless came to her house, Helen admonished him: "You were told not to be here." At that point, he began screaming at Helen: "You fuckin' bitch, you're breaking us up, we love each other." Vasso's father became so enraged that he threatened to break Ray's knees if he came near their house again.

Says Rosalind Wiseman, the director of Empower, a violence-prevention program given in the Washington, D.C., area schools: "You don't get between your daughter and the boyfriend. That's just what the manipulator wants you to do. He prefers to put *himself* between the mom and her child." When Helen forbade Ray to come to her house, her edict bound the couple more tightly.

Helen knew that Vasso was continuing to see Ray outside her home. Although she found him jealous and possessive, Vasso believed she still loved him. But eventually she would become tired of his constant checking up on her. It was only when Vasso herself tried to end their relationship that Ray's physically violent side would emerge and threaten her life.

"I WAS THE ONE PERSON WHO UNDERSTOOD WHO HE REALLY WAS"

At age fourteen, as a high school freshman in Washington, D.C., Rosalind Wiseman fell "totally in love" with the "pretty boy" of the class — "handsome, very wealthy, and incredibly charming." He was confident and seemed to have everything going for him. Although Rosalind came from a loving, supportive family and excelled academically and athletically, like many girls her age she felt ugly and insecure, "unworthy of his love." Yet the relationship bloomed. There were "roses in the locker," and for two years, the couple was inseparable.

But their "fabulous" relationship began turning abusive when Rosalind was sixteen. "He started controlling me, humiliating me. He constantly told me I was stupid, and he belittled everything I did.

"Although he presented himself very well to the world, I was the one person who understood who he really was. I knew about his insecurities." Rosalind realized that he was taking his anger at his family out on her. There were many nights when he would cry, with his head in her lap, because he thought he had failed in his family's eyes. He needed unconditional support and love from someone, and Rosalind felt special because she was providing that love.

But at that point it never occurred to Rosalind that she was being abused. Of course, it wouldn't have. She came of age around the same time my daughter did. Again the parallels strike me. Both Rosalind and Jenny fell for the "pretty boy." Although they were both smart young women, they based their attraction mainly on the externals, guys who were "so-o-o handsome," who inundated them with the inevitable roses. In the mid-eighties, what young girl ever heard of a boy exercising power and control over her, of an "abusive teen dating relationship"?

It would take two more years of increasing emotional abuse, overlaid with sexual manipulation and occasional physical violence, for Rosalind to admit even to herself that she did not have "the perfect boyfriend."

THE SELF-ESTEEM ISSUE

When I first studied the dynamics of dating violence, conventional wisdom seemed to say that only girls with poor self-esteem would become entrapped in an abusive relationship. Jenny, I thought, was an anomaly, the exception to this rule.

Although she still had braces on her teeth, by the age of fourteen Jenny had outgrown the awkward gangly stage and discarded her thick eyeglasses. Contact lenses showed off her large blue eyes; she knew how to style her thick blond hair and dress her slim, curvy figure with a flair all her own. More confident and poised than most girls her age, she became the center of a group of popular freshman girls. Many older boys were asking her for dates. By the time she met Mark Smith, the feedback she was getting told her that she was a beautiful young woman. In her case — and in the stories of many other girls I would subsequently interview — the seduction of the "ugly duckling" clearly did not apply.

"That scenario is myth," says Dr. Rawlings. "Some abusers delight in taking down a girl who has good self-esteem. It's mind control. They are masters at knowing how to tear down one's self-esteem, one's sense of self, one's identity."

"Low self-esteem can make someone more vulnerable," says

therapist Barrie Levy, "but *everyone* is vulnerable. Young girls are tempted to believe they can save these guys. Nine out of ten times, the young women are sucked in."

Dr. Noelle Nelson agrees. "Girls with high self-esteem, even cheerleaders, often get into abusive relationships. *I can change him,* they think, *because he's basically a good guy.* They're not attributing his abusiveness to a pattern. Then they get their self-esteem battered."

Tiffany, a smart and athletic eighteen-year-old college student, recalls her experience with her emotionally abusive boyfriend:

> *He wasn't physically beating or battering me at all. He just kept digging away at me relentlessly — calling me stupid and crazy and a whore. It was more subtle than physical abuse, but just as damaging . . . like having black-and-blue marks inside you.*

Lana, who at seventeen began what would become a two-year abusive relationship, describes her experience:

> *I think any girl, no matter how strong, how smart, can have her self-esteem drop to rock bottom because these guys are so skillful at hiding their true personalities in the beginning.*
>
> *I thought I was being strong by putting up with everything he did, by persevering and helping him with his problems, doing good things for him. The whole time, my strength was going down the drain. When he didn't get better, I thought it was my personal failure. I should have been working harder.*

Lana's mother, Judi, makes these observations about her daughter:

> *Lana was such a leader in school, almost bossy; she was the last person I'd ever suspect would be manipulated. He told her she wasn't good-looking or fun. He said she should be grateful to him for dating her. She believed it because no one else was around to disagree, because he had separated her from everyone else. Lana was just like a social worker. She thought she could help him. Then he just tore her down.*

Nina, at twenty-three, looks back with great insight on the abuse she suffered during her three-year relationship with her high school boyfriend:

I was very much one of those girls who said, "If he ever touches me, I'm out of here," but I scoff at girls who say that now — because by the time he gets anywhere near to hitting you, your self-esteem is gone anyway. Forget it, you're not going to leave. You know why? Because you are begging for any scraps he will give you. It's going to take you a lot longer than that first hit to figure out what is going on, and I applaud the women who get out then, but I just don't think it's reality.

Girls are not prepared for the kind of emotional abuse they are going to get from a man. They're prepared for the physical abuse because that is so much more dramatic and sensational (they see all the domestic violence warnings on TV).

And guess what? Physical abuse is not what you're going to be afraid of. The most damaging is the emotional abuse. Here are guys who know exactly what the girl wants to hear, how special and wonderful she is, they can say it with the straightest face — and then with the same straight face they can crush a girl without even touching her. Why aren't we preparing them for that? Instead, we're just telling them to go to a shelter if he hits you. "He said I was fat and worthless. I'm going to a shelter for that?"

THREE

PROVE THAT YOU LOVE ME
Sexual Abuse

UNLIKE DATE/ACQUAINTANCE RAPE, sexual violence in an ongoing dating relationship usually takes the form of repeated sexual coercion and sexually aggressive acts. Using psychological pressure, the abuser coerces the girl to have sex against her will.

Classic ploys are statements such as "If you love me, you will"; "You've been leading me on"; "You say no, but you don't mean it." Other timeless talking points are "You're not a virgin anyway"; "You're not a real woman"; "You're frigid."

We had been going together for months, and I knew he expected sex, but I wasn't ready for it. He respected that at first, but he kept hounding me about it. Then one night when we came back from a party, we had the same conversation. I kept saying no, he kept pushing and pushing, and I didn't back down but neither did he. Then, in the end, he just took what he wanted. I tried to think of all the reasons why it shouldn't be called rape . . . you know, maybe I had more to drink than I thought. Although I knew I wasn't drunk. I didn't want to believe that it had happened to me. He didn't see anything wrong with it. We never talked about it after that. It was kind of like, I wouldn't let something like that — rape — happen to me, so I couldn't think of it that way. You always think you could have done something to prevent it.

*After that, I tried to be willing; I didn't want him to force me
again, so I thought I might as well participate. I tried to say no a couple of other times, but I had no choice.*

Lana, age 17

TALK AND BEYOND

According to Karen Harker, "Sexual coercion is not necessarily intercourse or penetration. There may be a lot of sexual references
about her, calling her lewd names." In his book *The Batterer: A Psychological Profile,* Dr. Donald G. Dutton notes that the same four
names are used over and over: bitch, cunt, whore, slut. "All are sexual, and all are related to her imagined lasciviousness."

Beyond verbal manipulation, some batterers use physical violence or the threat of it to force a girl to participate in sexual behavior — petting, intercourse (with or without protection), oral or
anal sex — any act of intimacy that she does not want *at the time* or
finds repulsive. This sexual servitude can be extremely risky for the
girl — in more ways than one.

"Often the abuser refuses to let the girl use any sort of birth
control," says Harker. "Or he won't use anything to protect her
from sexually transmitted diseases."

"Sexually active girls are in denial about STD and pregnancy,"
says domestic violence attorney Sarah Buel, who has interviewed
hundreds of girls in the focus groups she runs. "They almost never
use birth control. Or protection against disease. 'Why not?' I ask
them. 'He's really a good guy,' they say."

Sixteen-year-old Caitlin Brummer* was one of the exceptions.
Says Caitlin, a tall, fresh-faced girl: "My mom and I always had this
good relationship about sex. She said if I ever needed birth control
to come to her. But when I did, she came down on me. She always
said she would never tell my dad, but she flipped out and told him
anyway."

"I had to tell my husband because I was so upset," her mother,
Gayle,* explains to me with an embarrassed clearing of her throat.
"Caitlin was in an unhealthy relationship, and we couldn't con-

vince her to break up with her boyfriend. He was a control freak and weird, but she could not see it."

Gayle finally did take Caitlin to her doctor for a prescription. "Any parent who thinks her child is in an abusive relationship should be sure to get her protection. I had been talking to Caitlin's friends, and I knew they were having sex whether or not they were on birth control."

"How did you feel about putting her on birth control?" I ask her, remembering my own distress and ambivalence when Jenny wanted me to put her on the Pill.

"It was hard," she admits, "but the thought of her bearing a child and forever being linked to a lunatic and his family was worse. The possibility of what could happen to her life if she became pregnant was awful. Either way you go, abortion or birth, will scar your child forever."

THE POWER AND CONTROL SPIRAL: SEXUAL ABUSE

Among the sexually abusive behaviors highlighted on the next whorls of the Power and Control Spiral (see accompanying illustration on page 34) are some of the following:

- Calling her sexual names
- Talking about the intimate details of the relationship to others
- Bragging about his past "sexploits"
- Flirting with other girls to make her jealous
- Comparing her to past partners
- Spreading sexual gossip about her
- Coercing her to watch porno videos and to pose or "act" in "home-porn" videos
- Threatening to show the "home-porn" videos to others if she refuses to give in to his demands
- Getting her drunk to have sex
- Coercing her to have what she considers "weird" sex
- Insisting on unprotected sex
- Date rape

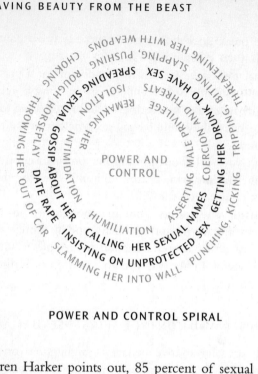

POWER AND CONTROL SPIRAL

As Karen Harker points out, 85 percent of sexual assaults are committed against teenage girls. They are the segment of the population most vulnerable to sexual assault by someone they know.

He would manipulate me into having sex with him whenever he wanted to, and maybe I didn't want to.

Kelly, age 18

I was a virgin, and I wasn't ready for sex . . . but my boyfriend just pushed himself on me. And I was scared I'd be killed right then, so I sort of allowed it.

Jayne, age 15

When I told my boyfriend no, he tied me to the bed and raped me.

Maggie, age 17

"If you're in an abusive relationship, you don't have the right to say no; you have abdicated consent, as you have in other areas of the relationship," says Rosalind Wiseman. "The way they like to demonstrate their power over you is by making you do sexually humiliating things."

In the introduction to her book *Defending Ourselves,* Wiseman recalled that when she was sixteen, her boyfriend would put her in his mother's bed and blindfold her. She wasn't allowed to do or say anything. If she spoke, he would tell her to be quiet. "Every time sexual abuse occurred, he would say, 'I love you. Why are you angry with me? I love you.'"

One time, my boyfriend took nude pictures of me. The next year, when I decided to break up with him because he was belittling me all the time, he threatened to show the pictures to my parents and to the other guys in school. I couldn't let that happen, so I stayed with him.

Alana, age 17

PERFECTION AND PERVERSION

Nina Grantworth* was a sophomore in a midwestern high school when she met Ethan,* a junior. "From the moment I met him," she recalls, "I really tried to get him interested in me. He was very attractive and in shape. Cute hairdo. I'd never had a boyfriend before, never dated."

Like several other young women I interviewed for the book, Nina, now in her early twenties, is eager to tell me her story. Tall, her blond hair tied back in a bandanna, she bounds into my living room wearing sweats and no makeup, a far different look than her professional appearance at work as the lead teller in the local bank. But either way, she is a pretty young woman.

We talk for four hours. I sense that all these girls find the interviews therapeutic; they don't want them to end any more than I do. And they are truly enlightening for me.

"I had always been the ugly duckling in middle school and during the first year of high school," Nina says, sipping her Coke. "I had a few hits, mostly misses, as a freshman. I'd ask guys out, and they'd say no."

But Ethan said yes, showing up at Nina's house on Valentine's

Day with candy and roses, and taking her out that night in his car to the mall. They soon became a couple, meeting each other at their lockers, walking each other to class, going to movies on weekends.

Nina's parents found Ethan to be a perfect gentleman, "much more so than I expected guys that age to be," says Nina's mother, Carly,* in an interview I have with her the following week. "And he brought Nina flowers. I thought, *Wow!*"

Just as Nina has described her, Carly is tall, thin, a young-looking "fifty-something," and "really cool." I sense the closeness between Carly and Nina, that they are really more than mother and daughter.

Carly recalls feeling "very excited" when Ethan took Nina to the prom because she herself had been "such a wallflower in high school. I had a circle of friends and a lot of guy friends, but I felt like I had missed something because I never dated. I didn't want her to miss those things I thought I had missed."

Nina was just as thrilled as her mom. "I got to go to the prom as a sophomore; not many of my friends were doing that, it was cool. Just his being with me built up my self-esteem — not that he ever told me I was valuable. And my friends got to that point where they said, 'We are sick of hearing how perfect he is, no one is, get over it.' He was perfect to me. That was the honeymoon period."

The honeymoon ended after a few months. Carly noticed the change. "There were no more flowers and little attentions. I think Ethan was becoming more comfortable; he thought he had made quite an impression on us. All of a sudden, instead of going to a show or out with friends, they were hanging out more in my home . . . in Nina's room — it was very large, with a TV, stereo, and stuff. It didn't bother me too much because we had the open-door rule."

The open-door rule did not prevent the couple's relationship from becoming sexual. "I remember we had done the usual high school fooling around in the car, but mostly in my room. My parents had this rule that I could be alone with him in my room if I kept the door open, but I just kept it open two inches so you couldn't really see anything."

As we approach the subject of her sexual relationship with Ethan, Nina asks in a little-girl voice if she may smoke. I nod. She will finish most of the pack before she leaves.

Between deep inhalations, Nina, her voice whispery, tells me how she and Ethan, in an attempt to save her virginity, began with anal sex — at his insistence. "He begged me — 'Please, please, please, please.' I broke down and said, 'Okay, sure.' We had it one time. Enough to know it wasn't for me.

"I've always been close to my mom, but I didn't tell her anything about that. It was the best-kept secret I've ever had in my entire life.

"Six months into the relationship, we started having regular sex. I was sixteen. It was horrible," Nina recalls. "I'm a hopeless romantic. I remember that my 'first' was in my bedroom, with my brother on the first floor watching TV and my mother in the basement watching TV. There were no candles, no beautiful nightgown, no flowers. We were fooling around and he said: 'I just want to put it in to see what it feels like,' and then he did, and he kept his promise, but then it was like 'I didn't feel anything, so let's try it again.' It was his first time too."

Their sexual relations would continue — unprotected — until Nina found herself three weeks late and thought she was pregnant.

"I will never forget how I found out that she was sexually active," says Carly. She too asks permission to smoke. "One weekend I noticed she had been very moody, not herself. Jokingly, I asked, 'What is your problem? You are being so strange. Are you pregnant or something?' She looked at me and said yes. I was stunned. And she just broke down.

"I had always prided myself on being such a progressive mom, trying to keep an open mind, trying to let my kids know that sex is a big step, but we can talk about this, I am always there for you. We had spoken incessantly about protection, birth control, the whole gamut. I was sure that Nina and I had a really open relationship."

Carly got the test for Nina. The result was negative. At this point, Carly decided complete openness was essential. "I told Nina, this is really not something I want you to get into, but if you think this is going to continue, then we are going to get you protection." Only later would Nina confess to her mom that being sexually active was not something she wanted either, that she didn't feel ready. But it was something Ethan wanted.

Once Nina was on birth control pills, she began gaining weight. "Ethan started making fun of me, calling me names. He told me I was lucky he was still with me, how no one else was going to want me, but he was putting on much more weight than I was." Looking back at the relationship, she now believes that he was projecting his own insecurities onto her. "He must have thought no one else would want him, so he better do what he could to hang on to me."

Experts agree with Nina's insight. In his book, Dr. Donald Dutton notes that insults about the woman's appearance are often a man's way of securing a more favorable power balance within the relationship. Dutton, one of the foremost researchers and clinicians dealing with assaultive men, points out that some men believe that the insults will guarantee "sexual exclusivity." Abusers make an all-out attempt to annihilate the young woman's self-esteem, to enslave her psychologically.

While Carly did not yet realize her daughter was in an abusive relationship, she did not like the way Ethan was behaving or the way Nina would allow it.

I think her thought process was: Well, he gave me flowers in the beginning. What happened? Am I not doing enough? Why did he change? I have to be better, I have to go along with what he says so maybe he'll be like he was in the beginning.

After those first few months, it was all downhill, but by then she was caught. The thing that upset me so much is that from the time she was in junior high school, she made National Honor Society every single semester — until Ethan. Ethan had such an influence on her that she was dropping out of school life, and her grades started to drop. There were times when she'd even skip school — I never thought she'd cross that line, because I'm a teacher. I could see the change in her. But I felt helpless. Nothing I did or said made a difference. I couldn't control the influences of Ethan.

As Carly tells me her story, I am drawn into it, reliving it with her, hearing how painful it was as she discovered each new disturbing facet of Nina's relationship and how her fear would grow. Carly is a likeable, intelligent woman who thinks and analyzes and agonizes over her own actions — or inaction. I relate to her "mother's guilt" syndrome.

Nina admits that she continually made excuses for Ethan: "He was having a difficult time because his parents were going through a divorce. He would cry, and I would think, *I can make it all better.* If he had a problem, I would always try to fix it. If he was mad about something, then I was mad about it too."

Carly believes now that the relationship became abusive "when Nina started sleeping with him. It gave him so much power. He played on her weaknesses. What really angered me was that he was making fun of her weight because she was on birth control pills. Because of him! And he was getting pretty pudgy himself. He would threaten to break up, then he wouldn't."

Another strain on their relationship came when Nina got a job at the pizza place where Ethan was working. "It was the perfect high school job," says Nina. "But I was valued there a lot more than he was, which made him feel bad. I was getting tons more hours than he was. He was the son of a lawyer, very arrogant, with an I-am-worth-more-than-this attitude, and people picked up on it. I was making more money than he was.

"His friends were telling him he should have control. Nobody knew the actual truth of what he was doing to me, but they knew he kept me in my place, and they thought he should. I think it was serious insecurities in all of them." Again, Nina shows insight. Guys who are insecure about themselves and are afraid they won't be loved have a need to dominate and control.

"Ethan became more and more possessive and controlling," says Nina. "He had to control me down to the point when I could have an orgasm. I made the comment a couple of times that sex was uncomfortable because he was so heavy. Of course, he told his friends, and it became a big joke."

Ethan's power swelled into more sexual demands, "everything

you can think of. The absolute worst was when he wanted me to have anal sex with him again. I said no. At midnight, he ran yelling and cursing from my house, saying he was going to kill himself. I called his mother before he even got home, I was so worried. The next day, I ended up having anal sex with him twice . . . he knew how to manipulate me. It was *psychological rape.*"

But more traumatic to Nina were the breakups. "He broke up with me quite a few times, but he always came back. Each time, it was heart-wrenching, major trauma. All my insecurities would come back. Insecurities from before I was with him. Then he would call, I would cry, he would cry, we would get back together."

As the relationship entered its third year, Ethan would take it to the next level — physical violence.

KISSED AND CHOKED ON THE SAME DATE
Physical Abuse

*One time, in his driveway when we were in his car, he was kissing
me, and then all of a sudden, I said something he didn't like, and he
started choking me.*

Eve, age 15

OF ALL THE GIRLS whom I have counseled or interviewed throughout the past fifteen years, not one has ever reported physical violence occurring at the beginning of her relationship. By the time
the battering took place, her boyfriend had already established a
pattern of verbal, emotional, and sexual abuse.

"It is crucial to remember that abuse involves more than physical
assaults, and it progresses very slowly and subtly," write the authors
of *Reaching and Teaching Teens to Stop Violence,* a curriculum developed by the Nebraska Domestic Violence Sexual Assault Coalition.
"Each time she voices disapproval with his 'rules' or attempts to
slow down the relationship, he increases his use of violence."

He then rationalizes his behavior as "love," defends his jealousy
as a sign of how much he cares, and justifies his hitting as his only
choice when "she acts like she doesn't love him." All aspects of
abuse — emotional, sexual, physical — become braided into a
thick coil of control.

"NO BIG DEAL"

A few years ago, Pat Greeley,* a woman who lives in Ohio, wrote me a six-page letter describing her daughter's abusive relationship. Initially, Pat was pleased when Mallory* found her first "real love" during her senior year in high school. Jon* was a big basketball star from a neighboring school. With his good grades and great looks, he was the "perfect boyfriend." Mallory seemed ecstatic — spending more and more time with Jon and his friends, going to basketball games and proms. She managed to maintain excellent grades herself — she was third in her class — and attend her own school's basketball games as a cheerleader.

But there were personality traits of Jon's that "just didn't seem right" to Pat. When she tried to mention them to her daughter, Mallory would only draw closer to Jon.

One day, Mallory was sitting on Jon's lap in her kitchen while Pat was at the counter peeling apples for a pie.

He reached over, with Mallory on his lap, and he carefully put the point of the knife under her chin. Then he put it by her right ear, then down and around to her left ear. She sat there quietly. I asked him for the knife, and he gave it to me right away. I told him never to do that again. He said I was making a "big deal" about nothing. I thought I was going to lose it . . . because I knew that activity like this was far from normal.

After that incident, Pat decided to keep a close eye on Jon every time he was in her house — "without plopping in the middle of them." One day, when she was in the basement and Mallory and Jon were upstairs, she heard a loud crack. "I went upstairs to see what was going on. Well, he had spanked Mallory and was wrestling around on the floor with her."

Pat immediately ordered them to stop and told them that spanking and wrestling were inappropriate behaviors. Again, Jon replied that it "was no big deal." Nor did it seem a big deal to Mallory, who, Pat would learn much later, was putting makeup on her bruises.

POWER AND CONTROL SPIRAL

THE POWER AND CONTROL SPIRAL: PHYSICAL ABUSE

Physical abuse is defined as any type of physical control over another person. In the accompanying illustration of the Power and Control Spiral, some of the forms of physical violence are highlighted in the outer whorls — a continuum of the emotional and sexual abuse. (See above.)

Violence often begins "innocently" with simple "play wrestling." ("We wrestled, and I won," as one abuser put it.) Then the "horseplay" segues into slapping, punching, pulling hair, arm twisting. At that point, the girl will ask him to stop, but he won't; she may hit him back, but he hits harder.

Other physical ways that abusers often show how much they "love" their girlfriends are slapping, pushing, grabbing, shoving, tripping, biting, punching, kicking, holding her down so she can't leave, slamming her into a locker, or throwing her across a room.

The violent episodes become more frequent and dangerous, and escalate to burning her with a cigarette, throwing her out of a car, choking her, or threatening her with weapons.

ALL IN FUN

Kate Landis began going with her boyfriend when she was fifteen and a freshman at a private school in Englewood, New Jersey. A year older than Kate, he was on the hockey team and played football and lacrosse. "Control was a big issue," says Kate, a tall, slender young woman with blue eyes, long, straight blond hair, and a vibrant personality. "Because of him, I drew apart from my friends who were my age, and I hung out with his."

Most of his abuse was verbal, but sometimes when they were having an argument, he would intimidate her by driving too fast, careening around corners. Other times, he'd yell at her to get out of the car.

There were times when his abuse became blatantly violent. Kate remembers: "We would be playfully pushing each other — then all of a sudden I'd find myself at the bottom of the stairs. Another time, at a party, he pushed me over a coffee table and started kicking me — in front of our friends." One girl told Kate she could no longer be her friend if she continued to date him.

ABUSE THAT SHOWS

Rosalind Wiseman recalls that it took two years before she realized that her high school boyfriend was destroying all her confidence — even in the areas of her life where she excelled. "I once got so angry at him for belittling me that I slapped him across the face. His response was to throw me up against a wall, put one hand around my throat, the other hand in front of my face and say: 'If you touch me again, I will kill you.' I really believed he would."

Sociologist Murray Strauss observes that in recent years, girls have been doing as much hitting as boys. He believes "cultural norms these days say it's okay for girls to hit boys," but he warns that hitting is "the wrong kind of equality for women. Although in half the cases of physical abuse, both sexes are doing it, a girl thinks: *I know I won't hurt him,* but any hitting has a big risk of escalation." And because of the difference in male and female muscle power and strength, "the injury rate is seven times higher when the boy hits back."

Barri Rosenbluth, director of school-based services for Safe-Place in Austin, Texas, agrees: "Girls are acting out aggressively, becoming increasingly tough, and sometimes it works in warding off potential abusers — but it heightens her risk of serious injury if she is already in an abusive relationship."

"Self-defense courses help only in a limited way," Karen Harker maintains, "because adolescent boys are larger and stronger than girls; they will escalate the violence if she hits back."

Rosalind Wiseman's relationship with her boyfriend was gradually becoming more violent, even though she was not retaliating. One day, when they were standing at their lockers at school having an argument, he hit her in the face. "He gave me a huge bloody nose. I didn't want to cover it up. I wanted him to see what he did — that he was injuring me in a way that *showed*."

OUR SECRET

"It started out more as play-hitting," says Ronna, who recounts her experience with abuse when she was sixteen for the Teen Dating Violence Project of the National Coalition Against Domestic Violence. But the "kidding around" took another turn when she and her boyfriend began to argue. (Jealousy was at the core of most of their arguments, she remembers.) He would begin by grabbing her and shaking her to make her listen to him. The grabbing would get tighter and tighter, to the point where it would leave bruises. If Ronna tried to get away from him, his violence would escalate. "I interpreted it as an act of love," she says. "It made me feel like someone cared for me."

Ronna notes that her boyfriend's violence actually built a closer bond between them because they experienced so much together. Not only were they sharing their most intimate thoughts, but "the violence you share is also very intimate — the secret just between the two of you." Their "secret" drew her closer to him than to family and friends.

DECONSTRUCTING A CONSTRUCTIVE SUGGESTION

Nina, whose relationship is described in chapter 3, recalls how her boyfriend's abuse exploded into the physical. The immediate trigger: what she thought was a constructive suggestion.

"I was getting sick of Ethan basically tearing apart my self-esteem with comments about how fat I was and how no one would want me. I am not model stick-thin; I have big bones. I was a size twelve, which I don't consider fat for my height. But when I suggested that we should *both* start working out — he was getting really heavy — we ended up in a fight so bad that he threw me against the front door. I had bruises from the frame. The bruises were easy to hide — but my self-esteem was in the Dumpster."

Although Ethan had also begun experimenting with drugs, Nina believes the real cause of his violent behavior was that he had seen his "pompous-ass lawyer" father push his mother around.

Nina knew that Ethan was planning to pick her up from school after a day of smoking pot.

I was not into that scene — the whole thing scared me. So I arranged to get a ride with someone else. But he came to pick me up anyway, and there was a huge fight. The end result was that I was backed up against the car with his hand around my neck. My friend was bold enough to grab him by the collar and tell him to let me go. With his other hand he shoved her up against the car. No one around the school did anything. I don't know if anyone even noticed. At the time, it didn't register to me that nobody did anything; maybe they thought it was no big deal.

Nina did manage to ride home with her friend. "Of course, five minutes later, Ethan showed up at my door: 'I'm so sorry, I didn't mean to, please trust me.' And we got back together, once again, because at that point he was still my world, he was everything. I had bought into everything he told me."

"LET'S JUST FORGET IT HAPPENED"

Lisa Vernon,* a popular, outgoing honor student, who in high school had dated many boys, was just seventeen when she entered the University of Illinois. Her first weekend there she met Bart.* He sent her flowers along with a note: "I want to have a date with the prettiest girl in class, and you are the one."

Lisa, now a young married woman in her early twenties, with expressive brown eyes and an engaging smile, seems a bit uncomfortable when we first begin the interview in my house. She asks if she may smoke. I nod, and she begins talking for what will be three hours, warming up as she continues. I can see a kaleidoscope of emotions playing across her face as she relives the experiences, her feelings of being trapped, her reasons for rebellion. I can sense the anguish about the broken relationship with her mother, a relationship that has not been repaired completely.

Although I have counseled other girls and their parents, I have never had such a vivid description of every torturous moment in a relationship painted for me by a girl who lived through it.

"At first," Lisa tells me, "Bart was everything I thought I wanted in a guy — he was *older,* he was *taller,* he wanted to be a schoolteacher, he was great with kids. And I love kids. I met his family. They were so nice to me, so laid back, so different from my parents. They had rules, but they were a lot less strict."

Although Lisa was very close to her mom — when she was in high school, they used to talk for hours after she'd return from a date — Lisa knew she would not approve of Bart. He was still in college at age twenty-five, an age her mother considered too old for her daughter.

Lisa's mom, Joanne,* disliked Bart from the moment she heard how he had escorted Lisa to her sorority Christmas dance — Lisa had paid for the tickets — and would not dance with her. "When they returned by bus to the campus at four A.M.," she says during our telephone interview the following week, "he just left her on the street. She had to walk back to her dorm alone. He put her in danger."

Joanne, a high school teacher, at first seems hesitant to reveal her feelings during the interview, and sensing that she is a private person, I wonder if I am irritating her with my questions. But as we speak, she becomes more forthcoming. Just as vividly as her daughter did, Joanne paints for me the picture of a parent caught up in a nightmare — her child's relationship with a brutal boyfriend. The more she talks, the more I begin to imagine myself in her place and to understand how wrenching these years were for her entire family, how the scars are still there. I myself had never been in the role of a parent trying to get her child out of a violent relationship. It was only after my child's murder that I learned the true nature of her situation.

Joanne's forebodings were reinforced by her first meeting with Bart and his parents, when she came to campus to pick up Lisa for break. Bart barely spoke to her, but his mother told her that Lisa was "the best thing that ever happened to Bart" and that she hoped "the kids" would make better choices than she had. Joanne would later wonder: *Was Bart's mother being abused, and if so, why didn't she warn Lisa?*

During summer break, Joanne would vigorously express her disapproval of Bart, and Lisa would argue constantly with her. And then phone Bart.

Joanne read excerpts from her diary to me, and I heard the hopelessness in those passages. "I just can't understand Lisa anymore," Joanne had written in one of them. "She says she sees a different side of Bart. She wants to get away from us and be with him."

"Because of him, the girl is under the delusion that the parent is the enemy," says Dr. Shelley Neiderbach, a clinical psychologist. "In a power struggle between the guy and the parent, the guy is going to win."

Bart won. Lisa decided to share an apartment with him the next semester. "My husband and I told her," says Joanne, "if you go live with him, that's the end of our money: no tuition, no room and board."

"I didn't care," says Lisa. "Bart's parents were wealthy. They paid half the rent. I worked part time as a waitress, and I got credit cards to pay for the tuition and everything else."

Once they began living together, Bart's controlling personality became more apparent. In *Dating Violence,* an anthology edited by Barrie Levy, Dr. David Sugarman and Dr. Gerald T. Hotaling point out that cohabiting increases incidents of dating violence because of "deeper and more intimate knowledge of the partner," including "higher levels of interaction frequencies" and the "likelihood of complications due to sexual jealousy."

Says Lisa: "He would play 'twenty questions' with me whenever I went out. He made me stop going to my sorority, to all my activities. The only friends we had were his friends."

He isolated Lisa from her family as well. He made it difficult for Lisa's mom to speak to her on the phone. Lisa was always "out or sleeping" when Joanne called. Lisa could call home only when Bart was not around.

When he wasn't bad-mouthing her mother, he was manipulating her. "He called my mom one time and told her he was worried because I had put on a little too much weight and asked her what he could do. I don't know what my mom said. I walked in about halfway through the conversation, and what I did hear made it sound like my mom was the one complaining about my weight while Bart was trying to defend me. So I got on the phone and yelled: 'How can you say that about your daughter?' I didn't believe her when she said Bart started the conversation."

"I'm still trying to understand why she accepted his word over ours," says Joanne. "One day, he told me on the phone: 'Lisa will never grow up; she needs me to help her.' In an odd way, I think she experienced a feeling of being protected. He was a big guy. Powerful. Demanding."

"Identity issues for girls can be extremely difficult. Separation from her mother is part of a girl's normal adolescent development," says Dr. Carol Eagle, who has authored *All That She Can Be: Helping Your Daughter Achieve Her Full Potential and Maintain Her Self-Esteem During the Critical Years of Adolescence.* "Lisa, no longer identifying with her mother, had given up her identity to this guy, merged with him." Even four years after the relationship ended, Lisa's mom sees much of Bart's personality in Lisa. It was "as if he had taken her personality away from her and blended it with his," says Joanne.

Bart convinced Lisa to drop out of her day classes to work as a waitress and go to school at night. But he "showed how much he loved her" by surprising her with an engagement ring. A big party followed at his parents' house. Cake. Presents. Bridal magazines. Lisa got swept away in the fun of planning, despite her family's less-than-enthusiastic reaction.

"I was anxious to set a date. I thought once we were married, I would have a say in what he did. I would get some control as his wife."

Lisa was wrong. Marriage, the experts agree, often triggers a more domineering reaction, a now-she-belongs-to-me feeling that exacerbates violence.

Bart's abuse so far had been confined to mostly yelling — loud enough for the police to be called twice to their apartment building, but "on the lower end of the physical scale, a little pushing. He would say things like, 'If you ever do that again, I'm gonna smack you,' and he did smack me a couple of times."

It was during Christmas break with Bart's family that his violence took a quantum leap. In his parents' house, overlooking the family room, there was a balcony on which Bart's dad had an office. Lisa was playing on the computer.

I stood up when we started arguing about something. He kind of pushed my shoulder a little bit, so I told him not to do that. He said, "I'll do it when I want," and pushed me again. I said, "Don't touch me anymore." I reached out to slap his hand away, and he just reached back and smacked me. I got mad and started yelling at him to never do that again. His mom was downstairs and heard us. She said: "If you guys don't cut it out, you will have to take it outside."

He kept coming toward me and backed me up into the railing of the balcony. He pushed me again, and I fell against it. I pushed again, he pushed again, and I went over the railing — flying over backward. Luckily I landed on the arm of the couch in the family room.

His mom came running in and wanted to know what had happened. I told her. I was crying and sobbing, and she couldn't understand. I was pretty much in shock. It was like, These things don't happen to me, I don't let this kind of thing happen to me. *Bart said, "She pissed me off." His mom said something like: "You can't be doing stuff like that." But she wasn't yelling at him.*

When Bart's mother drove Lisa to the hospital, Bart refused to go along. The doctors determined that Lisa had a concussion and a broken arm. Although there were laws against domestic violence in Illinois at the time, nobody questioned Lisa's explanation that she just fell. Bart's mother paid the hospital bill, but she never mentioned the injuries again. "Didn't say anything to him, didn't say anything to me," Lisa recalls. "Didn't say: 'I can't believe my son did this to you.' We just went back to their house."

"The parents of the boy usually have been hoping that the girlfriend will save their son," says Mary Ann Fremgen, director of counseling at Promoting Alternatives to Violence through Education (PAVE) in Denver. "The mother is in a pattern of rescuing her son. Her own image of herself as a parent is a motivating factor. *We can't let him fail*, she tells herself."

Bart never said he was sorry to Lisa. "All he said was, 'Let's just forget it happened.' He did a lot of stuff for me," says Lisa, "which I think was his way of apologizing. His dad came home from work that night, looked at me, and went about his business, never asked what happened. That's when I wondered if his dad does stuff like that to his mom too, and in this house, you just don't talk about it."

"If their fathers are already emotionally withdrawn or abusive, that doesn't leave much in the way of support. . . . There's no help here in sorting out inner states of dread or confusion . . . ," explains psychology professor Donald Dutton in *The Batterer*. "The message is simply to ignore the inner aspect of experience and focus on the outer world. . . ."

After her arm was broken, Lisa thought of calling her brother. "If you ever need me to come and get you, no matter where you are, call me," he had written on her recent birthday card. "But I decided no. My father had gone through open-heart surgery, and I didn't want to upset him."

Lisa spent the rest of the Christmas break never leaving Bart's house, Bart never mentioning the incident again. "I think it clicked in my mind that this was not somewhere I should be — but that I would deal with it later."

Back at school, everyone was asking Lisa why her arm was in a cast. "I said: 'I just fell.' I knew people didn't believe it, but they weren't about to confront me."

Although Lisa knew she had to leave him, Bart preempted her. He told her that she wasn't "living up to his standards" and asked her to return his ring.

"It pissed me off. I thought, *How dare he? He treats me like this and then he gets to break it off before I do?*" But Lisa saw his change of mind as an opportune way out.

The next day, after her cast was removed, she called her mother to ask for financial help to get back into the dorm. "There were times my mom just begged me to let her help me out of the situation. I always told her I was fine. I never wanted her to know she was right. It took every ounce of dignity and strength to call her that day." Through the residential life office, Lisa was able to find a room immediately.

When Bart got home from classes and saw Lisa's bags packed, he pleaded with her to stay, saying they could work things out. Lisa refused, and he became enraged. She threw his ring at him and ran out to the campus police, who drove her back to the apartment and helped her move. Bart finally drove to the dorm and dumped the rest of her stuff in the lobby. "Have a nice life," he said.

As he left the lobby, Lisa felt enormous relief — she would never see him again. Or so she thought. She would spend the next two years in fear as Bart stalked and terrorized her.

THE NURTURING PREDATORS

"If a girl is not getting enough nurturing in her home, she may be looking for it outside — even from the guy who abuses her," observes Dr. David Sugarman, professor of psychology at the University of Rhode Island, who has researched dating relationships in the Family Research Laboratory with Murray Strauss.

Lynn Ann Kenny believed that her parents, who both worked

long hours, were not around to give her the attention and praise she needed at fifteen. But a boy in her Baltimore suburb was. Seventeen-year-old Garry Leinbach, who studied astronomy, was "preppy-looking and well mannered, everything I thought I wanted in a boyfriend," and — at first — he catered to all her wants, even cooking dinner for her. But after three months, he isolated her from her friends and family, and would become wildly jealous when he suspected she was flirting with the only people he allowed her to be around — *his* friends.

In an interview reported by the *Washington Post* Wire Service, Lynn recalled that his first act of violence was a push. "I didn't think anything of it — a lot of guys push girls." But slaps eventually followed — hard enough to leave marks on her face — along with tears, his as well as hers, and his apologies and her forgiveness. The pattern would repeat — more and more intensely.

He would punch her on her arms and legs, in places she was able to cover up with clothing. When her parents did notice a welt or a bruise, she would lie: she had fallen or had tripped over something in school.

The violence escalated: once, he threw her across the room and choked her; another time, he knocked her unconscious. Three years into their relationship, Garry Leinbach beat her up so badly that she was hospitalized with a smashed nose, black eyes, a bruised kidney, and bites, blood, and bruises all over her body. Leinbach was sent to prison for assault and battery, blaming Lynn for knowing "how to press all [his] buttons."

Lynn sat next to me on the set of the *Oprah Winfrey Show* during the second half of the program on which we both appeared. She reminded me a lot of Jenny — her pretty face, blond hair, sweet nature. I saw her face swollen and battered almost beyond recognition in the blown-up photographs that had been taken of her in the hospital after the beating. I saw her mother in the audience sobbing.

At the next break, Lynn turned to me and said: "I knew about you, and I knew about Jenny. I had seen you on TV, but I didn't think it was the same thing that was happening to me." I was taken

aback. *Why were these young girls just not getting it?* For several minutes I felt despair and wondered why I was continuing to make TV
appearances and give my gut-wrenching presentations in schools.

During the next segment of the program, as Lynn described the
beating — how he was choking her, how she thought she was dying, *knew* she was dying, how her thoughts of what it would do to
her family made her fight all the harder, and how she saved her life
by jumping out of a moving car — I returned to my own obsessive
thought: *What did Jenny go through? What were her last thoughts?*
Jenny had no method of escape, she was so badly injured right
from the first stab of the knife. Oprah, ever empathic and wise, saw
that I was crying and quickly related insights she had gained from
previous interviews with burn victims and crime victims, in which
they stated that there was no pain or fear during the incident, that
the pain came later, that the body goes into shock, and that the
person is pain-free during those awful moments. I appreciated
Oprah's efforts to comfort me.

Like Lynn Ann Kenny, Kaisha Marshall* also felt nurtured by
her battering boyfriend at the beginning of their relationship.
Kaisha, a twenty-year-old petite Long Island woman of Jamaican
ancestry, whose straight medium-length hair frames her beautiful
mocha-colored face, relates in her gentle voice: "I was fourteen,
and he offered to look out for me. He took me out and bought me
things my mom never did. My mom and I didn't like each other.
He was twenty, but I lied to my mom that he was a senior in high
school."

Kaisha felt close to him because they had a common bond — an
unhappy home life. Neither had a relationship with a dad. Kaisha
had never met hers. Darryl* had an abusive father, who had left the
family years earlier.

Kaisha found Darryl charming and witty, but also too controlling — he frightened her by punching a wall in anger. After six
months, she broke up with him and began dating a boy from
school.

"Three months later, Darryl beat up my new boyfriend. I felt
terrible for the guy."

But Kaisha forgave Darryl because "he played on my sympathies. He told me his mom passed away — as if it happened recently. I didn't know she had died four years earlier."

Once Kaisha was back with him, Darryl became more controlling. And violent. "Once, he threw me across the floor, and my back hit the bedpost. He cried and apologized. But then he made me feel guilty for provoking him."

He soon became sexually abusive. "I was still a virgin at fifteen," says Kaisha. "One night, he forced himself on me in his car. He actually date-raped me. I cried afterward — but he made me feel as if I really wanted to do it."

Yet Kaisha remained in his thrall — even after she saw him pushing her mother while yelling profanities at her.

Seeing that she could no longer control her daughter, Kaisha's mother asked the court to assign her to the Persons in Need of Supervision (PINS) program. Kaisha was moved to a group home in another town.

But Darryl followed her, moving down the block. And Kaisha admits she was pleased. "He was there for me. 'Nobody loves you but me,' he would say."

She was allowed to have supervised visits with him in the group home, but she would sneak out to be with him alone.

Their sex life resumed, and so did his abuse. But the group home supervisors never saw signs of his violence. "He never hit me in the face. I had bruises on my thighs, which I hid."

But she could not hide her pregnancy. She was assigned by the social services agency to another group home for pregnant girls.

There, the father of her child was allowed to visit her. "He promised that he wouldn't hit me anymore. And he did stop for a while, but he was still manipulating me." When Kaisha was six months pregnant, she found out Darryl was seeing someone; they had an argument, and he pushed her and ripped the sweater she was making for the baby.

But again she forgave him. "Being pregnant, I was vulnerable. He said he would marry me; he even went to Lamaze classes with me." When she gave birth to her baby boy, he was her coach. "I had a drug-free childbirth," she says, "but not Darryl. He came into the delivery room high."

Kaisha, back at her mother's house with the baby, continued to see Darryl outside her home. Although he was doing off-the-books manual labor for a construction company, he refused to support his child. But Kaisha was still hoping they would marry. He agreed to go for therapy to "work on his hitting problem." But each time his aunt would baby-sit, he would break their counseling appointment and insist they go to the movies instead.

Because he was not "book smart," Darryl became jealous of Kaisha's ambitions when she started going to college to study advertising. "He tore up my graphic-design sketchbook right outside the campus in front of the teacher." At that moment, Kaisha had an epiphany.

"I decided that was it, we're breaking up." Kaisha went to remove the license plate on his car, which was registered in her name because his license had been suspended.

"As I was removing the plate, he started the car. I fell on top of the car and was flying off it as it was moving. I was so scared — humiliated that he did that to me in front of a whole bunch of people. The witnesses insisted on calling the police — I really didn't want to go to court — and Darryl was arrested."

His family put pressure on Kaisha not to press charges. "I stupidly listened to his aunt, and I said in court that I had jumped in front of the car. The judge dropped the case but issued an order of protection, allowing him contact — because we had a child — but stopping him from verbally abusing me and harassing me."

Darryl was remorseful. "I still wanted to see him," Kaisha admits. "I was still thinking we could work things out, that all he needed was therapy. I wanted a family for my baby." Because Kaisha had never known her father, she longed for one for her son.

Four days after she received the order of protection, Kaisha's dream of family life would become a nightmare.

TRAPPED AND TRYING TO TEAR FREE

ANOTHER PIECE OF "COMMON WISDOM" I found to be not so "wise" was the notion of how much easier it is for a young girl to break away from an abusive relationship than it is for an adult woman.

"Not only do teens lack experience in relationships," says Barri Rosenbluth, "but the media is training them to play extreme 'feminine' and 'masculine' roles. The boy demands respect from his girlfriend and his peers by showing physical and mental toughness; the girl, ultradependent on her 'man,' feels responsible for caretaking and solving the problems of the relationship."

Karen Harker points out: "Girls misinterpret messages of love. At the beginning, you are supposed to devote yourself completely to this person, if this is love; they don't realize that how we love normally gets less intense as the relationship continues. The girls believe that continuing passionate involvement is a sign that 'he loves me.'"

Rosalind Wiseman, author of *Queen Bees and Wannabes,* a book for teenage girls, finds that the primary issues for girls in abusive relationships are:

- **Autonomy.** It is more important than abuse. The greater fear is "If my parents find out, they'll take away my privileges, make me stop seeing him."

- **Privacy.** The kids really feel that they are in love — and at times the relationship *is* wonderful.
- **Social status in school.** School is their whole life. Having a boyfriend is totally tied to who they are in school.

"Just as an abused wife feels that her home is her world, teens feel that high school is theirs — and that's why it's often so hard for a young girl to give up an abusive relationship," says Wiseman. "Having a boyfriend gives her the status she craves. There is a disconnect between the ways a girl feels about herself. She may believe 'I'm smart, I'm competent, I'm athletic,' but at the same time 'I have to have a boyfriend — or else what will people think of me?' If she decides to break up an abusive relationship, it's very hard for her to see past two weeks and the worry of *How am I going to get another boyfriend?*"

She recalls her own experience with her abusive high school boyfriend in her book *Defending Ourselves:* "Once I had this relationship, I felt tremendous pressure to maintain it because I believed my social status depended on it. Very quickly, I began to think that I would be nothing without him."

Zeina Kinkel, age fifteen, slim, pretty, blond, with an engaging air, observes:

> You don't know how many times a girl wants a boyfriend, but then when she has one, she sees it isn't that great. She may not have that much in common with him, but her friends tell her: "Your boyfriend is so cute, so hot." When they see the PDAs — public displays of affection — it gives her social status. Everybody around you is doing the PDAs; you feel so happy when you are too.

Zeina, a high school student in the Washington, D.C., area and a member of the Girls' Advisory Board of Empower, Rosalind Wiseman's organization, is well aware of the danger signs of an abusive relationship, thanks to her father's frank discussions with her, but she also points out how a boyfriend can boost a girl's ego at the beginning of a relationship. "A girl may think she's fat, and her boyfriend says no, you're fine, you're *not* fat."

For many girls, there is no better coup than to have a cool boyfriend — "perfect" in everyone else's eyes. "None of my friends ever questioned the picture I had painted of him, because I was such a smart girl," recalls Nina, whose "perfect" boyfriend coerced her to have anal sex.

THE IDENTITY ISSUE

"Breaking up can be extremely difficult for teenage girls," says psychologist David Sugarman. "There are identity issues. Teens experiment with different roles. Often they will define themselves in terms of whom they're going out with. A girl thinks, *If I leave him, I lose not only the relationship, but a part of myself.* So she stays."

Boundaries were a big issue for Rosalind Wiseman, whose relationship with an abusive boyfriend began when she was fourteen and continued until she was twenty. By the time she had been with him for two years, she found that her identity was completely tied to his. She could make decisions only on the basis of "how they would affect the two of us."

For a long time, the question of abuse did not enter Rosalind's consciousness. "It was not denial about his abuse on my part," she says, "it was not knowing, not putting it into the context of my life. I hadn't seen any abuse in my parents' relationship. It was as if my relationship with him existed in a vacuum. And at fifteen, although my parents were loving and supportive, I didn't want them to know anything about my private life."

Rosalind's words about the abuse — the not knowing — were key, I believe, to my daughter's concept of what was happening to her as well — not knowing, not wanting her parents to know. Like Jenny, Rosalind came from a loving home in which abuse was never seen or even discussed in those relatively "innocent" 1980s. Neither Rosalind nor Jenny could see the control their boyfriends were exercising. For a while, it was "only" mind control. Neither girl saw it as abuse. There were no programs being presented in school. I am still saddened and angered that there was no one speaking out, doing the work I do today, the work that Rosalind does today. If there had been, maybe Jenny would be alive.

CAUGHT IN A CYCLE OF ABUSE

Many girls are trapped in the cycle of violent relationships, a cycle first described by Lenore Walker in 1979 in her seminal text *The Battered Woman*. Their teenage romance becomes a twisted version of the classic boy-meets-girl story, playing out like this:

- **Boy Meets Girl:** Instant magic, soul mates
- **Boy Spoils Girl:** Heady moments, roses, "honeymoon" stage
- **Boy Engulfs Girl:** "Only the two of us"
- **Boy Remakes Girl:** Her clothes, friends, activities
- **Boy Controls Girl:** Her every moment
- **Girl Sees Girls:** Needing her friends and space
- **Boy Blames Girl:** For making him jealous
- **Boy Berates Girl:** Tension builds
- **Boy Beats Girl:** Verbally and / or physically, sexually
- **Boy Loses Girl:** Momentarily or for a short time, she recoils, shocked
- **Boy Gets Girl Again:** Profuse apologies, tears, and promises of "never again," more roses and gifts, more magical moments, more intense passion, new "honeymoon" stage
- **The Cycle Repeats:** The spiral of control and tension builds; surveillance, threats, and abuse escalate; his apologies diminish ("You made me do it"); her guilt rises; her self-esteem plummets; the boy she loves has turned into a despot (See accompanying illustration of the Cycle of Violence on page 61.)

Rosalind Wiseman found herself trapped in the cycle for six years, trying to break up with her boyfriend and being persuaded each time to come back. "There would be honeymoon periods when we would reaffirm our love. I made myself believe that his love for me and the abuse were two separate entities, and that if I became 'perfect' — doing everything he wanted — he would stop the abuse."

Even when Rosalind was thousands of miles away from him — in college in California — he would continue to call her, especially

THE CYCLE OF VIOLENCE

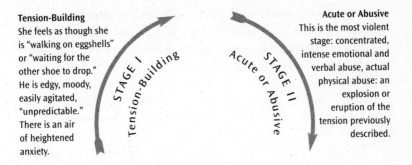

Tension-Building
She feels as though she is "walking on eggshells" or "waiting for the other shoe to drop." He is edgy, moody, easily agitated, "unpredictable." There is an air of heightened anxiety.

Acute or Abusive
This is the most violent stage: concentrated, intense emotional and verbal abuse, actual physical abuse: an explosion or eruption of the tension previously described.

"Honeymoon"
He says, "I'm sorry. I'll never do it again." He may blame her for his actions with "If you wouldn't . . . I woudn't get angry." He wants to make up with "hearts and flowers" or sex. She experiences many feelings from anger to love to confusion. She believes him and the cycle continues.

From *In Touch with Teens: A Relationship Violence Prevention Curriculum for Youth Ages 12–19* by the Los Angeles Commission on Assaults Against Women, 1992

when he was down. "The feeling was that no matter what I did or whoever I would see, I would always be involved with this relationship, that I was fated to be with him. I was making the same mistakes over and over again."

Rosalind believes that strong platonic friendships between boys and girls are especially valuable. "Many girls would rather talk to their male friends about a troubled relationship than to their girlfriends." She found an understanding male college friend in whom she could confide. She had to tell him over and over about her boyfriend's behavior before she realized how abusive it was. Each time she spoke of it, she felt shame and embarrassment.

As therapist Barrie Levy points out, shame is one of the most powerful emotions girls feel in an abusive relationship. "They have not only been emotionally undermined, but the majority have been sexually abused as well. They don't see it as rape; they are not outraged. They absorb all the shame and humiliation that a rape victim experiences, but they blame themselves, not him. She won't ever tell a parent or a therapist."

When Rosalind finally felt strong enough to break up with her abusive boyfriend, he cried to her that she was the only one who understood him and, from a telephone in Paris, threatened to kill himself.

"Threats of suicide are a very common type of control — a form of blackmail," says Janet Berger of the Teen Dating Violence Program of the National Council of Jewish Women in New Jersey. Berger advises the girl to resist the blackmail, get out of the relationship, and get adult help by calling a crisis line — anonymously.

"If the girl has strong rescue needs, a suicide threat is a very effective weapon in keeping her trapped in an abusive relationship," says Dr. Edna Rawlings. "It is the ultimate manipulation."

THE CARETAKER

When she first arrived at my door to be interviewed for the book, Kristy Broome* seemed hesitant, almost apologetic, as if she were thinking: *I see what you were trying to tell me the last time we met; I'm sorry I didn't follow your advice.*

Three years earlier, when she was fifteen, I had tried for more than two hours — at her mother's request — to counsel her about the abusive relationship she was in. Pretty, with thick chestnut hair, a quick smile, and bright blue eyes, Kristy struck me then as a highly intelligent girl — energetic, bubbly, communicative. Many times when I speak with young women, it is difficult to get them to open up. Kristy was instantly talkative, friendly, unusually poised and self-assured for a girl of fifteen, a seemingly independent thinker. I was careful not to preach to her in a motherly fashion. She was so intelligent that I thought all I needed to do was present the facts to her. But I had the feeling that although she was weighing and analyzing everything I said, nothing was clicking with her. The more we talked, the more the signs of her boyfriend's abuse became apparent, and I had a few moments when my stomach tightened with fear; I realized the situation she was in was dangerous. But I also realized that Kristy was not going to change her mind; there was no way she was going to leave this young man, even after I related the simple bare facts of Jenny's story. She expressed sympathy and nodded her head, but I could see that she did not connect Jenny's story to her own.

When she came for the interview three years later, the last thing I wanted was for her to feel guilty about not following my advice. There would be no I-told-you-so's from me! We hugged, and I welcomed her warmly and thanked her for participating in the project. In a few minutes, she was back to her bright, bubbly self, eager to tell me, in what would turn out to be a four-hour interview, the bizarre details of her relationship.

A passionate animal-lover, Kristy describes herself as having a "caretaker personality" — drawn to the wounded, whom she tries to "fix." But initially she was attracted to the charm and romantic ways of a boy she had met at a party three years earlier. Jack* was a grade behind her in their Iowa high school, and they both sang in the choir.

They started seeing each other every day, and after two weeks, they both "knew" they were in love.

> Everything was so wonderful for the first three months, movie-quality, that's why it was so hard to see it coming. The arguments started slowly, then came his yelling. He was always looking for an excuse to blow up at me. He would get angry with other people, but he didn't think he could blow up at them. But with me, he got comfortable enough to show his anger. I was the one person he could control. He trusted me to stay.

After six months, Jack's means of control became physical. He would start by grabbing Kristy by the arm and shaking her a little; then his grabbing would get harder, leaving bruises on her arm.

"But I would think, *Oh, he didn't mean to. He just grabbed a little too hard.* It would have been so much easier for me to see what was happening if it had been a real punch in the face."

Kristy did not dare tell her parents about Jack's physical abuse. "When I started to come to them with the little things he did, they would overreact. It was a shock to them. I thought, *Oh my God, if they carry on about this, what would happen if I told them anything else?*"

Kristy, an only child, believes that her parents played right into Jack's hands — fueling the fire with their harping — "How could you go out with him, how could you do this to us?"

"I had been a good kid," says Kristy. "But my parents were so hurt and angry that they started acting in an unloving way, criticizing everything I did. They were always chipping away at my self-esteem with *How could you?* The more my parents kept pushing, the more I shut them off.

"Jack played this whole thing over and over: 'If your parents really cared about you, they wouldn't do this.' You feel like he is the only person who cares about you. The only course of action is to stay and try to make it better."

And so the relationship continued — for almost three years.

When Jack and I had a huge fight and I would leave, I would just drive around for hours because I didn't feel like going home. Jack had separated me from my family and my friends. I had nobody to talk to.

In an abusive relationship, you are trapped — at least you feel that way. And part of you wants to be there because society tells you that you should be. I was listening to the radio, and every single station had something about a "lost love, how do I live without you . . ."; "I try to say good-bye, but I choke; I try to walk away, but I stumble." All this stuff. Little by little it chips away at your value as a single person. The music, the TV shows, everything tells you that you should have a boyfriend.

Kristy's ambivalence was resolved by her parents' ultimatum: *It's him or us.* "You feel there is no way out — especially if you are the caretaker because you feel he will hurt himself, that you will be killing him."

Jack turned one of his suicide threats into a piece of theater by leaving a party, banging his head against a wall until it bled, and returning to the party dripping blood.

"Women are suckers for losers who need us to take care of them. The guy is more likely to replay his family dynamics than to heal with her help," says Barrie Levy.

Kristy learned that Jack's father had badly abused him as a child and was abusing his mother. "If he has grown up around abuse," explains Levy, "the young man accepts the mistreatment of women as normal. There have not been enough sanctions in his environment to prevent him from doing it."

In Jack's house, crying was seen as a sign of weakness. "He was always afraid of seeming weak," says Kristy, "because he knew he really was. So whenever I would cry, he would get even angrier."

"Abused men can't tolerate weakness when they find it in themselves, so they manipulate the girl to think she is the dependent one because that is more the social norm," says Levy.

As time went on, Kristy and Jack's relationship cycled more and more intensely. "Sometimes, it was wonderful, sometimes terrible. It was getting more extreme, more turbulent. The good times were twenty times better, and the bad times were twenty times worse . . . though the physical abuse was not too bad. I didn't have broken bones or anything, mainly just bruises.

"Once, we got in a fight, and he stopped the car and told me to get out. We were in the country, miles and miles from town. I walked through the fields so no one would see me. All night. As bad as it was, it was also quiet out there, and I started to realize what I was missing, that peace."

Yet even after Kristy went away to college, she continued to see Jack on weekends. "One weekend, I stayed at Jack's house, and my parents didn't even know I was in town. I got very good at lying."

"Victims get very good at deception, especially at deceiving their parents," says Sarah Buel, founder and codirector of the Domestic Violence Clinic at the University of Texas School of Law in Austin. "They don't want to admit to their parents that they were right — that this person is a jerk — and they want to help this person so he will no longer be a jerk."

The breaking point for Kristy had not yet come, although "Jack was getting really angry and starting to get into some pretty heavy physical abuse. I don't think I ever totally realized that I couldn't fix him until the day he tried to strangle me. He had his hands around my neck, and I reached back and broke his nose and gave him a black eye. I didn't wait to see if it made him more angry, I just ran.

"I felt a void from being so entangled with him. My life had become Jack, and I used to think if I left him, my life would be over." Yet Kristy rejected all of Jack's efforts to get back, hanging up on him each time he called.

Like Rosalind Wiseman, Kristy found an understanding male friend. "The words of guy friends have more power than the parents and the girlfriends," says Kristy. "Girlfriends can support you and be there for you, but guy friends can tell you that you are beautiful, you are great, you deserve to be treated so much better than this. Then you think: *Well, he's a guy, maybe I won't be alone forever; there's one person who still thinks [I am] wonderful.*"

"ADDICTED TO THE DRAMA"

Kate Landis, the Englewood, New Jersey, girl whose boyfriend's abuse eventually became physical, broke up with him four or five times during their two-year relationship. Each time was "heavily traumatic." Yet she admits that she found herself "addicted to the drama of the situation." Some teenagers find a stable relationship boring, observes Dr. Edna Rawlings.

According to therapist Ginny NiCarthy, long active in the battered women's movement and a contributor to the anthology *Dating Violence: Young Women in Danger*, addictive love is often a component of an abusive relationship and implies an "urge far beyond desire." The young lovers believe their very survival depends upon the survival of the relationship.

Rather than admitting his neediness — even to himself — the young man typically expresses his dependency in terms of "control and criticism," while the young woman, more aware of her dependence, "narrows the focus of her life to concentrate on pleasing him." Her addiction causes her to ignore or make excuses for his abuse. Says Kate: "I would break up with him; then he would come over and apologize with roses; then I would tell all my friends about it. We thought that was the way a relationship should be." But Kate never told her parents of his violence or his heavy drinking.

Why the secrecy? "Part of adolescence is having a different life from your mother's," says Dr. Carol Eagle, who runs a group therapy program for young girls in New York City.

At times, Kate's parents knew, from hearing her side of the phone calls, that Kate and her boyfriend were having more than a love spat, that he was yelling at her, but Kate would always make excuses for him. She never asked for help from her parents, who were good friends of his parents. She did not want to disappoint or worry them.

After the breakups, there would be many late-night phone calls, as well as harassment in school. "He would sit behind me and talk to his friends about various acts of violence he found thrilling. My friends told me: 'Kate, if I were you, I'd be afraid to go to school.'"

The final breach came when Kate went into an empty schoolroom one day, and he walked in behind her with his hockey-player friends, "talking about me as if I wasn't there, making lewd remarks about my body."

A guidance counselor saw Kate running out of the room, crying. Hugging Kate, she invited her to talk. After Kate confided her problem, she suggested: "If you have some friends who know about his abuse, have them come to talk to me." Two boys and one girl corroborated Kate's account.

But Kate's boyfriend denied the abuse to a group of counselors. "He told them lies, and they believed him," Kate said. "He told them *I* was the alcoholic, that *I* kept showing up at *his* house — which was impossible because I didn't have a license to drive."

"There are two sides to every story," one of the counselors told her. "I think you are being a little dramatic, Kate."

Kate's mother, now aware of the problem, discussed it at lunch with her good friend, his mother. But she supported her son's version to the school authorities.

Kate's parents were considering getting a restraining order, but

Kate discouraged them. But the school did warn him to keep at least ten feet away from her.

He kept his distance but kept harassing her. When she would enter a room, he would say loudly: "I'm supposed to stay away from Kate," and he and ten of his friends would immediately leave. He would bang on the lockers when he'd see her passing in the hall. He would glare at her.

DATELESS AND FRIENDLESS

For the next six months, Kate's ex-boyfriend continued his harassment — from ten feet away. Kate was made to feel like a pariah. "Once you're out of the relationship, then you're out of the group you were part of. All his friends, who were yours too, pull away from you. A very difficult thing for a teenage girl," says Kate. Even the friends who had urged her to stop seeing him and had corroborated her story to the counselor avoided Kate. "One of his friends was in the middle — torn."

Kate would sit in her room and cry for hours. Normally outgoing and social, she had withdrawn from other friends. She no longer did well in school. Her passions — photography and cooking — lost their appeal. "I never attributed it to the relationship and its aftermath," she says. Nor did her mother, who thought at the time that she was acting like a moody teenager.

Girls, facing a void without *him,* without the friends and interests he made her give up, lose their sense of self. As one girl put it: "They manipulate you, so that you have nothing left; they suck your insides out." Many girls fear being alone more than the bruises.

"The peer pressure to be in a relationship is intense," says Dr. David Sugarman, "regardless of how damaging it may be. Some friends may even reinforce the idea that it's okay to hit her. On the other hand, if she does leave, as did Kate, she finds herself snubbed by even those 'friends' who told her to leave."

Programs such as Expect Respect teach the difference between healthy and unhealthy relationships and are turning that peer pressure around into a more positive force. Says Barri Rosenbluth: "We put up posters in the middle schools and high schools about teen dating violence, and friends and classmates of abused girls often refer them to us for counseling — as a whole group did recently when a girl came into class with a black eye. They become a support network, leaders. This is not a victims' group."

THE HOSTAGE

Maria Fedele, the sixteen-year-old sophomore from New Jersey, recalls *willingly* losing her friends when she began her relationship with her controlling boyfriend: "I was so much involved with him that I didn't mind — at first."

Maria was eager to help him through wrestling season. "But his weight loss and tiredness were putting a new burden on our relationship — mood swings and a nasty attitude. I became his number-one fan and, eventually, his only fan. He lost all his friends."

"Many girls, like Maria, have a natural nurturing need to help a boyfriend through stress," says Dr. Shelley Neiderbach, director of Crime Victims' Counseling Services in Brooklyn, New York. "She plays the good mommy, and he, the bouncing baby. She believes — mistakenly — that she can nurture him back to his 'true sweet self' with her love."

Maria's mission was not succeeding, and she realized that she was "without a friend to be found." She recalls telling herself, *At least I have him, right?* — "always with a question, always knowing it wasn't right.

"After he was ordered by the doctors to quit wrestling, he lost control of his life," says Maria. "I was the only thing he had, the only thing he could control. He was terrified of losing me. Then his manipulation became total."

His power peaked when they were shopping at a large New Jersey mall. "That cold day in March, he pushed so hard — the hardest mental push I had ever felt. 'Just put the shirt in your bag,' he ordered. 'Do it for us!' I knew he didn't need that $15 shirt; he had $135 in his pocket and a brand-new sports car that his parents had given him for his seventeenth birthday. But I was listening to his threatening words out of fear of his anger, a madness that would last for hours. And, sadly, I obeyed."

Suddenly there were police and handcuffs for both of them. "And tears," says Maria. "I cried and so did he. He looked into my eyes as the officer spoke, and he asked: 'Will we be all right?' I just turned my head in disgust, and every time our eyes met, he said, 'I love you.' It was my father's birthday, and he got a phone call from the police telling him I was arrested for shoplifting."

Dr. Edna Rawlings believes that Maria was at the beginning of a pattern that she identifies as part of the Stockholm syndrome (named after a bank holdup in Stockholm in which the hostages strongly bonded with their captors). "Emotionally, Maria was a prisoner, especially because she was isolated physically and sociologically, and didn't see the way to get out. And she had mixed emotions toward him because as the 'captor/abuser,' he showed kindness, love."

Maria was lucky to have been arrested, according to Dr. Rawlings, "since it was the first incident of her breaking the law. If the shoplifting had continued, Maria's thinking would have become distorted. Getting a person compromised with some kind of illegal activity draws her further into the Stockholm syndrome, strengthening her bond with the abuser."

Because she had never confided in them, Maria's parents were shocked to learn about their daughter's troubled relationship. On the way home from the mall after the arrest, Maria's father said only: "We trusted him to take you out and protect you. This is not the way someone shows his love."

As punishment for the shoplifting incident, Maria's parents did not permit her to see or telephone her boyfriend for the next month. "That month of crying and soul-searching was a blessing in disguise," says Maria. During that time, she often replayed her father's words in her head: *This is not the way someone shows his love.* "I now knew he had broken my heart. He had been running my life. I was exhausted, tormented by his demands."

"Maria's parents were wise to impose a separation period," says Dr. Rawlings. "They couldn't forbid the relationship completely, because it wouldn't have worked. But they took a stand for a month, and their ruling gave Maria space and time to think about the relationship."

During the break from her boyfriend, Maria only saw him at school, in some of her classes, and she admits she missed their closeness. "It was like an addiction. In school, he'd whisper: 'I love you, I love you,' but then say, 'Why are you wearing that?'"

After the month of enforced separation was over, Maria realized with great anguish and sometimes fury that it was time "to free myself of this so-called love that felt like a deadweight. It was time to put his commands into perspective — 'You can't wear that. Don't look at him.' I wanted to come home and have no one to call. I wanted to walk to class alone. I wanted to talk with some girlfriends. I needed to remember how to be myself. I had no identity. We had become one — one by his rule."

"It was to Maria's credit that during that time she saw what was happening," says Dr. Rawlings. "Her breakup occurred fairly early in the process."

"With rage, pain, and butterflies in my stomach," Maria told him of her decision to make the break permanent. "Together again, we cried for the last time. He said he couldn't let go. He swore he'd kill himself." Maria, terrified, tried not to hear him and walked away.

Maria's ex-boyfriend did not take his life. But he stalked her for the next few months, vowing he would find her, before he finally gave up. She found his behavior at the end of the relationship so stressful that she came down with mononucleosis and had to have home tutors for the last month of her junior year.

I WAS THE ONLY ONE — SO I HAD TO STAY STRONG

Ashley White's* seventeen-year-old boyfriend used the threat of suicide so many times that even his parents — his mother was a volunteer for the suicide hot line — shrugged off Ashley's warnings to them.

"Josh* told me that no one could help him except me," says

Ashley, who was fifteen when she began dating him, "so I had to stay strong." Josh's suicide threats were the bars that kept Ashley caged in their relationship for almost a year.

Ashley, now seventeen, is petite and pretty and has dyed blond hair, with just a hint of brown roots showing. Like my daughter Jenny, she is an honor student and loves dance — jazz, tap, pointe. Although she seems reserved, her mother, after my presentation at her church's mother–daughter luncheon, has assured me that she is eager to talk to me.

"Early in the relationship, Josh seemed like a normal kid," recalls Ashley's mother, Deb, a brown-haired, heavier version of her daughter, as we all drink iced tea in a nearby coffee shop. "I liked him a lot. He was on the football team, he got decent grades, and he worked at a local grocery store." Deb had worked with Josh's mother, a registered nurse, on a teen pregnancy task force. His father was a schoolteacher in their small Iowa town.

"Josh was so fun to be with," says Ashley, becoming more friendly and animated as she remembers the early part of the relationship. "We fell in love after a few months of dating. He was my first real boyfriend. I had some of the best times of my life with him and" — she bites her lip — "and some of the worst."

After three months of romance — flowers, gifts, expensive restaurants — Josh started issuing edicts and bans: Ashley had to drop all her friends; she was not allowed to dye her hair or even to cut it, to work as a lifeguard, or to talk to any other males. She could not leave her house without calling him first and getting his approval.

Josh would rage and call Ashley "horrible" names for the most trivial infringement of his rules. "I would cry and promise never to do it again. He would give me the silent treatment until he was satisfied with all my apologies and with hearing me say over and over how much I loved him."

The one rule Ashley refused to comply with was giving up her dance lessons. "He told me if I went to dance class, he would be waiting outside, and afterward" — her eyes widen with fear as she says the words he spoke more than a year ago — "he would shoot me dead." Deb, who was as unaware of Josh's threats to her child as I had been of Mark Smith's threats to Jenny, draws her child close to her. I take her hand.

Frightened, but keeping his threats secret, Ashley missed a few dance classes. During the next class that she attended, she asked the teacher to lie if Josh called, to say she wasn't there. For further safety, she asked her parents to pick her up after class.

But Ashley never told her parents why; she knew that if she did, they would forbid the relationship to continue. "I still wanted to see him," she admits. "I just wanted him to change and stop treating me badly."

Josh once admitted to Ashley that he found the violence in his football games a sexual turn-on. Off the field, his physical action segued into pinching and pulling Ashley's arms, grabbing her wrists and squeezing them, kicking her in the genitals several times, and once, slapping her hard across the face.

But truly terrifying was his behavior each time she tried to break off the relationship. After the tears, apologies, and promises to change came the suicide threats. "I would cry that I loved him and beg him not to do it. If he died, I would hate myself forever. He would always end up not going through with it — even after the note he once left in my locker: 'By the time you read this, I will be dead.'"

One summer day, Josh escalated his suicide gamesmanship during a heated argument with Ashley on the telephone.

He kept saying: "I'm going to kill myself, and not even you can stop me this time."

I heard him playing with his friend's gun in the background, making clicking sounds with the trigger. He told me he was loading it. Then he said, "I love you, Ashley." I heard a gunshot, and the phone went dead.

I have never been so scared in my entire life. I kept calling back. Nobody would answer. I knew his parents were out of town, and my parents weren't home. He lives way out in the country. I had no way out there except by bike. I rode for miles, fighting to see through my tears. When I finally got there, he laughed. He said he couldn't believe I fell for that. After he drove me back home, I threw up, then went to my room and cried.

Deb, aware only that Josh was too controlling, learned for the first time how violent he was when she told him one day that Ashley could not go out with him because of her chores. "He kept hammering on the door, demanding that we let him in. Then he came back with his pickup truck and dumped Ashley's stuff, her magazines and scrunchies and makeup, all over the lawn and started shouting obscenities at us."

Deb called 911. By the time the police arrived, Josh had disappeared, but he left a message for Ashley on the phone, threatening suicide once more. He was picked up by the police and brought to a mental-health facility.

The diagnosis was depression. Three times in the next several months, Josh would be admitted and released from the mental institution. During the last interval, when he was in custody for several weeks, Josh wrote Ashley 110 letters, pleading with her to "stand by me. I need your help."

But Ashley was no longer standing by him; she was dating another boy. The third time Josh was released from the institution, his love letters would turn to hate e-mail, his threats of suicide to threats of murder.

HOW NINA FOUND THE COURAGE
TO BREAK UP WITH ETHAN

After almost three years with Ethan, with her self-esteem at "rock-bottom," Nina found a job as a cashier at Miracle Car Wash.

The ratio of guys to girls was probably one hundred to three. All of a sudden, I felt attractive, sexy, desired. A lot of these guys were jack-asses, but it was the nice guys who really validated me. They recognized that I was a smart woman, pretty. I didn't need this loser latching onto me, telling me that if I left him, there would never be anyone else for me. Because here was proof that someone else would want me. It flew in the face of everything he ever tried to make me believe.

At this point, I was around them more than I was around him. I got my self-esteem back — I was no longer under his thumb. I broke up with him on my eighteenth birthday.

Two weeks after Nina broke up with Ethan, she saw him sitting in his car across the street from the car wash where she worked — stalking her. "And I suddenly realized that the problem all along wasn't with me, but with him."

WHY SOME BOYS CHOOSE TO ABUSE

ALMOST FROM THE MOMENT my daughter Jenny was murdered, I started to ask *why*. Why would Mark Smith do this? What caused him to become violent? I sat at his trial and learned that he came from a seemingly normal family. I learned that he had not been in trouble with the law. Apparently, he had been a normal kid, who just committed this horrible crime out of the blue. I couldn't buy that. I couldn't believe a person could one day just snap and become violent. The defense was psychiatric: "diminished capacity," a crime of passion caused by attention deficit disorder. But, like me, the jury didn't buy it.

I wondered if Mark had been born "bad." I wondered if his family really was as normal as it was portrayed at the trial. I secretly believed that Mark's home environment must have shaped him in a violent way, but I had no proof. His family denied any dysfunction. His siblings had turned out fine. But I have always wondered what really went on behind the walls of his home.

My wonderings led me into the broader question: Where do angry — often hurting — young men come from? Why do they become abusers? I read every book I could find on boys and violence, and I interviewed experts in the field who work with violent young men and their families, as well as men who had been abusive teenagers but had transformed themselves into loving mates.

From my research, a picture gradually began to emerge. The shadings and textures may vary from portrait to portrait, but there are common threads that weave through each tapestry of abuse.

THE CRAVING FOR DOMINANCE: IS IT EVOLUTIONARY?

Since the time of the caveman, violence has been one of the most effective means of gaining and keeping control. "Violence is used as a strategy by men because it works for them — but women do not have a history of it as a successful power ploy," says Dr. Edna Rawlings.

A young man's very maleness, the stronger upper-body muscle power that has developed through evolution, can be viewed in itself as a threat, according to Dr. David Sugarman, and it often gives him an intimidating attitude: "If I have the power, I can use it." Sugarman's research reveals that many young men purposely use violence against their girlfriends in order to "frighten or force her to give [him] something."

"Boys are not born that way," says Mark Green, who runs the Adolescent Training Group supervised by Dr. David Adams at EMERGE in Cambridge, Massachusetts — a group whose purpose is to provide an alternative to violence for men who batter their wives or domestic partners. "Violence is a choice. It is a learned behavior that can be unlearned once boys are taught to recognize the thought-patterns that lead to violence."

EXTREME JEALOUSY AND POSSESSIVENESS

"No other guy better look at her." These are the words that Jacey Buel of the Dating Violence Intervention Project in Cambridge, Massachusetts, hears regularly from young abusers. "They are very jealous," he says. "Girlfriends are possessions, not people — 'My girlfriend is there for my own use. *My* girlfriend.' Her body parts are *his,* not hers."

One young man that Buel worked with had hit his girlfriend because another boy had touched her breast. The boyfriend said: "Those are my breasts; no one else can touch my breasts."

EARLY CHILDHOOD INFLUENCES

The home of the violent teen may be an environment where one adult is abusive to the other, or where the adults are abusive to the child. The teen is repeating the interactions he has seen: violence as anger management and force as a way to set things "right."

Jacey Buel says that the home lives of the boys he works with are "unbelievable. These kids have never witnessed a healthy relationship between a couple, and they don't know how to conduct one themselves. They feel perfectly justified in hitting their girl to keep her in line.

"He thinks he is teaching her a lesson. It is like a parent–child dynamic, and he must punish her. He doesn't see them on an equal level. These boys have gotten the message that if someone does something you don't like, you hit them. As little kids, they were screamed at and hit when they spilled their cereal."

ONGOING MODELS OF AGGRESSION

"I grew up in a home where my father was violent," says Chad Roehner,* who is from a Minnesota city. "I watched my mother being hit; I would come home from school and see he had her by the hair, her cheek was turning blue. I said, 'I'll never do that.' When I was nineteen years old, I got into a relationship — and that's *exactly* what I did."

Emiliano de Leon, a native of Austin, Texas, also grew up in a violent home.

> As a child, I was aggressive with my siblings; I fought more than normal with them. I hit people. I was not a bully, but I was responding aggressively. This came from not knowing how to resolve a situation.
>
> I had stepfathers. As the oldest child, I was always getting clobbered by an adult man; he was modeling to me how I could respond when somebody upset me. I had ongoing models of aggression.

When Emiliano was a sophomore in high school, he had a girlfriend. "I was possessive, easily offended, verbally and emotionally abusive. I was acting nasty a lot of the time, getting into fights with her at school, embarrassing her, hitting her in public — in the halls of the school. Nobody ever said anything."

Emiliano, who recalls being skinny and small for his age, felt that abusing his girlfriend gave him a lot of power. "I pushed her at the mall, and nobody said anything there either. She started walking away from me. I ran after her and slapped her."

Again, nobody interfered, but the girl broke up with Emiliano. "To this day, almost ten years later, she won't speak to me. I don't blame her. Looking back at the situation now, I say, 'Good for her.'"

In the long run, it turned out to be good for Emiliano too. "But at that time it registered with me that there was this woman who would no longer be with me. I realized I was becoming like my stepfathers. At that point, I went for help from my school counselor and from people in my religious life."

THE SHAME-TO-BLAME TRAJECTORY

The experts agree that as painful as physical violence is — and as much as boys suffer from being frequently yelled at — there is nothing more damaging that a father can do to a boy than shame him.

> *My father is a martial arts instructor. From early on, I was one of his best pupils, but I was also on the receiving end of his violent temper. He used to beat the crap out of me, but his beatings didn't hurt me nearly as much as his words: he'd always tell me I was no damn good, I'd never amount to anything, I'd never do anything right. And that's what I've told every girlfriend I've had — she can never do anything right.*
>
> Ed, age 19

Clinical psychologist Donald Dutton's research shows that when boys are shamed by their fathers, their very sense of who they are is threatened. Shaming is perceived as an attack on the global sense of self — "soul murder" as psychiatrist Leonard Sheingold describes it. In *The Batterer*, Dr. Dutton writes: "If I had to pick a single parental action that generated abusiveness in men, I would say it's being shamed by their fathers."

When he becomes a teenager and is dating girls, the boy's sense of self is so fragile that he responds to the slightest affront with sudden rage — wildly out of proportion to the "provocation." Anger masks his shame as he converts it to rage, then to blame — blaming her, of course.

With his mind-set of projecting blame, he plays and replays what Dutton's batterers' therapy groups call the "bitch tape" in his head. He ruminates about the girl's "bitchiness" until he explodes, and then defends his violence as "all her fault."

Twenty-year-old Garry Leinbach, who was convicted of the assault and battery that sent his girlfriend, eighteen-year-old Lynn Ann Kenny, to the hospital, admitted at the time in a telephone interview reported by the *Washington Post* Wire Service that "he had a problem with his temper and sometimes resorted to physical violence," but he blamed her for "inciting him. Psychological abuse can leave scars too, you know," he said. "She wanted to be hit. Something wasn't right to her unless she was hit."

As another batterer put it: "She triggered my actions. Push came to shove and shove came to choking."

Here are some blaming quotes taken from the batterers' groups in the Alternatives to Domestic Aggression Program of the Catholic Social Services of Washtenaw County in Ann Arbor, Michigan:

She destroyed my calm.
She messed me up.
I picked up her bad habits.
We used a lot of verbal and it turned into physical.
She set me off.
I was trying to settle her down.
She pushed my anger buttons.
I felt like she was controlling me.
She asked me to hit her.
If she was a bad woman, she deserved a pop in the eye.

I was baited into it.

She was coming after me.

THE NONNURTURING HOME

Sometimes there is no overt physical abuse or covert shaming in the home; there's just simple neglect.

The lack of nurturing in both the early and later years of life, particularly in the teenage years, can be traumatic. The lack may be obvious — the loss of a nurturing figure through death or abandonment — but it can also be subtle. The nurturing person can be physically present but emotionally absent because of depression or substance abuse. Without knowledge of how to parent or to meet a child's needs, the person is unable to give emotional sustenance. The home, chaotic and neglectful, never provides the child a peaceful and ordered environment.

"Too little love and care and too much freedom in childhood contribute strongly to the development of aggressive behavior," says Dan Olweus, a psychologist based in Norway. He finds that parents of aggressive children spend little time with their kids, leaving them without a sense of being loved and without guidelines for appropriate behavior.

In a taped TV interview, years after he murdered my daughter, Mark Smith made this statement:

> There was no family thing there for me. It's like my parents had kids and then just let us raise ourselves. I never had a curfew. No one cared if I came home or not. No one ever said they loved me, not once in my whole life. The only time my parents stood by me, went all out to help me, was after I was arrested for murdering my girlfriend.

THE NEED TO TURN CHAOS INTO CONTROL

Neglected boys who come from chaotic families are more at risk of becoming abusers. Says Jacey Buel: "The feelings of unworthiness and the unexpressed emotional neediness come together in one overwhelming need — the need to get control of one's life. The thought process is: *If I can get control of this part of my life, of my girlfriend, then I am in control of my life as well.* The feelings of internal chaos are diminished, and a sense of worthiness is reached."

Ethan felt very insecure, so he took power to the next level — violence. Scaring someone into submission with threats of violence or by actually carrying out violence is the ultimate in control.

Nina

FEARING INTIMACY AND HER "POWER" OVER HIM

Many abusive boys crave intimacy, yet fear a girl's "power" over them, a power that leaves them vulnerable. As Dr. Donald Dutton explains, boys with fearful attachment "experience strong and unresolvable push–pulls in intimacy" and are "hypersensitive to rejection." This vulnerability stems from their early ambivalent relationships with their mothers, relationships characterized by great warmth, yet also by strong feelings of rejection during the times when she is absent, unavailable, or in a seemingly hostile mood. The boy's emotions seesaw between clinginess and aloofness.

He counterbalances his closeness with his girlfriend by dominating her. He is consumed by fear. On the one hand, she may leave him; on the other hand, she may swallow him up. "Dependence on girls is ridiculed by the group," says Jacey Buel. "In a few cases, it will look like he has a healthy relationship. He seems to care for the girl's needs. He buys her lunch, and he buys her prom dress for her. But if she talks to another boy, he hits her." The perceived sense of loss fuels his panic and rage.

FOSTERING EMOTIONAL ILLITERACY AND JOCK MENTALITY

"Whether intentionally or unintentionally, we tend to discourage emotional awareness in boys," write psychologists Daniel J. Kindlon and Michael Thompson in *Raising Cain: Protecting the Emotional Life of Boys.*

In *Real Boys,* William Pollack maintains that boys in our society feel free to express only half of their emotional lives — their tough side. "At school, even with parents, you can't act like a weakling."

Pollack speaks of the "boy code," an unwritten rule that says boys and men are tough and aggressive and that they must conceal their inner feelings for fear of being perceived as sensitive or weak. Boys learn, at a painfully young age, not to cry, that acting tough is the way to survive. With years of practice, a pattern develops and becomes a part of who he is.

Concurrent with the separation process from parents, boys experiment with the tough-guy image seen everywhere in the media and in the games they play. The role models boys adopt are action heroes that "kick everybody's butt" and don't feel a thing inside.

In suppressing his emotional life, a boy learns to be silent and to suffer alone with conflicting, scary, and painful feelings. The more he learns to shut down his feelings, the more he turns to anger to let those feelings out.

The child from a nonnurturing home is in an even more dire situation. Feeling unloved or uncared for, he thinks of himself as unworthy; he builds defenses, primarily with the development of a tough facade that holds other people, as well as his own emotions, at bay. The pain caused by facing them would be too great to bear. Eventually, he loses touch with his feelings. As one boy, using a quip for cover, admitted: "I wouldn't touch them with a ten-foot pole."

Allowing someone to get too close risks having her discover how unworthy he really is. Better to be tough, to be emotionally lonely, than to be found out. "Lacking an emotional education, a boy meets the pressures of adolescence with the responses he knows are socially acceptable, manly responses of anger, aggression, and emotional withdrawal," write Kindlon and Thompson.

CULTURAL EXPECTATIONS TO BE DOMINATING

Not only in the media but in many varying cultures, the male is expected to dominate. Emiliano de Leon explains the mores in his Latino family and Texas neighborhood: "A guy is supposed to have his way and be forceful when he's dealing with his girl. I grew up with that kind of mind-set; we called it machismo. By controlling girls, I got respect from my guy friends."

De Leon, who became a child advocate at SafePlace in Austin, Texas, recalls that relationships were at the center of male talk, which included "boasting about sexual experiences and how many women you were taking advantage of."

"They learn from the older men in their world that 'women are here for me,'" says Jacey Buel. "What she says doesn't matter; he never asks for her opinion. A girl is just a girl. Girls are interchangeable. Guy friends come first."

"Their one important rule," says Rosalind Wiseman, "is that your girlfriend cannot emasculate you in front of your peers. If it looks like she's doing that, you have to control her."

Although boys and men commit most of the violent acts in our culture, Wiseman stresses that boys are "*not* the enemy. At Empower, we do not link boys and men to violence. Rather, we link *how our culture defines masculinity* to violence. We teach boys about the status they feel they need to have: How am I going to get respect? My girlfriend has to act a certain way in front of my friends. If she doesn't, does that make me less of a man?"

"My father died when I was eleven," says Chad Roehner, now in his early forties, "but I followed many other people's examples — being a tough guy, stuffing my feelings. In the neighborhood in which I grew up, violence was an option. Being in control was part of being a guy. I saw friends being disrespectful to women — on different levels of violence.

"I also learned it in church: that it was my right to be the head of the household, and wives were to submit," says Chad, a tall, handsome man with a brown beard and a warm manner. "I was acting out the beliefs that I had, who a man should be and what roles women should play."

From ages nineteen to twenty-one, Chad lived with a girlfriend.

She called the police three times because she felt fear. The third time, I was arrested. It was all very embarrassing, the court process. I never had anything before but traffic violations. I was jailed. I didn't know that what I was doing was a crime. If I slapped somebody who was walking down the street, I knew that was a crime. But I thought slapping your girlfriend was part of the relationship.

Chad was put on probation and ordered to participate in a domestic violence program. "I stopped the physical violence, but I continued to be verbally abusive to her. I was not doing things to have a healthy relationship. I was not allowing myself to be vulnerable, to experience real intimacy," says Chad, who now coordinates a program for a men's nonviolence domestic abuse intervention project in the Midwest.

Kindlon and Thompson find that popular culture is a destructive element in boys' lives, but believe that "emotional miseducation begins much closer to home."

Dr. Donald Dutton's research shows that potentially abusive boys pick up on conflict-resolving messages touting power, control, and violence differently from those who are not likely to abuse. "Indeed, they look for negative messages about women in society."

As Dutton points out in *The Batterer,* "Boys who do have a secure attachment and identity take the cultural influences as they come, rejecting some outright, picking up parts of others."

On the other hand, he finds that "the boy whose personal identity has not been buttressed by his mother's warmth and his father's presence, is the one who is most susceptible to cast about desperately for aspects of the culture that will reaffirm or justify his abusiveness."

ADDICTION TO VIOLENCE

Some batterers actually admit that they find the physical action of battering pleasurable — almost like an aerobic exercise. If they have psychopathic personalities — a lack of conscience and the ability to distance themselves emotionally — they are able to remain controlled and focused, like a well-trained athlete. Battering also becomes an effective stress-reduction technique, releasing the body's built-up tension.

The abuser's rage, even if expressed only verbally, is what Dutton calls a "highly self-reinforcing emotion that carries with it built-in rewards." Anger energizes a young man and advertises his potency and determination. Consistent with his notion of manliness, it enhances his self-image. And it works! He gets his way.

Dutton stresses that anger also "short-circuits anxious feelings of vulnerability . . . For a man it is less distressing to be angry than to feel afraid."

TOO BARREN OR TOO FULL

Jacey Buel separates the abusing young men he sees into two categories: (1) the young men who come from abusive, barren backgrounds and (2) the middle-class young men who have been indulged.

"The kids who lead a barren existence have bad grades, no interest in sports, no job," says Buel. "They are not going to college. They have a negative relationship with their mothers. They have no father.

"You can't scare them, because there are no consequences for their behavior, nothing to hold over them. There is no hope for the future, no concept of what a nice life is all about. They receive only negative reinforcement in their lives, from teachers, parents.

"They are kids with nothing to lose. There is no fear that the girl will call the police. They live in neighborhoods where no one calls the police for anything. The lack of self-esteem is almost universal among them. They have internalized this feeling: *They don't respect me*. They feel they must scare women into staying with them. They are incapable of positive self-talk."

None of the kids Buel sees has received positive self-talk from the parents or adults in his life. "He has been taught that life is always bad." Buel tries to "rephrase things for them, put things in a positive way, because they don't know how to do it."

At the other end of the spectrum are the kids with the "frat boy" mentality. "These boys," says Buel, "have been indulged by their parents (but not nurtured, in many cases) and have developed a sense of entitlement. They are spoiled — 'I can have whatever I want' — and believe they *should* have it. They think life is to hang out, drink, take vacations, and get laid. They view girls as designed only for their own pleasure.

"The more affluent kids feel that they can get away with abuse because the girl will be too ashamed to tell or because she won't be believed. They are also counting on the fact that no one is going to say or do anything if they witness abuse."

ORGANIC BRAIN DAMAGE?

While most abusers can control their behavior, some experts believe there is a small minority that have insufficient control over their anger impulses. Any slight stimulus sets off a reaction of fury.

In *The Batterer,* Dutton describes the individual with "intermittent explosive disorder," or IED, as one who "bursts intermittently into an uncontrollable rage out of all proportion to what preceded it." The victim of these outbursts is typically someone he's very close to — such as a girlfriend. But Dutton disagrees with the interpretation of many of his colleagues. He points out that since "the violence only occurs in the context of intimacy and typically in private," it cannot be called "uncontrollable."

Neurological damage from prior head injuries — from early childhood abuse, even *in utero* trauma from the mother's drug or alcohol abuse — is sometimes seen as the cause of violent behavior. In every case in which Dutton suspected neurological damage, the abusers also had "rageful relationships with their parents. The neurology, by itself, was only part of the story."

ALCOHOL AND SUBSTANCE ABUSE

Most therapists and researchers have found that a large percentage of assaultive men abuse alcohol and drugs. Some studies find that when combined with their already volatile personality traits, it puts them at "an ever greater risk for violence," allowing them to lose all restraint. However, when the men say, "The alcohol — or the drugs — made me do it," they're blaming one symptom, violence, on another, substance abuse, which according to Dutton are two different aspects of an abusive personality.

SOLVING A MYSTERY

A year after her eighteen-year-old nephew had assaulted and raped his fifteen-year-old ex-girlfriend in California, Yola Feldman,* the mother of one of my son's elementary school classmates, called to ask if we could talk. *Why me?* I wondered. She knew I was a counselor . . . but she also knew Jenny's story. I had never counseled a member of a perpetrator's family — or wanted to. I was on "the other side," still trying to deal with my sometimes irrational hostility toward Mark Smith's mother, who had never even apologized to me. There were countless agencies for perpetrators' families, but something in Yola's voice made her seem needy. I agreed to meet her for coffee at a diner.

Although Mark Smith's mother had never apologized, Yola seemed to be doing it for her, admitting that she could not possibly compare her family's pain to the pain of the victim's family. But, beginning in a tentative way, she explained that her sister and brother-in-law were still reeling from the crime. And so was she. And she did know there were parallels between Mark Smith and her nephew Gabe.* Their respectable, intact middle-class family backgrounds. Their previous crime-free records. Their other siblings who were apparently leading exemplary lives.

As she drank her coffee, Yola seemed to be voicing her own thoughts rather than searching out any insight from mine. She was still utterly perplexed. How could her adorable, angel-faced nephew have committed this atrocious act? In her desire to stand by her family and in her enormous compassion and fear for a nephew sent into the prison system, she had let herself focus on Gabe's endearing traits — his charm and affectionate ways, his sense of humor. How he had always loved to help "Auntie Yolie" cook and garden when he spent a few vacation days with her.

But as she was speaking, she began adding other pieces to fill in the puzzle. Yes, her "high-spirited" nephew had been a difficult child at home. He had bullied the kids in his neighborhood for years and had a penchant for torturing cats. His parents — Yola was his mother's sister — had not been able to control him. Like Mark Smith's parents, they were told that he had attention deficit disorder. But Ritalin did not seem to help Gabe. Nor did his father. According to his aunt, his father frequently humiliated him in front of the extended family, calling him a no-good son of a bitch. Once, he accidentally closed the door on Gabe's fingers — then laughed.

Yola and I agreed: these events did not solve the mystery, but they gave telling clues.

As Dutton reiterates, the primary factors that produce an abuser are

- A shaming, abusive, or absent father
- A mother whom the child perceives as all-powerful, but who is only intermittently warm and available
- Ultramacho sex-role socialization

In combination, he believes they make a potent mixture for mayhem, putting these boys at a much higher risk for becoming abusive.

But he also finds that *most* men who grow up on this formula, while probably suffering from emotional problems, do *not* become abusers themselves. Like Gabe's siblings, they do not mimic the violent behavior they have been exposed to.

To complicate the mystery further, despite coming from toxic homes, some sons of abusive fathers become fervently nonviolent. Perhaps they are deliberately defining themselves as polar opposites to their hurtful parents. Another possible explanation: they might have been influenced by a supportive adult in an otherwise hostile neighborhood.

But the mystery remains. Along with parenting, some scientists believe that part of the answer lies in patterning — the sequencing of the DNA. Research indicates the possible presence of a "daredevil gene" exhibited in the risk-taking or thrill-seeking behavior of violent criminals — *and* war heroes.

As psychologist James Garbarino states in *Lost Boys: Why Our Sons Turn Violent and How We Can Save Them,* these boys are not born bad; they are born with difficult temperaments. They start out as cranky babies, difficult toddlers. According to Kindlon and Thompson, many have "conduct disorder" — bullying from the time they're young, violating societal rules and the basic rights of others. The signs are showing aggression to people or animals; destruction of property; deceitfulness; theft; serious violations of the rules.

Because these boys are so difficult to nurture, yet *nurtured* they must be, parents often find themselves — at best — running in place. Garbarino believes that morality *can* be developed if it is nurtured, that these boys can be taught to realize they have inflicted pain on someone else. He believes that they can develop an emotional conscience, that they can learn the skills of love and empathy.

Most of the experts agree: every behavior is influenced by multiple forces, ranging from biology to community.

PART TWO

WHAT A PARENT CAN DO

SEVEN

WARNING SIGNS
How to Spot an Abusive Relationship

MANY OF US FIND it hard to believe that our bright, accomplished teen daughters would actually allow themselves to be in an abusive relationship. "Even in this day and age, some people keep their heads in the sand when it comes to their own children," says Karen Harker. "These parents are the hardest to reach."

But even those of us who are aware of what's out there might not recognize abuse when it's happening to our own child.

Although Carly knew that her daughter Nina's relationship with Ethan had become sexual and was making Nina unhappy, like many other mothers, she never realized the relationship was coercive and battering until it was over.

But the experts concur that there are definite clues that parents can look for from the very outset of their teenager's romance.

Her boyfriend's love is very intense and begins at a whirlwind pace. "If he is saying 'I love you' and talking about 'our marriage' almost from the beginning, watch out! It is so seductive for her. You see this especially in an older guy–younger girl relationship," says therapist Barrie Levy, "but it happens with young teens too."

Two weeks after they started dating was the first time they said they loved each other. They were both fifteen! They hadn't even been

friends; she didn't even know him before. It was her first relationship.
To us, he seemed so normal in the beginning. I should have reserved
my opinion. I was too easily fooled.

Mim, mother of Kathryn, age 17

He checks up on her a lot, calling her constantly. "Notice this!" says
Levy. "If this behavior lasts more than three weeks, she is heading
into a controlling relationship — which leads directly to an abusive
one."

He is obsessed with her whereabouts, possibly even making her carry
a beeper. When he pages her, she must call him back immediately.
You may also find out that he is calling her siblings or her friends
to find out where she is and what she is doing.

Wherever she goes, he happens to show up. He will pretend it's co-
incidence, but his "coincidences" defy mathematical probability.

Whatever Jillian was doing, Matt would know. If she went out with
her friends for ice cream, he would join them. When we went shop-
ping at the mall, Matt would suddenly appear. He always seemed to
find out about her plans, even if she didn't tell him. He always knew
where she was.

Virginia, mother of Jillian, age 14

She seems afraid to anger him. You hear her on the phone, repeatedly explaining where she has been, whom she has seen, what she
is wearing, as if answering an interrogation. She is tense, frequently
crying and apologizing, perhaps denying that she has been coming
on to other guys.

You see or learn from others that he loses his temper easily, and when
under stress, he hits walls or smashes objects. You may have heard
stories that he has been violent to someone other than your daughter. She may be both flattered and appalled that he has struck another boy who showed interest in her. "This kind of explosiveness

is intimidating," says Levy, "and just as frightening as violence directly aimed at your daughter."

You have heard him yell at her or call her names — supposedly just kidding around. If he does this in your presence, you can infer how much worse the verbal abuse gets when they are alone.

He is prone to sudden mood changes, from laughter to fury. According to *Dating Violence: An Anti-Victimization Program*, a curriculum from the Texas Council on Family Violence, dramatic mood swings are "typical of men who beat their partners, and they are just another way to take control and manipulate a person."

> *All kinds of stupid stuff would cause his outbursts. One time, there was a huge fight because Kerrie bumped the volume on his CD player, but some things she thought he'd be furious over turned out to be no big deal. It was like she was living on a minefield; she could never predict what his reaction would be.*
>
> Angela, mother of Kerrie, age 16

He does not interact well with your family. He seems squirmy and ill at ease, especially when anyone asks him questions. Nor can he stand his own family, who, he tells your daughter, have abused him.

He lacks his own interests and goals and is overly dependent upon the relationship. Your daughter — "every breath she takes, every move she makes" — is his primary focus, his "career track."

> *He was putting pressure on her not to go away to college. He would say: "I need attention, I need someone here all the time."*
>
> Candace, mother of Klara, age 17

> *He just latched onto her as if his life depended on it. "I can't be everything to him all the time," she finally told me. "I'm not his mother. I don't want to be his mother."*
>
> Sharon, mother of Julie, age 17

She's becoming more distant from you and more secretive, avoiding eye contact. Sometimes you feel as if your child has been "stolen" and replaced by a giant peapod from whom this stranger has emerged.

> *We used to talk all night after she came home from a date, but when she started seeing Bill, she would tell me very little. If she would only talk to me, I'd say to myself, but I couldn't get her to open up. Everything about the relationship seemed so secret. It seemed as if we were losing her.*
>
> Julianne, mother of Lola, age 17

She cuts herself off from her friends, saying she has no time for them, or is suddenly finding faults with them. If derogatory remarks like "slut," "whore," and "lesbo" don't sound like your daughter's talk, she's probably parroting his.

> *The biggest warning sign to us was when she stopped hanging out with her best friends. Kristy was a child who had been blessed since she was tiny with a wonderful network of grandparents, best friends, aunts, uncles, cousins, and a web of music teachers. He isolated her from all of us.*
>
> Gwyn, mother of Kristy, age 15

She drops all her outside activities — clubs, family outings, church or synagogue. Your formerly high-energy daughter claims she has neither the time nor the energy for the things she used to love. An abusive relationship drains the girl of energy. She spends what she has left trying to please the abuser.

> *My daughter loved acting and singing in the Broadway musicals her high school would put on each year. She was hoping to major in theater in college. But when she started seeing Liam in her senior year, he convinced her that all the rehearsals took too much time away from him. He called the guys in the plays a bunch of "losers" or "fags" and the girls, "sluts." I could see in her eyes that she was dying to try*

out for the part of Laurey in Oklahoma! *or at least work on the costumes. But he demanded every spare moment of her time.*

Anne, mother of Brittany, age 17

Her weight either balloons or drops dramatically. Changes in weight, gains or losses, are a common symptom of abuse and are often caused by the stress and anxiety in the relationship.

Moira became very distant and irritable, and she started losing a lot of weight. She was not eating, we later learned, because he was telling her she was too fat and nobody would want her.

Paula, mother of Moira, age 16

Her grades begin to drop. She may even be cutting classes.

When my daughter entered college, she had been an A student. But then she started seeing Byron. By the time she finished her first year, she was put on probation.

Janet, mother of Larissa, age 18

He roughhouses and play-wrestles with her. Sometimes it appears to you that it is not as playful as it seems.

She apologizes for his behavior. She makes excuses for him or becomes defensive and hostile when you make the slightest criticism of him.

Her appearance dramatically changes. She may no longer take her usual care in dressing or wearing makeup.

I saw that she was dressing as a "college grunge," no more preppy style, just layers and layers of loose-fitting clothes or jeans and sweats. He wanted her to dress in a way that didn't draw attention to her body.

Jane, mother of Lynn, age 17

She wears clothing inappropriate for the weather — long sleeves, turtlenecks — to cover bruises. She gives illogical explanations for injuries that you can see — bruises, red marks (as from a slap), a limp, clumps of hair missing, torn clothes, burn or choke marks.

> *All of a sudden, after she had been seeing Brian for about six months, she became a klutz — tripping over furniture, slipping on steps, even getting her scarf caught in doors. Twice, she got hit on the head with a basketball. Everything was suddenly happening to her! It had to be more than sheer klutziness and lousy luck.*
>
> Susan, mother of Brooke, age 15

She finds it difficult to make decisions on her own. Abused girls may appear anxious about making independent decisions because they must continually "get permission" from their boyfriends.

She cries easily or overreacts to minor incidents. The girl who lives in fear of more abuse is under extreme stress, trying to second-guess her boyfriend's moods in order to avoid his violence. At home, she may explode about something minor.

> *I asked her to run over to the supermarket and get me another French bread for the company we were having for dinner. She bit my head off and then went slamming into her room in hysterics. This was not my sweet and generous daughter. Since she'd been seeing Paul, her whole personality had changed.*
>
> Ruth, mother of Amy, age 16

> *Julie and Mike were dating all through their senior year, but during that time, Julie seemed mad at the world. She stopped smiling and back-talked us. "You're angry all the time," I told her, but we never connected her moodiness with the way Mike was treating her. We really liked Mike. We just didn't see the abuse. Maybe it's because we wanted him to be as good as he appeared.*
>
> Sharon, mother of Julie, age 16

He's fascinated by violence and weapons, or hangs out with a crowd or comes from a family that is. As trauma psychologist Shelley Neiderbach observes: "More guys than ever before are packing heat these days." In his book *Protecting the Gift: Keeping Children and Teenagers Safe (and Parents Sane),* Gavin de Becker, a threat-assessment expert, describes the gun as a device that grants the young male "power and identity," makes him feel "dangerous and safe at the same time," instantly turns him into "the dominant male," and connects him to his "evolutionary essence." Although de Becker is not advocating government gun control, he emphasizes what should be obvious: "Teenage boys with handguns are more dangerous than teenage boys without handguns."

He regularly drinks and/or uses drugs. While alcohol and substance abuse are not the basic causes of abusive behavior, "it's like pouring gasoline on a fire," says children's advocate Emiliano de Leon. "It makes men who are abusive more scary — willing to be more violent." But typically they are able to choose the time and place of their violence — instead of acting out at the drinking party, they wait until they get their girlfriends alone.

It is well documented, says Barrie Levy, that male partners play a key role in initiating young women to drugs and alcohol. "Sometimes they drink together or use drugs together to sustain the connection between them or her caretaking role."

Emiliano de Leon observes that more young men are drugging women and taking advantage of them, "actually date-raping them. The women often blame themselves. They say they made a bad decision, and they continue to go with the guy because they still like him."

"Drinking, along with abuse and rape, is very prevalent in relationships on campus," says Sarah Buel. "The perpetrator will say to his girlfriend: 'We were both drunk, let's just forget it, it doesn't mean anything,' but she can't forget it. It has an impact on her studies. She often calls the clinic anonymously, afraid of giving her name, afraid he might be thrown out of school."

EIGHT

LEARNING ALL YOU CAN ABOUT THE RELATIONSHIP

IF YOU SUSPECT your daughter is in an unhealthy relationship, it is vital that you keep the channels of communication open with her in a supportive, nonalienating way. As immature as she may be, she thinks she is truly in love.

"What parents have to understand is that their daughter's feelings are real," says Shanterra McBride, director of education and programs for Empower.

McBride, who has degrees in sociology and public affairs, stresses that parents should never dismiss the importance of having a boyfriend.

Many girls believe that they must have a boyfriend to make themselves feel complete — no matter how accomplished they are in other areas. It is a true feeling. Moms shouldn't feel bad if they can't complete their daughters. No matter how many affirmations of their daughters' accomplishments and qualities they give them, they don't fulfill the desire to have a boyfriend.

McBride herself recalls how she dismissed her mother's affirmations when she was in high school — "Oh, you're just saying that because you're my mom."

"A lot of girls need someone who cares for them, who they can walk down the halls with holding hands. Parents belittle that fact. They forget about the pressures in high school."

"In high school, the focus on dating has never been greater," says Sarah Buel, who has been working in the violence-against-women field since 1977. "Even girls with strong career goals at prestigious colleges and graduate schools feel their top priority is having a guy."

"Teens don't tell their parents about the abuse, because they think they won't understand the intensity of the relationship," says Barri Rosenbluth. "So it becomes their own personal business." But as parents we need to make it *our* business to learn all about our child's relationship . . . in spite of the myriad distractions of our own lives.

Rosalind Wiseman recommends that parents focus on the interaction between the couple, the day-to-day situation. As Carly reflects:

There are a lot of times I wish I had been more aware — but I was in a fog, going through a divorce. My gut told me something wasn't right — Nina's grades were dropping, he wasn't treating her so well — but I had no inkling about the things he did to her. Later, when I found out, I thought, How could I be so blind? *Looking back, I think I should have followed my gut instinct and questioned her more about the relationship. But knowing Nina, I think she would have only told me when she was ready.*

"All parents have to be vigilant in observing their children's relationships," says Leah Aldridge, director of Youth Violence Prevention Policy and Training, a program of the Los Angeles Commission on Assaults Against Women (LACAAW).

The trend is that when they were young, we were superinvolved in their activities and play dates, but once they're in middle school — and especially in high school — we pull away, thinking they're self-sufficient. But that's the time we should step up our involvement. A parent must know whom she's going to the mall with, where she's going on dates. And get to know her child's boyfriend and *his parents.*

Sharon Hoberman* thought she knew her daughter's boyfriend very well. Julie* had been seeing Mike* for a year as part of a group of friends in their high school in an affluent town in Kansas. "They started out just being good friends before they dated. That's the way it should be, I thought," says Sharon. But Sharon did not know Mike's parents or his problems — he was living in his car throughout his senior year because his parents had kicked him out of their home. Sharon would not meet them until they appeared with high-priced lawyers, pleading with Sharon and Julie to drop charges of burglary and assault against their son.

HOW TO MORE FULLY ENGAGE YOUR DAUGHTER

Although your daughter's boyfriend's faults may be glaringly obvious to you, resist criticizing his appearance, manner, or lack of goals. Instead, encourage her to tell you what she loves about him. Ask her: "What does he do to make you feel so special?"

Shanterra McBride finds that girls will often say: "He is helping me feel good about myself, to feel beautiful when I'm around him." She urges parents to "understand that feeling, that need for the boy. It can be just as powerful as your own feeling that you want to protect her. *Hear* her when she says she really loves him." If you are being supportive — telling her that you love her and understand that she cares about him — she may feel free to reveal the times when he makes her feel bad about herself, when he tells her, for example, that she's dumb and ugly.

When that time arises, counter with: "How could someone who loves you talk to you this way? Would you have said the same thing to him? Does he have a different agenda than you?"

Make her aware of the kinds of behaviors that are not normal in a healthy relationship. If your daughter sees that you are working toward a more open relationship with her, that you value her thoughts and feelings and want to help her, you can try direct questions — framing them more in the manner of a self-test or quiz from a magazine rather than an interrogation: "Is he always checking up on you? Does he always decide what you both will do? Does he get jealous easily and have a violent temper?" Or you

RELATIONSHIP QUIZ

- Are you afraid of his temper or to disagree with him?
- Does he yell at you or make fun of you in front of your friends?
- Does he keep checking up on you several times a night? Or showing up unexpectedly wherever you are?
- Does he blame you for how he feels?
- Does he ever treat you roughly — grab, push, pinch, shove, or kick you to "get your attention," throw things at you or hit you?
- Does he tell you what to wear and how much makeup to use?
- Has he ever threatened you to get his way? Or threatened to hurt himself if you break up? Or to hurt you?
- Does he play with guns or use them to protect himself against other people?
- Do you keep things from him so as not to upset him?
- Does he put down your accomplishments or goals?
- Does he tell you that you are nothing without him?
- Does he try to keep you from leaving after a fight? Or leave you somewhere after a fight to "teach you a lesson"?
- Does he tell you which friends you can see?
- Have you been frightened by his violence toward others?
- Has he wrongfully and repeatedly accused you of flirting or making out with others?

This self-quiz needs no numerical scoring key. Any "yes" answer gives you an opening to define and discuss the abusive behavior with your daughter in a calm, straightforward way. Her "no" answers to the questions involving physical violence may be less than truthful; revelations of battering might be too embarrassing to her and might make her fearful of your reaction.

can actually use the Relationship Quiz shown in the sidebar on page 103.

"Many times," says Barrie Levy, "the physical violence is a small part of an abusive relationship, but the *threat* of violence is great. And the emotional undermining is more damaging."

"I DIDN'T SEE THE CHANGE"

When Jennifer Coleman was a sixteen-year-old Brunswick, Maine, high school junior and cheerleader, she fell in love with the seventeen-year-old captain of the football team. They were both athletes — on the track team together. And he had no problem being away from Jennifer when she worked part time at the Pizza Hut: "He liked spending the money I made," says Jennifer, a tall redhead with a well-toned body and a vibrant personality. Now in charge of the satellites for the Smithsonian Observatory in Boston, Jennifer wrote about her relationship for *Teen Ink: Our Voices, Our Visions,* a collection of essays by teenagers from the magazine of the same name.

> *It was a slow process, but in the next fourteen months I became a whole new person. I went from being energetic and bubbly to a quiet person who had withdrawn from the world. I was so wrapped up in the thought of having an older, more popular jock for a boyfriend that I didn't see the change.*

Nor did Jennifer's parents. They loved her boyfriend, and because he came from a dysfunctional family and lived with an older sister, they parented him and bought him gifts. Slowly, Jennifer began to notice:

> *It was that first summer that all my goals, values, and dreams were crushed. By this time I didn't need to be my own person. I had someone running my life for me. I didn't need to make decisions for myself. I was told what to wear and where to wear it.*
> *That was the first time I sensed something was wrong, but by then*

I was so scared, that I couldn't stand up to him. He had his list of people with whom I wasn't allowed to talk. If I was caught chatting with anyone on this list, he would punch walls, windows, anything in reach, anything but me. Because I "loved" him, I didn't want to make him hurt himself, so I obeyed his stupid rules.

He had become abusive and was getting more and more physical. Not just gritting his teeth, he was now pushing and threatening me with his fist in my face. Although he never hit me, he had his ways. Otherwise, I wouldn't have had a reason to be scared.

Jennifer's best friend, whom she was no longer allowed to see, had told her at the outset that something wasn't right, but at that time Jennifer was too much in love to notice. And she would not share her concerns with her parents — not until he was threatening and stalking her, and she felt her life was in danger.

STRESS THAT YOUR DAUGHTER NOT KEEP ABUSE SECRET

In *A Parent's Handbook: How to Talk to Your Children About Developing Healthy Relationships,* a pamphlet written for Liz Claiborne, Inc., Richard Gallagher, Ph.D., the director of the Parenting Institute of New York University's Child Study Center says:

Tell your kids that while it's okay to have special shared thoughts or memories in a relationship, girls in particular need to learn that secrecy that isolates them from friends and family is not acceptable. In fact, too much secrecy in a relationship can be the first sign of manipulation and coercion.

"And of danger," adds Barrie Levy. "Although they keep secrets from their parents, they will tell the boy anything."

"The more that your daughter keeps the emotional, sexual, and physical abuse secret from family and friends, the more ashamed she becomes," write Levy and her coauthor, Patricia Occhiuzzo Giggans, director of the Los Angeles Commission on Assaults Against Women, in *What Parents Need to Know About Dating Vio-*

lence. "As a parent, by maintaining your communication and connection with your child, you may be able to interfere with these attempts to isolate her."

Assure her that you're there to help her — not to judge. Tell her that you would like to brainstorm together, to aid her in solving the problem, not to force her to stop seeing him — *unless you believe she is in imminent physical danger.*

"If you have a good relationship with both young people, sit down with your child and ask her if you may talk to her boyfriend," suggests Karen Harker. "Do this *with caution,*" she warns. "You must ask her how he will react to it. If she agrees, talk to him separately. Sometimes it works, it helps break the isolation, to let him know that other people know what he's been doing."

"Many boys are just as confused about relationships as girls are," notes Rosalind Wiseman. "Many boys who are abusive don't even know that they are — and don't really want to be."

No matter how open and helpful you try to be, there is no certainty that your daughter will talk to you about her relationship in general, or about the violence in particular. But in order for you to be effective in helping her stay safe, "you need to know what she is dealing with, and she needs to know that you can help. *Communication between you is essential for her safety,*" write Levy and Giggans.

If her side of the communication is monosyllabic or hostile, they suggest you express your own uneasiness about the relationship by making empathic observations. For example, you might say: "I hear you apologizing over and over to Todd on the phone, and you sound so unhappy. I'm worried about the impact all this is having on your self-esteem." This will let her know that you know and care — without putting her on the defensive, as her boyfriend is always doing — and perhaps get her to assess the situation more realistically herself.

LEARNING INDIRECTLY ABOUT THE RELATIONSHIP

If your daughter remains uncommunicative, you may have to use other sources to get information.

The experts agree that it is a good idea to try asking her friends.

At first, they may be reluctant and feel that they are betraying her. It may be necessary to ask more than once. Tell them how worried you are about her. Although they may be torn — between their loyalty to her and their own discomfort about the abuse — they may be relieved to unburden themselves to you. And so may your daughter. "After ending battering relationships, several girls have told us they were relieved their friends told their parents about the violence, even though at the time it made them mad," explain Levy and Giggans.

Very often, a girl's siblings will know more about the abuse than the parents. While Sharon and her husband were completely un-aware that Julie's boyfriend, Mike, was hitting her and shoving her around, Julie's younger sister was not.

Bailey,* who was fifteen at the time, vividly recalls the day she eavesdropped on Julie and Mike when her parents were at work. "What else does a nosy little sister do?" says Bailey. She heard Mike raising his voice and then "the most hideous sound ever. I heard Julie say: 'Michael, you can't hit me. Remember we talked about this?' and I could tell she was in pain." Bailey barged into the room and confronted Mike.

> Mike was standing near Julie; he looked like he was trying to apolo-gize. "I'm only going to ask this once," I said. "Did you hit her?" Mike approached me. "You little witch. How dare you walk in here and accuse me of that." He moved closer. "Get out of my face, you stupid jerk," I said, as I walked over to Julie. He got right in my face and said, "Don't ever back-talk me." When I spat out, "I'm not your toy, so don't tell me what to do," he raised his fist as if to hit me. "Go ahead, hit me, I dare you," I taunted. "No! Mike, don't touch her," Julie said. I could tell she was surprised she'd stood up for me, but I was glad. "Get out of my house and don't ever touch my sister again," I said. I was no longer scared. He turned to Julie, and she pointed to the door. He walked out, and I heard him sniffle.

Julie thanked Bailey and begged her not to tell their parents. "I can't keep this quiet," Bailey said. Julie pleaded: "He promised not to do it again." Bailey told her: "If he touches you again, I'll tell

Mom and Dad." Mike did "touch" Julie again — many times — but Bailey would not learn of it until her sister believed her life was in danger.

Teachers and other adults at school may notice a girl's boyfriend abusing her, but assume the parents are aware of it. "Many adults who see abuse still feel that if it's not their child, they shouldn't intervene — but some schools have implemented programs to see that there's less interaction between her and the perpetrator," says Karen Harker.

Elmont High School on Long Island is anything but a "why should I intervene, it's not my child" school. Principal Diane Scricca explains:

> We have a policy in Elmont School District to report everything — from sexual harassment to dating violence. If teachers notice abusive behavior in hallways or on school grounds, they must report it to the administration. I enforce this policy. We try to identify the issue before it becomes serious.

It is usually a third party who reports the abuse, says Scricca. "Many times, friends of the abused girl tell a teacher, or a teacher may overhear that a girl is being stalked. We call the girl and the boy in separately, then together."

Scricca and her assistant principal carefully investigate the validity of the charges. Once they are convinced of their credibility, they warn the abuser and write up a report, which goes on his school record. "And we let the parents of both the boy and girl know — even if the girl doesn't want us to because she's scared of her boyfriend. Even if she denies the abuse, I would absolutely tell her parents. Sometimes the parents do have a clue, but sometimes they are not aware."

As principal, Scricca cannot press criminal charges unless the abuse is done to her personally. "Bringing criminal charges is up to the parent," she says.

She stresses that the effectiveness of the school policy depends on the level of enforcement. That level is high in Elmont High School because of her vigilance and the heightened awareness of the students. Not only is dating violence part of the health-class curriculum, but each year, one hundred children are trained by Pamela Linker, the school's health instructor and counselor, to become peer helpers, who counsel other children in the school.

Even if you have heard nothing from the school about your child's relationship but suspect something may be amiss, you can take the initiative yourself and contact the principal, the vice principal, a counselor, or a particular teacher who knows your child well. You can ask if they've noticed any changes in her behavior, seen any incidents of abuse by her boyfriend, or heard about incidents from her friends.

"SNOOPING RIGHTS"

"Snooping is a parent's right because she has to protect her child," states Dr. Edna Rawlings. Dr. Carol Eagle agrees. "In spite of the mess in her room, go into it. The diary that a girl leaves on top of her bureau is asking to be read. She may be too embarrassed to tell her mother directly about her sexual activity. Anything that's left out is left out for a purpose."

As conflicted as you may be about respecting your child's privacy, you may even have to listen in on her telephone conversations or check out her e-mail.

Both Dr. Eagle and Dr. Rawlings agree that it is vital for mothers to be aware of what's going on in their children's lives. "Many parents are too busy these days to get to know their adolescent," says Dr. Rawlings.

Or to realize the danger she may be in.

Gwyn Broome,* the mother of Kristy, whose story you read in chapter 5, tells how she confirmed her suspicions about her daughter's boyfriend:

I read her journal when she was fifteen; first and only time I've done it. I hated it. It made me sick. When she and her girlfriend got in, I had the journal sitting on the kitchen table, I was right up front. I said to her, "I was afraid you were getting hurt, and I went up and read it and this is a problem."

NINE

EARLY INTERVENTION

ONE OF THE PRIMAL EMOTIONS you will feel when you *know* your child is in an abusive relationship is rage. Another is fear. *Distraught* would not be exaggerating your state of mind. The truth can be all the more shocking "since so many adults don't realize that their teenager is in an intimate relationship as well as an abusive one," observes Rosalind Wiseman.

> *I think parents want you to lie to them. They really don't want to know that something wrong is going on with their kid. Once the parents and the kid open up to each other, once the parents get over the initial shock, I think they can really help. They need to realize that their child needs them to be strong, to take a real nonjudgmental approach, not to fall apart.*
>
> Nadine, age 17

HOW TO INTERVENE EFFECTIVELY

Resist the impulse to give her an ultimatum: "You are never to see him again!" "To an adolescent, nothing is as romantic and devastating as forbidden love," says Dr. Noelle Nelson.

"Parents should realize the risk of forbidding the relationship," says Barrie Levy. "You will get into an escalating power struggle with your daughter as intense as the struggle she is having with him. Parents can end up pushing the girl toward the guy. The stronger the parent–daughter relationship, the more conflicted the girl will feel. Parents should find the line where they are using their *influence* as a parent, not their *power* as a parent."

There is of course a caveat to this advice. If your daughter is in immediate danger of serious injury, if her life is in jeopardy, Levy recommends that you take radical action (like taking her far from home to live with relatives, particularly when the girl does not want to go). Dr. Shelley Neiderbach concurs: "Put her in the trunk of your car and drive her across the country."

TAKE TIMELY ACTION

"If the abusive relationship isn't broken up quickly, it gets worse," Dr. Neiderbach stresses. "The longer the relationship goes on, the harder it is to break the pattern."

Use reason and subtle persuasion. Rather than setting up a Romeo-and-Juliet scenario, New York City teen psychologist Carol Eagle recommends that both parents seriously discuss the relationship with their child. "Dating is one area in which input from Dad can be very beneficial. He can 'demystify' the male sex. He can offer some insight on how boys typically think and what healthy behavior would be. But the girl has to discover the truth of the relationship for herself."

Teach her the dynamics of abuse. "Girls need this basic education," says Los Angeles attorney Meredith Blake, who recalls her own innocence about the subject during her first relationship:

> *I was fourteen, he was sixteen. It was in the mid-eighties. At that time I had never even heard the words "domestic violence" — or any talk of it at home. I didn't know that my boyfriend was being abusive when he told me I had to be home when he phoned, that I couldn't go out with my friends. I bought into his controlling behaviors. He*

told me I was lucky to have him, that I wouldn't find another boyfriend. I thought everything wrong in the relationship was my own fault. Then his emotional and verbal abuse became physical.

Meredith was embarrassed, yet considered herself fortunate when a "good guy friend" confronted her about the abuse. "The end of the school year and my subsequent move to live with my dad (my parents had divorced several years prior) helped me to walk away from that relationship." After this experience, Meredith still thought "dating abuse was not a subject to be spoken about."

Again I am astonished when I think about the parallels between Meredith and my daughter Jenny: both teenagers in the mid-eighties, both surrounded by the same wall of secrecy and shame.

In college, however, Meredith "started hearing stories. I realized it didn't just happen to me — this wasn't just about my not knowing how to be a good girlfriend. It had happened to many others."

Now the director of Break the Cycle, a Los Angeles–based organization that targets its relationship-violence prevention programs and legal services to young people from ages twelve to twenty-two, Meredith Blake finds that there is still widespread unawareness about the dynamics of abuse. "Kids couldn't be more surprised to learn that verbal and emotional abuse are part of an abusive situation," she reports.

Teach her the rights she should have in a relationship. Many teen dating violence programs throughout the country have formulated "Bills of Rights" for dating teens. From them, I have put together an amalgam of "rights" I believe parents should emphasize. (See the sidebar on page 113.)

Engage in a continuing dialogue with your daughter. Says Leah Aldridge: "Try not to be judgmental," — admittedly difficult — "since parents tend to criticize their child's messiness, hairstyle, study habits."

If your daughter declares that her relationship is healthy because it is not physically violent, Aldridge suggests that you say words to

BILL OF TEEN DATING RELATIONSHIP RIGHTS

- I have the right to be treated with respect.
- I have the right *not* to be abused — physically, emotionally, or sexually.
- I have the right to say no and be heard.
- I have the right to express my own opinions.
- I have the right to private time and my own space.
- I have the right to have my needs considered as much as my partner's.
- I have the right to have friends of my own.
- I have the right to pursue my own special interests — and not be criticized for pursuing them.
- I have the right to accept a gift without having to give anything in return.
- I have the right to hear about my strengths and assets.
- I have the right to ask others for help if I need it.
- I have the right to live a violence-free life.
- I have the right to change my mind — to "fall out of love" and live with no threats.

Adapted from "Male and Female Rights and Responsibilities in a Dating Relationship" by the New Jersey Department of Community Affairs — Division on Women, the Office on the Prevention of Violence Against Women, and the "Teen Bill of Rights" from *Reaching and Teaching Teens to Stop Violence* by the Nebraska Domestic Violence Sexual Assault Coalition.

this effect: "Okay, so he doesn't hit you, but he calls you names and yells at you and decides where you can go and what you can wear. That doesn't sound like a healthy relationship to me."

"'You don't deserve to be abused' is the most effective thing adults have ever told girls — words that really get through," explains Sarah Buel. "That declaration came as big news for a lot of girls in my focus groups," she says.

Check your own relationship as a model for hers. "The parents may have to examine their own relationship, how they are modeling it — so the child doesn't come back with: 'Well, you let this happen to you,'" says Aldridge.

Don't be afraid to set limits, curfews, and rules. "Although we want our children to flourish, to learn to be independent, able to make decisions — and they want that too," says Aldridge, "parents must decide what the time limits and the parameters should be — in a course of negotiating them with the child. If you're not strong enough, your child can slip away."

Nina's mother, Carly, reflects on the relationship her daughter began when she was fifteen years old:

> *If I had to do it over again, I would trust my initial instincts and put my foot down: "No, you are spending too much time alone." But I was so afraid of ruining my relationship with Nina. There are times when you are so into being their friend that you give up some of your parenthood.*

"Be a parent to your daughter," says Mary Ann Fremgen. "She won't hate you forever. Children want limits; children are testing all the time. They will rebel. It is a process that starts very early. Parents must always keep the roles straight. Remembering 'I am an adult' is sometimes very difficult to do. Many adults don't want to be an adult."

Tiffany, a seventeen-year-old high school student in Illinois, explains the role that she and her friends believe their parents should play:

> *If our parents tried to make us stop seeing the guy, it wouldn't work. But as much as we complain, we really want them to give us rules. Their limits and curfews and stuff even help us to say no to the guy when he wants us to do something or go somewhere we don't want to. We just blame our parents — the "geezers." He can bad-mouth them all he wants, and we can laugh at them too — but down deep we know how much they care about us.*

"The relationship between teen and parent must already be close," Karen Harker points out. "If these girls never had boundaries set, and you suddenly set them, and this is the guy that loves them, whom do you think they'll listen to?"

Dottie Thompson, a domestic violence court services director in Newton, Iowa, has culled this advice to parents from support groups of teens who have been in abusive situations:

- Don't hassle your kid.
- Talk to your daughter as a friend.
- Don't threaten to punish her because of the relationship.
- Let your daughter talk.
- Try to see the situation from your daughter's viewpoint.
- Realize that your daughter really wants you to help — although she may deny it.

Encourage your child to communicate with people other than you — a relative, a family friend, a teacher. Rosalind Wiseman advises a parent to say: "I am really worried about you. If you can't talk to me, that's okay; talk to Aunt Sue."

I had my aunt; I could talk to her about what was going on. My aunt was nonjudgmental, she built up my self-esteem, and she would help me with suggestions. She'd say: "I don't agree with this, but let's see what will help to keep things calm in your family."

Klara, age 16

"The person your child turns to for advice should be an adult," stresses Mary Ann Fremgen. "Talking with peers is just shared ignorance." (This of course does not apply to those peers who are in a school program *led by an adult* in schools across the country — such as the Elmont High School Peer Initiative on Long Island.)

No matter how hip they think their mom is, girls often find a conversation about sex too embarrassing to have with her . . . especially if there has been coercive sex or forms they may feel ashamed of. Even in our sexually immersed culture, many parents are in denial that their child is having sex. "We know what's going on around us today, but we want to believe that our child is the 'good one,'" says Sarah Buel.

Shanterra McBride notes that after being in a sexual relationship, some of the girls are so emotionally attached that they cannot leave. Or they fear the boy will tar their reputation by telling people she is a "slut."

Encourage her to stay involved in skill-building activities. The experts suggest that parents stress all their daughter's talents and skills, rather than focus on her deficiencies, as her abuser exults in doing.

"We have to become a powerful advocate on our daughter's behalf," says Dr. Carol Eagle. "As exasperated as we get with our adolescent girls, we need to remember that they are still developing children who need lots of our praise and love."

Eagle stresses that we must never forget to praise our daughter "if she brings home a good test paper, if she plays well on her team, if she is helpful around the house, or if she handles herself especially well in a difficult situation. If she tries hard to achieve something, but fails, she should also be praised for trying."

We should remind her where she has shown strength in other areas . . . and in the baby steps she may be taking in dealing more assertively with her boyfriend now. Encourage her to continue to pursue — or to pick up — her previous passions, sports, music, drama, art, computers. Try to arrange some fun mom–daughter time together. Relay compliments that other people have given you about her. And give her your own sincere positive comments. (Children know what smacks of mere "mom-and-dad boosterism.")

Of course, her boyfriend will be discouraging her from spending any time away from him. It can be an uphill battle — but worth the sense of accomplishment she will feel, no matter how many obstacles he tries to put in her way.

He was always trying to ruin things for her. One time, she was doing a play, and he went backstage before the performance, got her incredibly upset, and was kicked out by the teacher. But in spite of him,

Cammie was great and won the "best actress" award. Afterward he didn't want her going to the cast parties, and she didn't.

Glenda, mother of Cammie, age 17

Explore her fears — and yours — together in frequent heart-to-heart conversations. Many times, a girl knows she wants to break off the relationship but believes he will "fall apart" if she leaves him, especially if he's going through a crisis in his home, at school, on a sports team, or at a job. After hearing a presentation I had given at a South Carolina high school, one of the teachers, Vivi Reardon,* called me about a problem in her own family. Vivi's fifteen-year-old daughter, Jade,* admitted to her that her boyfriend was "getting to be too dominating and demanding" and that she wanted to be free. "But how can I do it now?" Jade asked her mother. "He needs me — his brother is dying of cancer."

At my suggestion, Vivi discussed the natural feelings of guilt Jade was having about "deserting" him in his time of need. With patience and persistence, she was able to convince her daughter that a fifteen-year-old girl is not equipped to provide the guidance and support that can only be given by people trained in dealing with families in terminal illness and bereavement situations.

Vivi and Jade decided to work together. "Each time he called and asked to speak to her, I'd say: 'This is Vivi. Jade can't speak to you anymore.' I'd ask him about his brother and suggest helping organizations.

"Jade is still worried about him, but she allows me to deflect the phone calls," Vivi reported to me. But Jade was not as forthcoming with her mom as she should have been, and Vivi would soon have to intervene more dramatically.

Be supportive when she wobbles. Ambivalence is part of the crazy quilt fabric of many abusive relationships. The girl is torn between defending her boyfriend and wanting protection from him; it is very confusing to be in love with someone who hurts you. She goes through periods of anger toward her boyfriend; she decides to break up, she decides to stay. There is only one thing she seems to be clear about: she wants the abuse to stop.

Empathize with the difficulty of loving a boy who can be so adoring sometimes and cruel at others, and emphasize that she does not deserve to be treated this way. Try to get her to see the truth: that while it may *feel painful to leave, it is far more dangerous in the long run to stay and risk repeated and more serious abuse.*

Making a decision to change her life can be frightening for her, difficult, overwhelming. It can also be, as she has yet to discover, empowering.

But, most professionals agree, parents should not pressure her into that decision.

STRATEGIZING WITH COMMON SENSE AND CREATIVITY

YOUR DAUGHTER AND HER ABUSER are now a "settled-in" dating couple. And his abuse is escalating. But she seems trapped, unable or unwilling to escape his power and control, which is becoming stronger and more invasive — in her life and in yours.

EFFECTIVE TACTICS

Impose a moratorium or cooling-off period — with no contact allowed. "This will give her time," says Dr. Edna Rawlings, "to get back her good sense. When a girl is abused, her thinking becomes distorted."

Maria Fedele, the New Jersey teen whose controlling boyfriend ordered her to shoplift, is thankful that her parents imposed a moratorium of a month when she could no longer see him after school or speak to him on the phone. (She would still have to see him in class because their small town had only one high school.) That month — filled with tears, rage, and sometimes longing — allowed Maria to reexamine her relationship. "Daddy's words — 'This isn't the way someone shows their love' — got through to me," says Maria. "I saw that my boyfriend was a manipulative tyrant with an ugly need to overpower me. All his 'I love you's' and his 'I'm sorry's' and his tears lost their power."

The enforced separation cleared Maria's mind of any remaining romantic notions about "being high school sweethearts and having a graduation engagement." Now she wanted her friends back; she even decided she wanted a different prom date. The moratorium gave her space to regain her perspective — and her identity.

Put together an intervention. "Sometimes there is nothing more effective," says Dr. Shelley Neiderbach. "Call aunts, uncles, grandparents, friends, and neighbors. Gather them together. Sit your daughter down and say: 'Just listen, we are each going to tell you how we feel about your relationship. Then you can decide what to do.' This gives her the element of choice, rather than coercion. According to Dr. Neiderbach, "'deprogramming' can work."

Contact his family. His parents may be willing to try to get him to stop his behavior if they can — or they may deny his abuse. Karen Harker finds that denial is more probable. "Just as some people don't want to believe that their daughter has been abused, some people don't want to believe that their son could [be an abuser]." Usually, the boy himself will deny his violence and blame her, and his parents will want to believe him. Or they may think boys will be boys. But at least her boyfriend and his family will know that your daughter is not isolated, and that he is being watched. Barrie Levy notes: "Sometimes parents are afraid of their sons and think their son will be better off if 'she' stays in his life."

Keep up communication even when your child is hostile to you and protective of her abuser. For the girl whose toxic boyfriend has turned her against her parents, choose a strategy that will work, advises Levy, not one that will isolate her further. "You want your daughter to talk to you. You must acknowledge the love she feels at the same time you're acknowledging the hurt he has inflicted upon her. Of course, she is ready to defend him. Romantic love is powerful; he is her light against the world; the two of them don't need anyone else. You can't believe she picked him, yet she continues to live in your safety net." This is just where you want her to stay — you don't want to risk a full-fledged rebellion, which could result in her running away with him.

"Never cut her off," says Levy. "Inviting the boy into the home to mix with the family is an idea that could work. It would keep a connection with your daughter, and she may see that he doesn't 'fit' well with the family."

Joanne, whose daughter, Lisa, found herself trapped in a controlling and eventually violent relationship that began when she was seventeen, reflects on her situation three years after it ended:

I wonder if I should have been more welcoming to Bart, invited him home. Lisa is so close to her brothers, maybe she would have seen Bart's interaction with them. Maybe she would have seen that Bart just didn't fit in. Maybe she would have taken the truth better from them.

I wish I hadn't given her such a hard time about him. She got so upset that she wanted to stay at Bart's house. She told me she liked Bart's mom a lot and that she would visit her even without Bart. That hurt!

She said she would do college all on her own, didn't need us to help. She worked at Walgreens and a restaurant to pay the bills. We never wanted her to work, we wanted her to study.

Joanne stresses that although she had cut off college tuition and board money when Lisa decided to move in with Bart, she always kept in contact with her — as difficult as it was.

If you lose contact with them, whom do they have? Lisa knew we would still take her collect calls. She called about once a week. I could tell a lot from her voice. And there were many times when she cried about Bart, moments when she saw the truth. It was okay for Lisa herself to say bad things about Bart, but when I asked too many questions, she would get defensive and hang up on me.

Lisa herself recalls:

My mom actually saw how unhappy I was, but I was locked in this confrontation with my parents that Bart was encouraging. At the time, I hated them when they refused to pay for college as long as I stayed with him. Why aren't they there for me? *I thought, yet I didn't let them know there was any reason to be there. I know my mom didn't like to do what she did, but it was one of those things where kids have to learn on their own and deal with the consequences.*

Get her into therapy as soon as possible. Try to find a counselor experienced in dealing with domestic violence. Ask for referrals from your local women's organizations, shelters, and hot lines.

Some parents find that the best way to get their daughter into therapy is by going to counseling as a family. Pat Greeley, who describes how she witnessed her daughter Mallory's boyfriend "playfully" spanking her and running a knife near her throat, explains:

Mallory seemed happy, but my husband and I knew things just weren't right. Jon was getting more and more jealous of her friends. He was angry with her for having some senior pictures of some guys in her class. We told Mallory that if he loved her, he would want her to have friends, he would not be so jealous. We asked her to think about what kind of person he was. After that, she started to be very distant and irritable, and she was losing a lot of weight. Time went by, and we were losing our daughter, but we didn't know what to do.

In a doctor's office one day, Pat happened to read a magazine article about my daughter and other teenage girls who were abused and murdered by their controlling, obsessive boyfriends. The danger signs really hit home, she says. She remembered seeing me on a TV show telling Jenny's story. Suddenly "it all came together" for her. Pat asked a friend to refer her to a psychologist.

When my husband and I consulted with Dr. Bob, he gave us this advice: We were not to try to talk her into breaking up with Jon. Instead, we should suggest that she see him [Dr. Bob] — only for the purpose of discussing relationships.

Mallory agreed. After seeing Dr. Bob several times, she started to open up to us. She revealed all the emotional and physical abuse Jon had inflicted on her, how she put makeup on her bruises, why she was not eating — because Jon said she was fat and no one would want her. . . .

The psychologist gave her the tools to help herself, but Mallory was the one that had to do it. She broke up with Jon, with a lot of grief from him and support from us.

Do something therapeutic for yourself. Knowing your child is trapped in an abusive relationship is a wrenching experience. Lisa's mother, Joanne, remembers: "I was always on pins and needles with her. I cried a lot." Lisa, away at college at that time, was completely in Bart's thrall. A counselor in the school where Joanne was teaching suggested that Joanne keep a journal in which she could release her feelings. She found that the very act of writing down her emotions allowed her to vent them before they imploded. And she was able to temporarily disengage.

"[Keeping a journal] had a certain therapeutic power for me. After coaching the cheerleaders one day, I wrote in my journal:

Here I am, having fun with other high school girls, the same fun Lisa and I used to have, but because of Bart, I can't talk to Lisa anymore. She just yells at me. I can't let her hurt us anymore. I must put a wall around myself to distance myself from the Bart stuff. We will miss Lisa at Christmas.

"THREE YEARS OF HELL"

Let your daughter know that you are on the same team with her — not the opposing one. Gwyn and Dan Broome* learned this lesson the hard way during the "three years of hell" that began when their only child, Kristy, fell in love at fifteen with a boy a few months younger than she.

"Just as Kristy says, Dan and I played right into her boyfriend's hands," says Gwyn, as I interview her and her husband in their Iowa home. Although her profession is writing steamy historical romance novels, Gwyn looks like "the mom next door" who might have won a prize in a pie-baking cook-off. Rather than appearing sleek and soigné, she wears simple, low-fashion clothes and no makeup; yet her face, flushed with genuine interest and caring, has its own beauty. She has such a loving way about her that sometimes I think she should have been the mother of ten kids. Gwyn finds every animal she sees adorable and adoptable . . . and every friend of Kristy's worthy of her total attention as they pour out their problems to her. Gwyn writes her novels at home so that she is always available for Kristy and all her friends. For years, the role of "every kid's mom" was one she relished — until she became the "enemy" in Kristy's eyes and, consequently, in the eyes of Kristy's friends.

"We made ourselves the enemy," Gwyn admits. "We closed Kristy out with our reactions to Jack, and yes, our reactions were absolutely understandable. He was ultrapossessive and manipulative, he stalked her, and he did have a rage disorder. The more we attacked him, the more stakes she had in defending him to prove herself right. When I said: 'Be careful. What he's doing is weird,' it was my fault. I was incredibly hurt not only because I was losing touch with her, but because I was afraid; I could see all these warning signs, and there was nothing I could say or do to protect her."

After reading Kristy's journal and learning that her child was being pressured into sexual activity, Gwyn and her husband, Dan, decided much stricter rules were in order: they forebade Kristy and Jack to go up to her room. "Dan and I even told them: 'You guys have the downstairs, we'll go upstairs. We won't be coming down to check on you, you'll have privacy.' We also told Kristy she was not to go to Jack's house. We found out afterward that she was sneaking out to his house all the time, and his parents knew."

Dan contacted Jack's parents several times. "His dad admitted he knew she wasn't supposed to be there, but she was coming anyway," says Dan. "They turned it all around, making it sound as if Kristy was unbalanced, a stalker."

At one point, Gwyn and Dan decided they would no longer "give the kids the chance to play Romeo and Juliet." They would be more accepting, more open with Jack. Dan invited him to a restaurant.

Although he is no more than average height, Dan, a cabinet-maker, has a middle-aged tough-guy look, softened by gorgeous blue eyes and a great smile and sense of humor. An earring and slightly longer hair than most men his age give him a touch of eccentricity. Yet he considers himself a "man's man"; he loves guns, hunting, testing his survivor skills in the wild, taking friends camping with him, and cooking for them. I believe that he has a sensitive core, which he has difficulty showing. He recounts to me:

> It was so hard to sit down with this boy and tell him, "I know you had sex with my daughter while I was sleeping in the next room, and I know it wasn't consensual, and you know what, that really makes me angry!"
>
> He was afraid of me. It was great. I bet he thought: He's going to kill me. I just wanted him to know that I had his number.
>
> I told him, "I'm willing to overlook all that; we can all be adults here, right? We have to trust each other again. I'm willing."
>
> So we opened up, asked him to please come over more so that we could get to know each other better. The more we brought him into our family, the more he self-disintegrated: we were no longer giving him an excuse to bad-mouth us, so he tried to escalate his behavior to get a reaction from us — and we wouldn't react. Then he couldn't blame us anymore when Kristy herself saw him for the ass he was.

But Gwyn didn't count on the sense of shame that abused girls feel. "They have defended him for so long against you, and then, when they finally see the light, it is so humiliating that they keep trying to make the relationship work."

Kristy explains: "I thought my parents were just trying to prove a point, not help me get out. I didn't want them to know they were right, and besides, Jack wasn't pure evil, like they thought. If my parents could have recognized his humanity, it would have been a lot easier to get out."

But Kristy herself did manage to break up with Jack several times. Gwyn recalls a particularly stark incident after one breakup:

Kristy went to a weekend thing downtown with the other kids. Jack came looking for her. He got into a physical fight with one of Kristy's guy friends, and the cops broke them up. The kids went to another place, and Jack showed up there, all bloodied, his forehead gashed open because he had banged his head against a brick wall. He said he was upset that Kristy had broken up with him.

Kristy went nuts and left with him. He was this kid who had hurt himself multiple times. Whenever they would get back together, it was always after some major dramatic stunt that pulled her back in.

Gwyn and Dan tried to put thousands of miles between Kristy and her boyfriend during the summers. "We sent her to France. We sent her to England to get away from him, but it didn't work. When she came home, they would get back together."

One summer, Gwyn stopped working completely. "I felt I needed to devote time to my child. I dropped everything; I literally spent the whole summer with Kristy." But not quite literally. During that time, Kristy and Jack got back together again.

When school began, Gwyn went away for a few weeks to visit relatives and "de-stress." At that time, Dan rarely saw much of Kristy "because she just separated herself from us. Every day when she would leave the house, I played the whole thing out in my mind, her running off with him, us not knowing. I feared that if she did stay with him, I was going to lose my daughter, I was never going to know my grandkids."

Then Dan's rage took over. This interlude of attempted "tough love" is one that Gwyn and Dan recall with horror:

GWYN: Dan and Kristy always had a gift for pushing each other's buttons. While I was gone, Dan and Kristy got into this huge fight about Jack, and she wrote this "Dear Dad" letter.

DAN: I told her, "If you don't come home, I will turn your car in as stolen."

GWYN: That's the thing, the escalation, to ridiculous proportions, and neither one of them would give in.

DAN: All I wanted was to get her away from him, and I was willing to put her in jail to do it.

GWYN: But her reaction was that she was afraid of Dan.

DAN: Oh, the voice that came out of me that one night, it scared me. The most evil, loud voice. It was a roar; she said her girlfriends heard it in the next room. I was petrified.

GWYN: She told me later that her dad was scarier than Jack was. She was terrified of her dad.

DAN: There was a time when Gwyn and I were upstairs and Kristy and Jack were downstairs, and I could hear them arguing. So I said: "I need a Pepsi." I got my pistol and stuck it in the back of my pants, top of it sticking out, walked down the stairs, said, "Excuse me," got a Pepsi, and went back upstairs. It got deathly quiet.

GWYN: Dads need to be real. You say, "If he ever touches you, I'll kill him," then she can never tell you if he hurts her because she is afraid you will go off and do something wild and then Dad will be in trouble.

DAN: I worried that if anything happened to Kristy, that I couldn't go after him because then Gwyn would lose both of us.

Kristy's situation was affecting her parents' relationship. "Your child's problem will reveal every crack in your family," says Gwyn, "make it much worse." Because Dan ran out of patience much faster than Gwyn, she found herself playing the role of peacemaker between her husband and child. Family counseling (Kristy's sessions were separate) provided a place to talk.

After four months, Dan saw no change. "It's like watching your child drown. You throw her a line, and she won't take it." He found that keeping a journal helped him. "I could get all my feelings out, and Gwyn and Kristy didn't have to hear them."

Finally, Kristy seemed to have broken up with Jack on her own. She was going to an out-of-town college, three hours away, and Jack was still in town, entering his last year of high school. Gwyn and Dan both remember seeing Kristy go off to college as being traumatic in more ways than one:

DAN: I was so emotional when I dropped my little girl off at college that I could hardly talk. But we made ourselves believe that once we got her up to college, she would be safe, and we didn't have to worry about him being there.

GWYN: We were breaking our hearts over missing her, trying to be strong.

DAN: And then to find out a week later that he goes up and gets her and brings her back to town! To his house! And she doesn't even give us a call!

GWYN: We don't even get to see her.

DAN: It was like someone laid me open. I had to pull into myself. You feel such a sense of betrayal. I felt abandoned by Kristy.

GWYN: Kristy was never naturally deceptive, even as a child. Then with Jack, she was lying to me all the time. And it was awful for her, to have to live that way.

DAN: She used to say, before Jack, that whenever she was upset about something she could go to Mom and talk it out. Now she couldn't because of the lies.

GWYN: We did try to communicate, but it was such a hot, raw thing, and I was so scared and she was so defensive that it was really difficult.

DAN: It was really devastating to realize that in some ways he had more control. We were so out of the loop. She had broken up with him so many times that she just didn't want to tell us what was going on anymore.

GWYN: Dan and I, we had to face up to the fact that we turned her into a liar by reacting the way we did.

It was at this time that Gwyn and Dan, with their own relationship more and more strained, heard about my work in the dating violence field from a mutual friend and contacted me for help. As I have already related, I saw Kristy first and concluded that no one could convince her to end the relationship. No one but herself—eventually.

Then I was faced with suggesting to her parents the only option I knew would work, the very thing I knew Gwyn and Dan did not want to hear. I managed to say straight out: "I can see that Kristy is not going to give Jack up. You must back off and let her continue to see him." As I spoke, I could not even look at them. I felt guilty that I had no magic to seduce Kristy away from this boy.

All I could give to Gwyn was this dictum, backed by my experience counseling other parents and my research in the field: instead of acting on an impulse to "rescue" her, it is far more effective to empower her — to give her the strength to make the choice to leave. I offered to help her work out a safety plan for Kristy, and I gave her several books, some to which I had contributed.

After conferring with me a few more times and reading and rereading the books I had suggested, Gwyn and Dan made a complete turnaround in their behavior.

Gwyn recalls: "Dan and I sat down and said, 'Okay, she is not the enemy. We are a family, we love each other, and even though she may not believe it, we are on the same side. So we have to find ways to maintain our family bond as best we can.'

"We had a code word, Dan and I; if he would be losing it in front of the kids, we had a way of signaling each other, as a reminder to help each other get through it."

"There were times when it would have been better if Gwyn had just hit me with a bucket of cold water," says Dan. "That's how strong a signal I needed sometimes. A man is supposed to protect his family. I just wanted to take Jack out to a cornfield and gut him."

"We sensed that she would keep going back with him," says Gwyn. "I guess that was the surrender — after two years — when we realized that what we were doing was not working. We actually told her that, we said: 'Let's make an agreement not to lie to each other anymore.'"

"As soon as we took ourselves out of the equation as villains," says Dan, "and stopped giving him things to use to make us the enemy, things changed for the better. It went from 'You aren't going out with him' to 'Call us if you need help.'

"We told her, all we want to know is where you are because that is just common courtesy when you're living in someone's house. If she wasn't going to be home by midnight, she had to call to tell us where she was going to be, and then if she was going to drive home, she had to call us when she started out."

With this change of tactics, Gwyn and Dan were putting into practice not only my advice, but the advice of many relationship abuse experts. Barrie Levy describes the strategy this way:

> *Acknowledge that she is ready to stay with him, but point out her needs, her safety. Help her to be safe today and tomorrow, to be prepared to deescalate what could end up in a confrontation. She knows this guy better than you do. Ask her, "Can you ever tell when the tension is building, when he is going to explode? How can you protect yourself before he explodes?"*
>
> *For example, if she knows that he always gets abusive at parties, then she learns not to go to parties with him. If she sees that he is angry, she knows not to get in a car with him.*
>
> *Parents need to help her develop quick-thinking skills. Help her build a process that works on strength, teach techniques on deescalating the anger — don't do something to make him madder; don't yell back; don't get in his face; instead, count to ten, picture a peaceful scene, and so on.*

"We talked with her about a safety plan," says Gwyn. "We talked about the things she should be careful of, when she shouldn't be with him alone, what she should do if he started losing it: 'You call us anytime, anywhere, no questions asked, no judgment.' There was nothing we could do other than: 'Here's the cell phone, we love you, call us if you need us.'" (Specific safety plans are discussed in the next chapters.)

"It's almost impossible to do this at first," Gwyn admits. "You can read what to do, but there's the terror of letting go. All parents want to hang on so tight.

"I would be up all night until she got home. I was a wreck. Before, if we tried to limit her and she lied (because she was going to do what she was going to do anyway), then we wouldn't have known where to start looking. At least this way, even if I didn't like it, I knew where she was. We checked her story a couple of times, and we found out she was being honest.

"I made a lot of bargains with God, knowing that it could have gone wrong. But it was less likely to go wrong the new way we were handling it."

Looking back, Gwyn, Dan, and Kristy give their thoughts on this strategy and the way parents can use it to help their children:

KRISTY: Parents have to be very careful to act from love toward their children, rather than from fear. It is the hardest thing in the world to do because their fear is overriding.

DAN: You have to pick your battles, so you have to let some things go.

GWYN: Keep those lines of communication open. You are their only advocate, the only possible anchor they have. Their friends can't handle it; they aren't equipped. Even though she says she doesn't need you, you have to remember you are the only one. You are it.

DAN: No matter how upset or how much you disapprove.

GWYN: It was hard, when you feel your child is in jeopardy, when you are just waiting for the phone call to come, the other shoe to fall.

KRISTY: It forced my mom to stand back and let go.

GWYN: It doesn't make it any easier once you start letting go; you are still terrified. You are letting them go out with somebody you know could hurt them. I played out the scene so many times in my mind: *I let my daughter go with this dangerous kid. If something happens to her, how can I ever forgive myself?*

DAN: The scariest thing of all was knowing that if she were at his house and he did something to hurt her, his family would not intervene and help her. They would help him hide it.

GWYN: There was no safety net for her there, and yet we had to admit she was going to him whether we let her or not.

KRISTY: When I got out of the relationship, my mom had finally stepped back and said: "I love you. I'm always here for you," and that was when I could really come to her and talk to her.

GWYN: The reason Kristy came out as strong as she did is she went through the whole process — we didn't jump in to make things better.

DAN: People who hear about this going on in your life, they think: *Well, I wouldn't have let my daughter do XYZ, or I would have done XYZ.* They are trying to make themselves feel safe. You teach your daughter about the big bad wolf, but it never occurs to you that she could be the one letting him in the door.

ELEVEN

ACTIVELY CONFRONTING THE VIOLENCE

When you are in an abusive relationship, you learn a skill: you can shut off everything, like pulling the iron curtain across, and nothing anybody says or does gets through. You don't care. You go to a different place because it is just too painful to think that someone who loves you is hurting you. You just shut off.

Kristy Broome

AS WE HAVE SEEN, rather than trying to replace her boyfriend's control with their own, which proved to be counterproductive, Gwyn and Dan Broome finally allowed Kristy to take back her own power, to make her own decision. It was, as Gwyn said, dangerous, but Kristy "was already doing dangerous things."

When your daughter is in an abusive relationship, *how far to empower her — without endangering her —* is a point of debate among the experts themselves.

ZERO TOLERANCE

Mary Ann Fremgen is a voice at the far right of the spectrum. "Parents of girls in abusive relationships must stop the relationship immediately," she asserts.

"They must get restraining orders if necessary. Restraining orders are very effective; they provide a consequence for the offender." (We discuss the advantages and disadvantages of restraining orders later.)

Fremgen elaborates her position:

> *Kids do not live in a democracy. They don't have the right to continue a relationship if their parents want it to end. Kids have a right to the bare essentials, that is all.*
>
> *Some parents have stripped their child's room. The child must ask each day for clothes to wear, and only by good behavior earn back their stuff. It is not their stuff! If the child is provoked into anger, then the parents should call 911. These techniques have proven to be effective.*

THE AMORPHOUS "FINE LINE"

"You want to make sure you're not being abusive in combating the abuse," warns Karen Harker. "Parents must walk a fine line when they're approaching their child."

> *I would never tell my mom that I needed help, but I really hope she notices and does something about it.*
>
> Tara, age 15

The teens themselves seem to be torn — not sure which side of that "fine line" they really want their parents to be on . . . especially when they view their abusive relationship from the perspective of historical distance.

"Why didn't you just put me in a monastery?" Kristy asked her parents as she was apologizing for all that she had put them — and herself — through. Gwyn replied, "Because you would have fought us tooth and nail, and you never would have learned a lesson; you would have just gone back to him or found another relationship just like it."

Lisa, whose boyfriend pushed her off a balcony, reflects a few years later: "My family never knew about anything physical going on. You hope your parents will figure it out, but of course, you will deny it. I think I really would have wanted my parents to come up to college to get me and bring me home, but I would have fought them if they'd done it."

WHAT BALANCE CAN PARENTS FIND TO HELP THEIR DAUGHTER?

"This is the most controversial question," says Barrie Levy. "I think every situation is different. I often encourage parents to try the bold strategies on the chance that their daughters will respond with some relief that their parents are there to help (even if their daughters are ambivalent).

"When taking strong steps to help their daughters get away from the abuser, the parents' attitude is very important: it should be respectful rather than judgmental and controlling, calming the tension between parent and child rather than escalating it.

"If their daughter does fight them, and the intervention fails because of it, at least they have made an effort and made it clear to their daughter that they are worried about her safety and will do what they can to keep her out of danger."

Levy reminds us of the possibility of unintended consequences: the extremes that girls may go to after their parents try to get them away from the abuser — for example, running away or staying away from home even more.

LAISSEZ-FAIRE?

At the polar opposite of strong intervention is almost complete laissez-faire. Says Karen Harker: "A lot of parents think teens are old enough to take care of themselves. 'It's your life' is one type of parental mind-set."

"If I had to choose between the overpermissive approach — 'let the relationship run its course' — rather than the overforceful one, I would choose the latter," states Leah Aldridge. "It would be better than thinking, *I didn't do enough.*"

Having met several parents like me whose daughters were murdered by their boyfriends, I agree.

CONFRONT THE CHILD
IF YOU THINK SHE'S BEING HIT

"As a parent, the notion that somebody may be physically assaulting your child makes the mother lioness in you rise up," says Aldridge. Here is one approach she recommends:

> *Tell her, "We need to talk." Say, in a loving way, "Has he hit you, sweetie? I promise I won't get angry. I won't do something drastic." Children need to know this. They fear backlash against them or their boyfriends.*
>
> *Get her to give you more details. "How has this person been hurting you? Is there a pattern to this behavior? Of intimidation, pushing, restraining, slapping . . . ?" If there is, she will make excuses for him — he was in a bad mood because he didn't make the football team or because she spoke to another boy or because she wore that short skirt. She will blame herself, or she will say: "He would never do it again."*

This is the time to explain the Cycle of Violence, along with the Power and Control Spiral, to your child, as well as to simply say straight out, as Karen Harker suggests, "Honey, this beating you up isn't love."

You must let the child know, with a firm statement, that violence is unacceptable — under any circumstance. You can't be too emphatic about this: *there's no excuse for violence in a relationship — not alcohol or drugs, financial pressure, depression, jealousy, or any behavior of hers.*

"Ninety-five percent of abusers can control their behavior," says Sarah Buel, who believes that the phrase "a planned pattern of coercive control," coined by Dr. David Adams, a specialist in teen battering relationships, most aptly describes how abusers work.

What can we, as parents, impress on our daughters? Sarah Buel recommends two strong assertions:

1. *I am afraid for your safety.* "She is in denial — she's thinking of the promise of change, how much this person is in love with her."

2. *You don't deserve to be treated like this.* "He's using mind control."

As Leah Aldridge maintains, you can't repeat the "mom's mantra" too often: "You are my child, and I love you. You deserve to be in a relationship that is healthy."

But she warns that parents, in trying to bring the relationship to a close, must try not to seem to be taking on the same I'm-in-charge-here role as the batterer. "If you are disempowering the victim to make choices, then you are acting just like him.

"Together with your daughter, develop a strategy for terminating the relationship," says Aldridge. "Ask her to help you work out a clear, uncluttered plan to keep her safe.

"But never minimize the power of the relationship," she stresses. "Your daughter has an emotional investment. She may not be at all clear about wanting the relationship to end." Her boyfriend can also be very caring, and they've had a "history" of really fun times together.

Even after an incident of physical violence, she may not want to break up; she may prefer to attempt to work through the "problems" in the relationship.

"Begin by reevaluating the relationship together," suggests Aldridge. "Assess the risks when he becomes upset. See where his level of violence is on the 'danger scale.'

"Here are specific questions to pose: When 'stress comes to shove,' does he 'only' smack her with an open hand and push her (Level One)? Or does he punch with his fists, kick her, and throw her against the wall, or rip out part of her hair (Level Two)? If she admits he has already reached Level Two, give her a reality check: 'Don't you see? He is escalating the violence.'

"If she says, 'I punch and kick him back,' ask her: 'Do you want to be in that kind of relationship, kicking and punching each other?'

"Suggest to your daughter: 'Let's make a time line. Let's say by Friday you will tell him what he has to do if he wants to continue to see you: recognize your rights in the relationship and give you more than promises. He must admit that he has an anger-management problem and be willing to attend regular sessions of an abuse intervention counseling group." (You will have supplied her with alternative-to-violence resources from a local domestic violence hot line or teen line.)

Her boyfriend may decide she's just not worth the trouble and find another girl to abuse. "Some young men are users; they really do break up and move on to someone else if she makes it hard for him to stay," says Barrie Levy. "Many times, the young woman knows this, and she can't tolerate being apart from him. When she realizes that he will just find someone else, she will resist all attempts to break them up." Or she may promise not to see him until he makes changes — but she still loves him.

Karen Harker advises parents to strategize as much as possible with their daughter about ending the relationship but to be realistic: "You can say to your child: 'I don't want you to see him. But I know you are going to try to see him because you care for him.' In a small town, like many of those in Nebraska, with three thousand people and one high school, both have the same friends. That's the reality. She is going to see him."

She suggests some parameters that a parent can set while the child is still in the unhealthy relationship: time limits, when and where the couple may see each other, the necessity of double-dating, rather than just getting into a car with him and taking off to wherever he fancies. She adds, of course, that teens often get around the rules — and that's why she recommends a safety plan in case they do.

Leah Aldridge also emphasizes safety planning "because you don't know what they're doing when they're away from you. Sometimes a girl has two sets of clothes with her — one she's wearing to go to school and one she's changing into to cut school and go out with him. Or she could crawl out the window in the middle of the night.

"There are two types of safety planning — one for while she is still in the relationship (see the sidebar on page 139); the other for after she has broken it off," Aldridge explains. (The protocol for the latter is given in chapter 12.)

SAFETY PLAN WITHIN THE RELATIONSHIP

Even if your daughter is still in denial about being in danger, make sure she knows what to do in an emergency. Here are some safety steps — adapted from several domestic violence groups' recommendations:

- Get her a cell phone. Make sure it is always charged.
- Let her know you will pick her up at any time or place, no questions asked. Carry a pager.
- Decide on safe places she can go to in case she can't get home.
- Figure out ways she can get home safely if violence starts while she's out with him and can't reach you.
- If he's threatening her in a public place, tell her to yell "fire" as loud as she can to get bystanders' attention.
- List people whom she can call on and go to in emergencies.
- Prepare for emergencies — with spare keys, cash.
- Make backup plans for vulnerable times, for example, asking friends to accompany her going to and from school.
- Establish a safety net of people who will look out for her. Initially, you and your child may feel embarrassed about revealing the situation. (Will someone criticize your parenting skills or your daughter's common sense?) But it is important that everyone — your friends and hers, family members, teachers, school counselors, neighbors, members of the clergy — be aware of the problem and become involved.

Together with your daughter, you can create — and practice — an additional, even more specific plan in case of further abuse, an Individualized Teen Safety Plan. Begin by choosing a code word.

HOW THE "CODE WORD" WORKS

Let us say that the code word you choose is "reindeer," which can mean *call 911* or *have someone come get me.* Once your daughter has set the code word with you and with other concerned people, Leah Aldridge recommends that you rehearse the steps she should take the next time she sees her boyfriend's tension building and senses an explosion is imminent.

"If she's at a party with him, and she doesn't feel safe," explains Aldridge, "she can say, in the middle of a conversation with a friend, 'reindeer.' Or if he's getting nasty, she can tell him she has to go 'pee' and give the code word to friends or phone it to her parents." Make a copy of the Individualized Teen Safety Plan (see the sidebar on page 141) and have your daughter fill it in.

HER BRAIN IS HER BEST DEFENSE

"Your brain is your best defense" is one of the mantras of the Los Angeles Commission on Assaults Against Women.

During an argument, when it seems that her boyfriend is about to choose violence, a normal level of assertiveness could be dangerous. An underassertive response is what the potentially explosive situation calls for.

In *What Parents Need to Know About Dating Violence,* Levy and Giggans write: "If she escalates the argument . . . If she doesn't allow him to cool off or to leave if he needs to, she may be endangering herself."

Aldridge stresses another point: "Although you are constantly reinforcing the fact that the abuse is not her fault, your daughter still needs to be made aware that to a certain degree she can control the use of violence against her." How? By talking the batterer down.

In their safety plan, the Nebraska Domestic Violence Sexual Assault Coalition advises that if the situation becomes very dangerous, a young woman must use her "instincts and judgment to do whatever is necessary to be safe. This may mean giving the abuser what he wants to calm him down." For her safety, she may even have to submit to his sexual demands.

INDIVIDUALIZED TEEN SAFETY PLAN

Although I can't control my abuser's violence, I do have a choice about how to respond and how to get to safety.

- I will make up a code word for my family, teachers, or friends, so they know when to call for help for me. My code word is _____.
- When I feel a fight coming on, I will try to move to a place that puts me at the lowest risk for getting hurt, such as _____ at school or _____ at work or _____ in public.
- If I feel unsafe during an argument inside a house, I will try to move to a room without weapons and away from the bathroom, kitchen, garage, or rooms without a door.
- When he calls and I feel threatened, I can ask my parents and other family members to screen my calls and visitors. Or I can screen my calls with an answering machine.

Adapted from *Reaching and Teaching Teens to Stop Violence,* Nebraska Domestic Violence Sexual Assault Coalition and *Teen Dating Violence Resource Manual,* National Coalition Against Domestic Violence. (More information on safety plans is given in chapter 12.)

Once physical violence has started, there is no way she can deescalate it. Only he can stop it. According to Dr. Donald Dutton, acute episodes of rage are "solely under the control of the person who acts out the rage . . . He is driven strictly from within. The physical action is even pleasurable . . . it releases the pent-up tension. . . . It's the only way to rid himself of his bad feelings."

MAKE SURE SHE GETS PROFESSIONAL ATTENTION

If she has been physically or sexually assaulted, Dr. Noelle Nelson, like most experts, recommends prompt parental action: "Take her immediately to a medical doctor," says Dr. Nelson. "Do not speak to her in terms of the boy, but rather in terms of 'I am frightened for you.'"

Thea Johnson* happened to walk into the bathroom when her seventeen-year-old daughter, home for Thanksgiving from college, was taking a shower.

I couldn't believe what I saw. There were bruises all over her torso. When I confronted her, she told me she fell. But I could see that a fall wouldn't leave a pattern of bruises like that. Someone had beaten her up. Samantha* finally broke down and admitted it was her boyfriend. When she had tried to break up with him, he beat her. Then he apologized and cried and said he couldn't live without her.

Samantha told her mother she would never think of reporting him to the campus authorities; he was a brilliant preengineering student, and she would not want him to be expelled from college. She had rationalized the violence: he only did it because of his great love and need for her. "And besides," she said, "it's really nothing. It's all healing."

When Thea herself reported the incident, all that the on-campus professionals could do was suggest that she educate her daughter about abuse and work out a safety plan with her. (Another option of course would be to withdraw all financial support — but as we have seen, in the case of Lisa and her parents, that maneuver might drive her more desperately into the arms of her manipulative boyfriend.)

Since battered girls like Samantha tend to minimize the extent of their injuries in order to protect their boyfriends, your daughter may insist her bruises are "nothing serious."

"If she is black-and-blue all over her torso," says Karen Harker, "there may be internal injuries. Take her to a doctor. That's a high priority." An extensive medical examination and X rays may even turn up a concussion or a broken bone.

Even if her injuries are not serious *this time,* Dr. Nelson stresses the necessity of getting her into counseling. Since battered girls are often resistant, she suggests using an indirect approach. "The key is to express *your* fears. 'I am so scared for you, I need help.' Immediately call a battered woman's shelter. Then take her with you to the counselor they recommend. Through a third person who can be objective, she may see the danger for herself."

Why are many young girls — with no ties of marriage, children, and financial dependency — so desperate to continue a battering relationship?

Jeanine Pirro, a pioneering advocate for battered women and district attorney of Westchester County in New York, sheds light on teens' attitudes toward dating violence. Says Pirro, who started a Domestic Violence Unit in 1978, one of four of its kind in affluent suburban communities in the nation funded by the U.S. Department of Justice:

> *Just as battered wives in the late seventies and early eighties didn't know it was wrong for them to be assaulted, I liken today's teenager to the battered woman twenty years ago who had no idea of her rights. She believes the man has a right to hit her if she has done something wrong — or something he considers wrong — such as speaking to another guy. You're dealing with a very impressionable young girl whose self-concept is dependent on this relationship.*

Karen Harker hears many girls explaining the violence this way: "'He's only doing it because he loves me.' In the rap songs and in the media," says Harker, "the message is *love is supposed to hurt,* and boys get that message nine times stronger than girls. If he's not hurting her to keep her in line, to his friends he's a 'wuss' or even worse, a 'girl.'"

Sarah Buel has found that the girls in her focus groups who are in abusive relationships believe all men are the same; there are no good guys around. "If you stay in this relationship, how are you going to know?" she challenges them.

But lethargy and cynicism aside, the girls have more compelling reasons for not breaking up a violent relationship. "It is both seductive and terrifying, the messages they get from their boyfriends," says Buel. "Seductive: 'I can't live without you.' Terrifying: 'I will kill you if you leave me. I will make sure that you are never safe on this campus.' Some even threaten her with gang rape."

USE A WIDE ARRAY OF RESOURCES

Not all specialists in the teen dating violence field are social workers and psychologists. Many are attorneys who work in conjunction with mental-health professionals.

When she was volunteering at battered women's shelters, Meredith Blake found that all their resources were geared to adult victims. In 1996, one year after she got her law degree, Blake started Break the Cycle in Los Angeles to give free education, legal advice, and representation to young people, ages twelve to twenty-two. Break the Cycle, which has grown from a one-woman operation to a large, well-funded nonprofit organization, also works with parents who bring their teen children in.

Blake advises a parent who is concerned about her daughter's violent relationship to urge her child to get professional help:

> Say: "It will really mean a lot to me if you see the attorneys. They can help you understand your options but won't require you to do anything you're not willing to do."
>
> We educate the child about abuse and tell her we're here to support her with the decision she makes — from doing nothing to going to court. We give free representation for kids needing restraining and protective orders. A girl may come in and say: "I'm not happy in the relationship, but I'm not ready to do anything now." Then three weeks later, she may be ready to go to court.

Although Break the Cycle is now looking at expanding nationwide, the protections that exist in California are not widely available to teens in many other states. (In Nebraska, for example, a girl would have to be cohabiting with her boyfriend in order to seek a restraining order.)

"In New York State a teen has the right to bring her case into the criminal court if she is being threatened and stalked," says Jeanine Pirro. "At fifteen (or younger) she can bring criminal charges. Perpetrators would have to be sixteen for criminal court; if the charge is rape, fourteen. The trouble is, the girl won't testify against him."

"HE DIDN'T MEAN TO"

Even if a young girl has sustained serious physical injury, Pirro finds that she is often reluctant to have her abuser prosecuted. "In cases where one victim may not want to go forward in pressing charges, the abuser goes on to the next victim after he's finished with her."

She cites one case in which an Ivy League–college girl's nose was broken by her boyfriend, but the victim said she would never bring charges. "It's not just about you," District Attorney Pirro tried to convince her without success — even after she checked up and found that the boyfriend had a prior conviction. (Many teenage girls are involved with men in their twenties who have amassed "priors.")

In an even more egregious case, a girl who was brutally beaten by her boyfriend and left for dead on a roof refused to testify against him after her unexpected recovery. "She begged me not to call her as a witness," says Pirro. "She testified for the defense that he didn't mean to. . . ."

Pirro now has instructed her assistant district attorneys to train the police on how to convict a perpetrator without the victim's testimony — by taking a Polaroid of the victim's injuries and a signed statement by her at the time of the incident.

LEARNING THE LEGAL OPTIONS

It is essential for parents and children to learn about the laws pertaining to violence against women in this country. All states consider physical assault a crime — a misdemeanor or a felony depending upon the seriousness of the injury. Karen Harker explains the difference succinctly: "If he punches her in the jaw, it's a misdemeanor; if he breaks her jaw, it's a felony."

Many boys are not even aware that dating violence is a crime. Sarah Buel, who was once a prosecutor in juvenile court in Boston, believes that they have often been "scared straight" by a probation officer or police officer. "When a mother would say: 'I am terrified for my daughter's safety,' the officer would talk to the boy and let him know that what he was doing was illegal, and if he did it again, he would be prosecuted." With a felony on his record, Buel points out, a young man would not be accepted in the armed services or even be able to "flip burgers in a hamburger joint."

"Assault and battery are felonies," says Meredith Blake. "There are enhanced penalties if they take place on a school campus. Schools have to be involved and aware. More are now — in the wake of Columbine."

THE PRIMARY AGGRESSOR

Women hit men all the time, and when the police come, they're both
gonna walk out of there, but he's the one in handcuffs, right?

Brian, age 18

Barri Rosenbluth asserts: "While they may be in unhealthy relationships, I have never seen boys who are in serious danger physically."

On the other hand, Rosalind Wiseman points out: "Girls are strong these days. They can hit really hard, and they know how to take a punch."

Cases of "mutual combat," in which the abuser makes counterclaims against the victim, happen all the time, according to Jeanine Pirro. "Many times, both abuser and victim are injured. New York State now has a Primary Aggressor Law. Before this law," says Pirro, "whoever got to the police first was the one who was the complainant.

"Now it's not the person who comes to you first, or even necessarily the one with the most serious injuries, it's the one who crossed the line of violence. We determine which injuries are defensive, and who has more credibility. We also build a 'scheme' case against the person who inflicted prior intentional injuries, so that we can contradict his claim that she was the one who started it."

"Primary or predominant aggressor laws have been enacted in many states," says Sarah Buel.

HOW PROTECTIVE IS AN ORDER OF PROTECTION?

How effective are restraining orders, or orders of protection, as some states call them?

"A law is as good as how well it's obeyed," says Meredith Blake. "Restraining orders are more effective with young people than in the adult community."

Blake also remarks that it is difficult to enforce a restraining order against your daughter's boyfriend if she resists it.

If the parents feel they too are in jeopardy from her boyfriend, they can get restraining orders for themselves. Court protection covers the entire family, including pets, if they have been threatened or if there's been vandalism. "While the law is a powerful tool to protect them, it's not a bulletproof shield," says Blake. "They have to be responsible for their own safety."

ADDITIONAL PARENTAL PERSUADERS

If your child has been beaten by her boyfriend, Leah Aldridge believes the parents' best approach — after getting their child a medical checkup — is "to say to her: 'How about if I work with you? Do you want to call the cops?'

"Weigh the consequences with her, the level of risk of having him arrested. Restraining orders for minors are pretty effective, but it depends on how much the guy respects the law. If he's been running with a gang, been shot, been in jail before, it will be nothing to him." Nevertheless, incidents of violence should be reported to the police.

Sarah Buel finds from her focus groups that it is rare that girls want to file complaints.

If your child is under eighteen and refuses to work with you in taking any action against his abuse, Aldridge suggests a more forceful approach:

Tell her: "This violence is not only hurtful to you, but it is a crime. Therefore, I cannot allow it to go unreported. I am required, by law, to protect you. My options are: (1) I can call the police and have him arrested; (2) I can ask you to go for counseling." In California, a parent can get a court order making her go for counseling.

Aldridge explains:

Just as her teacher is required to call child protective services if she sees bruises, if a minor is injured by a boyfriend, the parents may be accused of child abuse because the law requires them to take action. A parent can say she had no idea about the abuse in the relationship, but then she may be asked: "Why didn't you know that this has been going on with your child?" There are many creative city attorneys in California.

ANOTHER RESOURCE: A SUPPORT NET

The experts agree that it is vital to get your daughter into a support group — and to join one yourself. It helps to hear other teens' or other parents' experiences.

Domestic violence shelters have weekly drop-in groups, as well as ongoing ones, and there are support groups forming in more and more schools, mental-health clinics, religious organizations, and online.

"The counseling situation (whether they talk to me one-on-one or join a support group) is very powerful," says Karen Harker. "It breaks the isolation; it lets them know they're not alone."

Like many other experts, she gives this caveat about couples counseling: Your daughter and her boyfriend should *not* be counseled together. *Couples counseling can be intimidating or even dangerous for the battered teen.* "I never sit down with both kids for counseling," says Harker. "It's unfair to that teen not to expect a backlash if she's telling me all about his violence in front of him. On the way home in the car, he may give her a right to the jaw."

Barri Rosenbluth also believes that students find tremendous value in the work of the twenty-one Expect Respect groups in middle schools and high schools in the Austin, Texas, area. "We work with many children who are dealing with abusive issues (other types of violence too) and, at the same time, help them deal with dating relationships.

"We don't involve parents unless the child is in danger. In the context in which we are working, it would limit a child's ability to participate. There is a high incidence of underreporting of violence . . . in the group, but when they realize the facilitator is on their side, they open up."

Recently, a survey was given to members of the Expect Respect groups. Some comments from the girls after twenty-four sessions were

> *I liked the group because of the way all of us openly discussed the topic. I figured out that there are lots of people that feel the same way I do about some things.*

> *I loved how everyone in the group was very helpful in dealing with your problems. They were always understanding and never judged you.*

> *I liked the fact that I knew the girls had some sort of experience like me, and I could really relate and know that abuse . . . is not my fault.*

> *We learned about good relationships and how to handle bad ones. We also learned that there are different ways of abuse.*

> *Just because you love someone doesn't mean you can be treated like shit.*

> *If someone is doing something bad and telling you to do it, you don't need to if you don't want to. There's help out there, and it's okay to leave a bad relationship.*

Says Sarah Buel:

> *There is still a tremendous amount of work to do, but lots of progress is being made. In many schools there are "Image Enhancement*

Groups" for girls. We don't use "dating violence" in the title, but we talk a lot about it — and we also have guests to talk about hair and nails. In boys' groups — they're never called "Abusers'" or "Batterers'" Groups — we try to make them see that once they get a conviction for a violent crime (and rape is a felony), their future is in jeopardy.

TWELVE

HELPING YOUR DAUGHTER
BREAK AWAY SAFELY

WITH YOUR SUPPORT, your daughter has finally seen the light. On her own. Making a decision to change her life has been empowering but also difficult — and dangerous.

It is at the end of the relationship that the abusive boyfriend poses a major threat, when his "love" may become lethal — even if there has never been physical violence before.

"This is the time when the control he was using through emotional manipulation may escalate to physical violence," says Dr. Edna Rawlings. Or the physical violence can reach life-threatening levels.

"Girls who leave a battering relationship are emotionally vulnerable and possibly in physical danger for a long time after the breakup," agrees Barrie Levy. "Parents must recognize that their daughter is going to be ambivalent. They should watch out for every mood change. They must realize that it is not a process in which the girl decides to break up, does it, and then gets over it. It is always push–pull after a breakup. He will call; he will show up where she is. He may be trying to plead with everyone she knows to help him. He may be threatening suicide. There may be moments when she feels a strong pull to go back, when she feels bad for his suffering."

Levy also explains that a girl who breaks off an abusive relationship often lives in a state of heightened fear. "He has scared her in the past when she talked of breaking up; she already knows how enraged he gets. A threat against family members is very powerful to young girls. They feel it is up to them to keep their family safe."

An immediate escalation of lethal behavior is not universal, Levy finds. "Some men will stay away for a while, then resort to stalking, lashing out, threats. It *is* possible to leave safely," says Levy, "but it must be carefully planned."

SAFETY BREAKUP PLANNING WITH YOUR DAUGHTER

Stress that she must make the break definite and final. She should say to him on the phone: "I don't love you. I don't want to see you. Don't call me anymore." But he will call her. Constantly. He will want to persuade her to come back to him or at the very least agree to "still be friends."

Gavin de Becker, the nation's leading expert on predicting violent behavior, maintains: "We have to teach young people that 'No' is a sentence." He believes that the worst mistake a girl can make is "letting him down easy."

In his book *The Gift of Fear,* de Becker gives this firm advice for girls who have broken up with their abusive boyfriends:

> Do not negotiate. Once a woman has made the decision that she doesn't want a relationship with a particular man, it needs to be said one time, explicitly. Almost any contact after that rejection will be seen as negotiation. If a woman tells a man over and over again that she doesn't want to talk to him, that is talking to him, and every time she does it, she betrays her resolve in the matter.
>
> If you tell someone ten times that you don't want to talk to him, you are talking to him — nine times more than you wanted to.
>
> When a woman gets thirty messages from a pursuer and doesn't call him back, but then finally gives in and returns his calls, no matter what she says, he learns that the cost of reach-

ing her is leaving thirty messages. For this type of man, any contact will be seen as progress. Of course, some victims are worried that by not responding they'll provoke him, so they try letting him down easy. Often the result is that he believes she is conflicted, uncertain. . . .

ONCE-AND-FOR-ALL BREAKUP SAFETY PLAN

Here are other tips incorporated from expert sources, such as the Nebraska Domestic Violence Sexual Assault Coalition's *Reaching and Teaching Teens to Stop Violence* and the *Teen Dating Violence Resource Manual* from the National Coalition Against Domestic Violence:

- Insist she avoid all direct contact with him — even for a few minutes to return or receive possessions. "No stuff is worth the risk of collecting it," says Dr. Edna Rawlings.
- Tell her she must never meet him, get in a car with him, or allow him in the house — especially if she's alone, but even when she's with her family. You need to explain to her that she might be kidnapped, held against her will, or hurt.
- Warn her to never let her guard down, even if he appears remorseful, apologizes, promises, or pleads. Remind her of the Cycle of Violence.
- Tell her *not* to allow mutual friends to carry notes back and forth.
- Have the locks on your house changed in case he has a key. (He may have had a copy of hers made that neither of you are aware of . . . as my daughter Jenny's ex-boyfriend, Mark Smith, did.)
- Alert the school counselor, security officers, teachers, and principal that she may be in danger from him. Ask that he be kept apart from her and that her class schedule be changed.
- If she is in college, have her dorm room changed, as well as her class schedule.
- Make sure you know where she's going to be.
- Give her a pager and a cellular phone.

• Use an answering machine at home to screen calls and record any harassment.

• Inform your neighbors and, if she has a part-time job, her employer that she may be in danger.

• Warn her to stay away from deserted places in case he "happens" to show up.

• If, in spite of your firm advice that she break up with him on the telephone, she feels she must speak to him in person, insist that she meet him in a public place, such as a busy restaurant, and have friends nearby. She must make it clear that the relationship is over.

• Help her figure out how she can vary her daily habits. Her ex-boyfriend knows them all too well.

• Make sure she is not alone at school, home, her job, on the way to and from places, or in any other situation. Have a friend or relative accompany her whenever possible while her safety is still in question.

• Warn her to take his stalking and any threats he makes seriously. Insist she share them with you.

CONTINUING "RESCUE EFFORTS" AFTER THE FINAL BREAKUP

Give your child ongoing support. Says Barrie Levy: "She has been totally cut off from her friends; they are fed up or they just don't get it. She can't even express 'I miss him' to anyone." Jennifer Coleman, the redheaded Maine cheerleader whose football-hero boyfriend made her withdraw from everyone she knew, wistfully recalls: "It was a lonely summer for me after we broke up. I had no friends anymore."

Levy stresses that nothing will feel that intense to the girl again. "He took a constant amount of her attention; there is a big hole when he is gone. There is nothing quite as dramatic as him. The longer they were together, the harder it is to get over. Let her know that you will be there to sort out her feelings."

MORE ON TELEPHONE TIPS

Most experts suggest that a young woman stalked by an ex-boyfriend should immediately change her number to an unlisted one. But Gavin de Becker and his associates recommend a different strategy. From experience, they find that the stalker always manages to get the new number. In *The Gift of Fear,* de Becker writes:

> A better plan is for the woman to get a second phone line, give the new number to the people she wants to hear from, and leave the old number with an answering machine or voice mail so that the stalker is not even aware she has another number. She can check her messages, and when she receives calls from people she wants to speak with, she can call them back and give them her new number. Eventually, the only person leaving messages on the old number is the unwanted pursuer. In this way, his calls are documented (keep the messages) and more important, each time he leaves a message, he gets a message: that she can avoid the temptation to respond to his manipulations.

Get her into counseling. Experts agree that intense counseling is often needed to get her over the urge to call him. "The more she can talk about it, the better," says Levy. "Parents must know that she could do an about-face in the middle. Sometimes a move to a new school, a physical break of some kind, where she is too far away to act on impulse, can help, but there is no guarantee. The more support she receives from her family, the more likely she is to stay away for good."

Encourage her to rebuild her life. Parents should plan carefully with their daughter how she is going to restructure her life without him. Wean her from her dependence on him by encouraging her to renew former interests and friendships and to take part in healthy new activities. Include lots of people and projects that will engage her: extended family, volunteer work, family vacations.

After a daughter's breakup with an abusive boyfriend, Dr. Carol Eagle suggests that the mother make Herculean efforts to take the girl on family outings and to search for challenging, skill-building activities for her — even more than she did when her daughter was little. "Although at first the girl may resist, the parent must persist. What parents say seeps through over time, not immediately."

Eagle expresses surprise "at how parents who knocked themselves out to book extracurricular activities for their daughters when they were in elementary school, suddenly stop when their daughters become adolescents. Although it's true that adolescents often feign lack of interest in everything, out of a wide range of activities there are bound to be one or two that will pique your daughter's interest."

CHOOSING LEGAL OPTIONS

When the ex-boyfriend persists in unwanted contact, there are legal options that the teenager or her parents can take. Under the law in most states, abuse is considered to be not only physical violence, but also threats of injury, forced sex, extreme embarrassment or humiliation, damage to her property, and stalking (now a federal crime). Issued by a judge, a restraining or "keep-away" order — or an order of protection — orders the abuser

- Not to contact, attack, molest, strike, threaten, sexually assault, telephone, or e-mail her
- To stay a specified distance away from her, her home, her work, her school environment, her car
- To attend batterers' treatment programs, counseling, and anger-management classes

If restraining orders are violated, the abuser is subject to arrest. Evidence of the violation may include

- Taped telephone threats
- Threatening notes (even unsigned) and e-mail
- Photos taken of him near her home or school

Temporary restraining orders usually last for two to three weeks. In order to issue a permanent order of protection — good for as long as three years — the court must provide notice to the offender and have a full hearing.

RESTRAINING ORDERS REVISITED

"In many cases, a restraining order is a very effective tool," explains attorney Diana Krause-Leeman, education director of Break the Cycle. "It says you are in trouble with the law. It works especially well with the first-time offender, for boys who fear going to jail and may not understand — until the judge tells them — that what they're doing is not only wrong, but illegal."

"Restraining orders are an added protection for an abused girl," says Sarah Buel. "But I always say to the victim: 'I don't know if your abuser will obey this order. We have to plan as if he will *not* obey it.'"

Yvonne Groton* discovered personally just how helpful a restraining order can be. A coordinator of dating violence prevention programs for middle schools in a southeastern city, Yvonne became greatly worried about the safety of her own seventeen-year-old daughter when she broke off a relationship with her boyfriend after eight months. "The relationship wasn't a classic case of controlling," says Yvonne. "*He* was dependent on *her*. She got him a job. But he definitely did not want her to go to an out-of-town college."

He began to beep her constantly and to stalk her. Yvonne spoke to his father, who did not believe that her daughter really *wanted* to break up with his son.

Then came his beeped message: "I am going to kill you!" Yvonne went to court and obtained a temporary injunction. The boy was served with a restraining order, and his father could no longer deny the situation.

"We got a permanent injunction after that," says Yvonne. In addition, Yvonne used safety precautions: she installed a burglar alarm, drove her daughter to school, made sure her daughter was with her friends most of the time. She admits she was uneasy when her daughter attended the senior prom, fearful that the boy would come after her daughter. But he obeyed the order and stayed away.

But some specialists disagree about the effectiveness of restraining orders. Gavin de Becker believes they work best on "the person least likely to be violent anyway . . . the reasonable person who has a limited emotional investment," that is, a man who has been dating just a few months as opposed to a husband of many years.

"Orders of protection? I call them 'orders of illusion' when you live in a free and open society such as ours and someone is hellbent to hurt you," says Jeanine Pirro. "Young people who have total disrespect for the law will disregard them. It depends on the individual."

But Sarah Buel looks at them differently than Pirro does: "When you're a prosecutor, all you see are the violations." Buel, a former assistant district attorney in Massachusetts, cites a study done for the School of Public Health at Harvard University by the commissioner of probation in Massachusetts showing that more than 70 percent of restraining orders are obeyed.

Buel and Pirro do agree that restraining orders can act as a deterrent to boys with ambitions. "And the police like restraining orders," says Buel, "because they get the power of automatic arrest."

"Sometimes just the threat of filing charges will deter abusers," says Pirro. "They know that if they break this order of protection it will be a matter of record."

THE ONLY WAY THEY COULD "GET IT"

When Mallory Greeley, with the support of Dr. Bob, the psychologist her mother, Pat, had consulted, decided to break up with her battering boyfriend, Jon, he ratcheted up his harassment and threats to kill her. Her parents tried talking to his parents, but they put the blame on Mallory for being unstable.

There was only one thing that got through to them and their son: the powerful message conveyed by the restraining order that Mallory and her parents filed — his behavior was criminal. Jon, a top student who had just received a basketball scholarship to a prestigious college, immediately stopped all contact with Mallory. The last her family heard about him was that he had gone off to college somewhere in the East — on his basketball scholarship. "And we were free to put all our energy into helping Mallory," says her mother, Pat.

RESTRAINING ORDER PLUS SAFETY PLANNING

One thing that the experts are all in agreement about is the need for safety planning in conjunction with the restraining order.

Meredith Blake explains: "If we go to court, we sit the girls down and say in very clear terms: 'You need to understand that the restraining order is not a guarantee of safety — so we have to do safety planning. We have to think ahead of time.'

"We can go with our client to the school administration and discuss moving the kid from one class to another. We ask her: 'What shift of part-time job do you have? Are you alone there?' We call her employer to see if her shift can be changed. We do everything to enhance her safety."

"I KNOW WHAT YOU ATE LAST NIGHT"

When seventeen-year-old Jennifer Coleman decided to break up with her abusive boyfriend, a restraining order was the one thing that stopped him from stalking, harassing, and threatening her.

"When I got fired from my job because of a fight we had in the parking lot — he put his fist through the window — I knew it was over. But he refused to accept my decision," says Jennifer. "He called every night at two A.M., and every time he drove by my house, he leaned on the horn. Sometimes he would throw a rock up at my window." Just as she had never told her parents about his abuse during their fourteen-month relationship, Jennifer said nothing to them about his harassment.

But her cheerleading coach saw him stalking her. Although he had already graduated — he turned down a college football scholarship to be near Jennifer — he would come into the stadium during games and sit down in front of her. Her coach made sure that he was escorted out. But he continued to show up everywhere she went.

At first, she understood his anger — "but then he started threatening me. He swore that he would hurt me and kill anyone I went out with."

Jennifer did go out with another boy. "The next day, I received a call letting me know that he knew where I had been, who I was with, and what I had done. 'I know what you ate last night,' he said. He even told me the flavor of ice cream I had ordered. This scared me. I wondered how often he had followed me. I began to worry."

Two weeks later, Jennifer was at a party with her cheerleading friends, dancing in the backyard, when one girl noticed someone in the woods. "We laughed at her," says Jennifer, "but when I was leaving, I had an eerie feeling in the pit of my stomach, and I asked a friend to walk me to my car. There he was in his truck, across the road. I went back inside and called my parents."

When her mother arrived, he seemed to have gone away. "But as we were saying good-bye, he appeared from the woods in a rage. He screamed he was going to get me, that he would be sure I would never have another boyfriend."

Jennifer's mom and her friends called the police. And she herself filed a restraining order. "I wasn't going to let him control my life anymore."

Once they found out about his violence, Jennifer's parents were very supportive of her. And the restraining order did work. He never contacted her again. Jennifer eventually returned to her lighthearted self and was able to have healthy relationships with other young men.

Her ex-boyfriend, however, continued his downhill slide. "He started all over again, dating a high school sophomore, and he became worse with her. I heard that he broke into her house. And he was arrested for violating the next restraining order filed against him."

FILING CHARGES FIRST

Sometimes the restraining order comes after the encounter with the criminal justice system. When her seventeen-year-old daughter Julie ran away with her high school boyfriend, Sharon Hoberman was amazed. "We had never criticized Mike or wanted to stop the relationship." At that time, Sharon and her husband were completely unaware that Mike had been hitting Julie, although Julie's self-named "nosy little sister," Bailey, had witnessed the abuse.

"I knew exactly where they were — her friends told me — in an apartment in town," says Sharon. "Julie just thought it would be glamorous living together . . . and she could take care of him there." (Sharon had no clue that Mike had been living out of his car because his parents had evicted him from their house.)

Sharon turned to a very good psychologist friend and asked if they should follow their first instinct: to drag Julie out of that apartment. "He said: 'You do nothing. You know exactly where she is. And she's still showing up at school.'" Mike was attending school, too.

Three days later, Mike called Sharon from the emergency room: Julie was having trouble breathing. "She was having an anxiety attack, hyperventilating. They needed us to give permission to treat her — she was only seventeen."

After she received treatment at the hospital, Julie told her mother: "I didn't know how to come home; the anxiety attack helped me get away from him." She revealed to her parents that Mike had been slapping her around. "That was when we said they could no longer see each other."

Three days later, when Julie was home alone, with all the doors locked, Mike broke in through the garage door. (One neighbor saw him and never thought of calling the police. She had assumed that he was still Julie's boyfriend and had probably lost his key.)

Suddenly, Julie saw Mike looming over her. "You're not going to break up with me," he was saying. "If you don't leave, I will," she told him. He twisted her arm, trying to restrain her. Managing to wrest herself free, she reached for the telephone. He tore it out of the wall and threw it at her. She ran out into the street, and he ran after her.

Another neighbor saw her. "I need help," she said. "Call 911."

The police came immediately and arrested Mike. The district attorney charged him with breaking in and assaulting Julie. "All Julie had to do was give a written statement," says Sharon. "Mike's mother begged us not to press charges, but it was out of our hands. There was the evidence, the broken garage door, the hole in the wall where he threw the phone, Julie's injured arm. He went to court. All of a sudden, his parents were there for him with expensive lawyers.

"Mike was sentenced to ninety days in jail, and the judge imposed a permanent injunction against him. He was ordered to have no contact with Julie. Ever. 'If we get one phone call that you're even near her, I'll give you much more than ninety days,' the judge warned him. Mike never got in touch with Julie again — although some of their mutual friends still see him in another town."

Julie went on to college, but Mike, who had been a top student like Julie, never returned to high school. Instead, he got his GED. So far, he has not gone to college, possibly, Sharon thinks, because of the felony on his record. "I hear he's been doing some construction work," she says, "and that he has a new girlfriend."

"GO BACK TO BED, SLAVEY"

In 2001, after I gave a presentation for a Missouri high school district, Annyjean Holder,* who had just gotten out of an abusive relationship, responded to my invitation to be interviewed for this book. She and her mother subsequently spoke to me on the telephone about their experience with a battering boyfriend and the law.

A seventeen-year-old senior in a rural high school, Annyjean had been dating a nineteen-year-old farmer, who fell so much in love with her that he eagerly traveled the forty-five miles between their homes almost every day. But after three weeks, he became controlling. Says Annyjean: "He wouldn't let me talk to another guy. He was always telling me what to do — 'Eat these brussels sprouts and like it. Don't smoke.'"

Her mother, Wanda,* thought this advice, while good for her daughter's health, was being delivered in a domineering way. Annyjean excused Chuck's bossiness as "concern out of love for me."

But Wanda was unaware of Chuck's volatile temper. "Sometimes he would blow up and get crazy. He would fight with his mom and get mad at me," says Annyjean.

Wanda, learning that Chuck was having difficulties at home, felt sorry for him and said he could stay at their house until he worked things out with his mom. (They would later hear from Chuck's mother that he was threatening to kill her.)

Once Chuck moved in, he tried to place a wedge between Annyjean and her mom. "He called me 'slavey' because I did chores around the house before school — to help my mom because she went to work early. When I'd get up at seven A.M., he would yell, 'Go back to bed, slavey.' One time, he threw me on the bed and hurt my arm so bad it had to be in a sling for a week."

Wanda had always assured her daughters that they could tell her anything. "Mom is my best friend," says Annyjean, but she admits she "did hesitate to tell her what was going on. *What's she going to do to me?* I thought. *She might freak out about the arm — because she cares.*" Her arm, she explained to her mother, had been injured in a fall.

"Chuck was screaming at me more and more and shoving me around. One day, I got really scared," she says. "When he left the house, I locked all the doors and called my mom at work. He came back, but I wouldn't let him inside."

Wanda called 911 and stayed on the phone with her daughter until the police took him away. When they booked him, they discovered he had a prior conviction for harassment. The judge warned him not to contact Annyjean again.

Three weeks later, Chuck called her. "He said he was in more trouble, that rape charges were being pressed against him. 'Why are you telling me this? I don't want anything to do with you,' I said. He stays away now. He knows my family will inflict some hurt on him." Annyjean's uncle, a strapping 6'7" farmer, with a voice that seems to come from the soles of his shoes, made that clear.

CONFRONTING THE SECOND AMENDMENT

Fifteen-year-old Jade was willing to accept her mother's aid in breaking up with her manipulative boyfriend, but she had not confided completely in her. While she had revealed his family's tragedy — his brother was dying of cancer — she never mentioned his family's hobby — target shooting.

Always polite and compassionate, Jade's mom, Vivi, never lost her patience when speaking to the boy. But he did. He was becoming more and more furious that Jade was "blowing him off." He began to follow her after school and plead, then demand, that she stay with him — or else. . . .

When Jade finally told her mother about the implied threats, Vivi, a South Carolina teacher, remembered that she and I had spoken after one of my presentations, and she still had my card. We spoke again on the telephone, and at my suggestion, she contacted the boy's family — but they were too distracted by their other son's illness to recognize the potential for danger. As for guns, they were a law-abiding family.

I consulted with Barrie Levy. "If I were Vivi," she said, "I'd get information from the police. I'd report that he's stalking her and get a restraining order. I'd try to get access to anyone who has influence over him besides his parents — to request that they help to monitor him. I'd do what I could about his access to guns. And I'd prevent him from having access to my daughter. I'd change her school, or I'd even send her out of town to live with relatives."

But just how much could be done about his access to the guns? Attorney Meredith Blake says:

> If Jade were living in California, she could, as a minor, get a restraining order against him. But it would mean that before the judge orders the family to turn their guns over, he must decide what has happened in the relationship. Have there been threats of violence? There has to be a credible reason to believe he can do harm to her — has he beaten up other boys or other girlfriends? Does he have a police record?

Vivi learned from the police that Jade's boyfriend did not have a record, but as Blake points out: "The fact that a nineteen-year-old has no criminal record does not mean he has never done criminal things."

If Jade were living in New York, the situation would be different, according to Sergeant Lori McIntyre of the Nassau County Police Department on Long Island. "Criminal action can be taken —

an arrest — for threats and stalking. If a girl has articulated fear, at the time of arrest we take his guns, even his father's, even licensed guns. We remove them all, *then* we do an investigation. Police departments are becoming very careful these days; many have been sued. The order of protection would come *after* the arrest."

Sergeant McIntyre, who has had more than a dozen years' experience as a liaison to the district attorney's office regarding domestic violence and boyfriend–girlfriend incidents, finds that teenagers are in relationships that are "very scary these days — that there has been an increase in this type of violence reported to the police."

McIntyre admits that when they arrest a perpetrator of a domestic incident "there's always the chance that when he's released, he'll become crazier." But she finds that 90 percent of the arrests and protective orders are effective. "You read about the ones that don't work. But most people are afraid to go to jail."

Vivi realized that in her state she had no control over his access to guns, but she did listen to Barrie Levy's opinion, which seconded mine. She made sure that the boy had no more access to her daughter; she sent Jade to live with her aunt and uncle in New Jersey for the rest of the year and the following one.

BREAKING AWAY AT COLLEGE

When Kristy's ex-boyfriend turned up the next year at her college as a freshman, her parents were "petrified." But they applauded how Kristy handled it.

Dan relates: "As soon as she knew he registered, Kristy went to the school counselor and told her what had been going on, that he was dangerous and she was afraid."

"When a girl reports to the college authorities that she is in danger from a boyfriend, their only option is suspension or expulsion from school," says Sarah Buel. "This is a much more effective sanction in college than in high school."

The next day, Kristy's ex-boyfriend left the college before he had even unpacked his bags.

But that wasn't the last Kristy heard of him. He turned up online. She recently told me:

I think every now and then he tries to contact me in college, but I have him blocked on my e-mail, blocked on my instant messenger, and I know all of his screen names for the computer.

Actually, I did talk to him once. He instant messengered me, and I said: "What the hell are you doing?" He said, "Well, I'm in therapy and one of the things they told me to do is to clear the air with this, and I'm really sorry about what happened, it wasn't right. I don't expect you to forgive me, I don't deserve it, but I'm sorry. I just had to say that."

It sounded like a very "therapist" thing to say. I don't know if it was a genuine apology or not, but I figure it didn't really matter because it gave me a chance to tell him off.

AN ADVANCED DEGREE IN ARROGANCE

"Some college men have a sense of entitlement over others, and that's a really powerful factor in their choice to batter," says David Garvin, director of Alternatives to Domestic Aggression, an agency of Catholic Social Services in Ann Arbor, Michigan. The fact sheet from the Centers for Disease Control indicates that the prevalence of dating violence in college is 50 percent higher than in high school. Garvin describes the ego-driven preppy batterers with high "S.A.T.s" — superarrogant traits — as "self-centered and righteous young men who put their rights and desires ahead of everyone else's, who think they are the center of the universe."

Lisa Vernon says this is the perfect description of her ex-boyfriend, Bart. The day she had the cast removed from her broken arm, she moved out of his apartment and into a dorm, with her mother's now eagerly given financial assistance. Lisa thought she was finally free, that she would never hear from Bart again. But just to be sure, she had instructed the dorm not to give her phone number to him.

"He kept calling the residence hall and leaving messages," she says. "It was almost like stalking. I was afraid to leave the dorm because I thought I might see him, and he might talk me into coming back. I didn't trust that I had enough strength, and he was so used to getting his way."

"The girl is ending a relationship with an intense traumatic bond," says Barrie Levy. "There will be moments when she misses the good parts. The worst time is two weeks to two months after the breakup. If she sees him again during this time frame, he can suck her in again."

When Lisa finally went back to her classes, Bart showed up outside and wanted to know what she was doing and why she hadn't called him back.

"I was scared," says Lisa. "*No matter what he does, I am not going back,* I decided. I was adamant. I had a guy friend walk me to and from classes. Bart thought he was my new boyfriend and threatened him a couple of times."

Although Lisa had never told her mother that Bart had pushed her off a balcony, Joanne believed her daughter was in physical danger when she moved into the dorm so suddenly. "Bart tracked her down there. I was scared. At first she didn't have a phone. I couldn't even call. Lisa told me at the time, 'Bart wants me to go out and eat one last time; he wants us to still be friends.' I said, 'Please don't get in a car with him.' She didn't argue with me; she must have been scared too."

Since Lisa's dorm was coed, it was easy for Bart to get into the elevator. At 2 A.M. he would pound on her door, saying, "We can work it out, everything will be fine."

Two weeks later, Lisa got an empathic roommate and made two new friends — her roommate's boyfriend and his lab partner, Tim, the man she would eventually marry. "But at that point I was sure I was through with men." Because Tim and his study buddy often worked together at the girls' place, they soon became a foursome. "I finally told them what happened with Bart," she says, "the first time I ever told anyone. After that, I was never by myself. They made sure of that."

Bart demanded to know who Tim was, where he was staying, but Lisa refused to tell him. "I was afraid for Tim, so I said: 'He has nothing to do with you and me.'"

But Bart would continue to stalk Lisa — and make prank phone calls to Lisa's new telephone number. (As Gavin de Becker states, the stalker always manages to get the new number.)

For no apparent reason, Bart's harassment suddenly stopped. (As Barrie Levy explains, sometimes the abuser temporarily changes his tactics.) Several weeks later, Bart asked Lisa if she would allow him to come up to her room and "talk just a little while because there were some things he wanted to tell me. It was the first time I thought he was being honest, not yelling, but calm." De Becker warns against this kind of ruse that ostensibly offers closure. "For this type of young man, any contact will be seen as progress."

Lisa, however, agreed to give Bart a half hour — but she did take additional safety precautions. She alerted Tim and his roommate and the girls next door to stay there and to call downstairs if they heard any yelling. "So they sat there. I hadn't had friends like that in a long time who were willing to do that for me. It felt really good.

"Bart and I did end up just talking, but when his half hour was up, I asked him to leave. As I went to open the door, he stepped in front of it and blocked me. I told him there were six people in the room next door who would come over and drag him out. Didn't faze him at all. So I started yelling so they could hear next door. They called security, and he was escorted out."

Although she never officially pressed charges against him, she made sure that every residence hall manager on campus had his picture posted behind the desk with instructions to call the police if he entered the premises.

Yet he continued to stalk her. "Everywhere I went, he would show up. Somehow, I made it through the rest of the school year."

Lisa decided not to go home for the summer because she was ashamed. "My parents were right about Bart; I didn't want to face that."

Knowing that Bart had graduated, she took an apartment with two girls. "He was supposedly living at home with his parents, in Chicago, but I would run into him on campus all the time. Said he was seeing his friend in grad school."

It took two weeks for Bart to find Lisa's apartment and pound on the door. To protect her, Tim moved into the extra bedroom. During the next year, she moved to four different apartments, and

Bart found the phone number at each one. "He didn't pound on the doors, but we would get prank phone calls."

Exactly one year after they broke up, Bart found the phone number of Lisa's newest on-campus apartment, which she was sharing with Tim and his friend. "He would only call when the two guys were gone, so he must have been outside watching them — and me."

Lisa never thought of having Bart arrested for harassment, but her parents did after he made prank calls to her family. Although the calls were traced to a pay phone two blocks from Bart's house, Lisa's parents decided they would rather not face him in court.

When she learned that Bart was applying for a teaching job, Lisa's mom, a teacher herself, considered sending a letter of warning to all the school districts in Illinois. But she backed off. The last they heard was that he was working in an elementary school — not a good place for a man like Bart to be, says Joanne — presumably using all of Lisa's childhood books, which she had lent him and which he refused to return, in his class library. But Joanne is grateful that Lisa is now happily married to Tim, whose character is diametrically opposite to Bart's.

THIRTEEN

TERROR/COUNTERTERROR

BEATING, BREAKING IN, STALKING, threatening, terrorizing — these behaviors put the abusive boyfriend very near the center of what Gavin de Becker calls "the predictive circle" of murder.

According to the Centers for Disease Control, homicide is the second leading cause of all deaths among children (14 percent) after car crashes (42 percent).

"While it is true that all batterers are dangerous, some are more likely to kill than others, and some are more likely to kill at specific times," the Pennsylvania Coalition Against Domestic Violence points out in *Assessing Whether Batterers Will Kill*. Although they admit that "assessment is tricky and never foolproof," they give certain guidelines to help investigating officers evaluate whether an assailant is likely to kill, regardless of whether there is a protection order in effect.

Among the indicators are threats and/or fantasies of homicide or suicide, access to guns, context of previous violence (the more calls to the police, the greater the potential danger), separation violence, and access to his girlfriend.

Jacquelyn Campbell, Ph.D. and RN, who is a professor at the Johns Hopkins University School of Nursing, has put together a risk-factor scale based on research conducted after murders have occurred. While Dr. Campbell says that she cannot predict what will happen in each case, she believes young women should be aware of the danger of homicide in situations of severe battering and of how many risk factors apply to their situation. She suggests rating incidents according to the following scale. (The numbers on the scale rise according to the severity of the abuse.)

1. Slapping, pushing; no injuries or no lasting pain
2. Punching, kicking, bruises, cuts and/or continuing pain
3. "Beating up"; severe contusions, burns, broken bones
4. Threat to use weapon; head injury, internal injury, permanent injury
5. Use of weapon; wounds from weapon

Other risk factors are increase in the frequency and severity of the physical violence, attempts to choke, access to guns, forced sex, substance abuse, violence to others. Dr. Campbell suggests that the young woman never undertake this risk assessment without the help of a professional in the field.

"Whatever the risk level," says Barrie Levy, "I immediately work on a safety plan based on the kind of danger possible, where and when. If the danger level is high (violence is imminent, say, as soon as she leaves my office), the safety plan must have immediate strategies, such as not going home, going someplace safe, not being alone, involving the police, et cetera."

"THIS BOY IS CALM NOW; HE WANTS HIS LIFE BACK"

The first time that Ashley White's suicide-feigning boyfriend was released from the mental-health facility — he had only been kept there for two days — the Whites were given no more than forty-five minutes notice that he was out.

Ashley's mother, Deb, spoke to the school authorities. "My daughter's scared," she said. "We told her we're no longer allowing her to see him. But he has access to her at school."

Deb insisted that the counselor change Ashley's entire program of classes. But lunchtime remained the same. "Finally," Deb reported, "we got the principal to change her whole schedule, but he acted as if my daughter were part of the problem. He suggested conflict-resolution sessions between Ashley and Josh!"

Josh was working on his own conflict-resolution scenario via nonstop telephoning. Realizing that the Whites had Caller ID, he would go from pay phone to pay phone, trying to speak to Ashley, but Ashley's father would answer most of the time and hang up on him. "We tried to keep her away from him," says Deb, "but we were afraid she would eventually give in."

At times, Ashley did give in — when Josh managed to play on her sympathies: his dad beat him, he was depressed, he needed her. "Sometimes I hated myself for seeing him," Ashley now admits. "I really did love him, but I think it made everything so much worse. He told me I would never be free."

Deb's neighbor reported to her that she saw Josh following Ashley down the street, calling her obscene names. When Deb called Josh's mother about the abuse, she said: "It looks to me like your daughter wants to be with him." Deb replied: "My daughter is not the one driving by his house."

After learning that she was seeing Josh surreptitiously, Ashley's parents put her on "lockdown." They drove her to and from school, monitored all her phone calls, never left her alone (Deb is a stay-at-home mom). They even went so far as to nail her window shut because Josh suggested she climb out and meet him. "I don't think she would have actually done that," says Deb, "but the window was above the carport, and Josh was an athlete. We were afraid he would climb in."

"I know my parents are just doing all this because they love me and don't want me to be hurt, but I feel I'm being punished for the things Josh has done to me," Ashley wrote in her diary. After she showed it to her mother, Deb took her to the crisis center in their town for counseling.

Josh was also getting counseling — during his second institutionalization after he had stolen a gun from a friend and sent Ashley a flurry of threatening e-mails and another suicide note.

Several weeks later, without receiving any word of his release, Deb saw him at her door one night looking for Ashley, who was on a date. "If she doesn't talk to me, she'll be sorry," he warned Deb. He then threatened to kill Ashley and her best friend.

"He will never leave me," Ashley admitted to her mother. The next day, they went to the county attorney to get a restraining order. Because of Josh's mental condition — he was reinstitutionalized — no criminal charges were brought against him. However, he was required to enroll in another school district at the time of his release.

Together with the counselor at the crisis center, the county attorney formulated another safety plan for Ashley, one that the school authorities agreed to follow should Josh ever set foot on their grounds.

Six weeks later, hearing that Josh had been released from the mental-health institute, Deb accompanied her daughter to school and headed for the principal's office, with the no-contact restraining order in hand. "I wanted to make sure the safety plan was in effect. I didn't trust the principal to follow it."

In the hallway, she saw Josh's mother enter another office. They said nothing to each other, but Deb was becoming suspicious. Deb wondered: *Is she trying to get her son reinstated in this school?* The woman, a public health director, had great influence in the community.

"This boy is not supposed to be back in this school," Deb declared to the principal.

"This boy is calm now," the principal insisted. "He wants his life back; he wants to play football again." Deb thrust a copy of the no-contact restraining order into his hand and reminded him of the safety plan. As she drove away, she thought she saw Josh prowling around the school grounds. Unshaven and rumpled, he looked anything but calm. From her car, she called the principal's office.

But Josh had already entered Ashley's classroom. The teacher, unaware of a safety plan, gave him permission to speak to Ashley in the hallway. When Ashley refused to follow him, he gripped her neck and began strangling her in front of the entire class. The teacher pulled him off of her, and Ashley escaped and ran to another room. He tried to enter that room too and was stopped by another teacher.

Before the police arrived, Josh asked Ashley: "Are you okay?" She had claw marks on her neck, bleeding from the scratches his fingernails had made.

Josh was arrested at the school. The county attorney pressed charges for violation of the no-contact order, as well as stalking and assault.

"The school administration buried their heads in the sand," says Deb. "Not the teachers, they cared and would have done whatever they could have to help her, had the principal only let them know. With all the recent media attention on school violence, you would have thought they would have been more careful with my child's life. They were more concerned about *his* rights. Where was my child's right to feel safe in school?"

(Regarding a lesser crime, sexual harassment, in 1999 the United States Supreme Court ruled in *Davis vs. Monroe County Board of Education* that under Title 9 of federal law, guaranteeing equal educational opportunities for both sexes, schools can be held liable if they are aware of a harassment pattern and do not protect the victim.)

Josh was sentenced to five years, but never spent time in jail, just a few more months in the mental hospital. Upon his release, he was required to leave the community; he went to live with his grandparents in Illinois. Deb heard that he was harassing girls in their area too — that he had wrestled one through the plaster wall of her house.

One year after the assault, Deb was shocked to see Josh with his parents and grandparents at Ashley's dance recital. He said nothing to her, but the Whites called the police afterward. They learned that the no-contact order had expired and that Josh would have to "do something again" before they could get another one.

Since our first meeting, Deb, who lives in a town several hundred miles from mine, has kept in touch with me. Recently, she let me know that Ashley has been taking precollege courses at the community college in town, and she just learned that Josh will be attending the same college. "And guess what courses he registered for? Criminal justice!" The irony made us both laugh — but only for a moment, to cover the fear. Although Deb was assured that the college has a zero-tolerance policy for dating violence, I suggested that after high school graduation, she send Ashley to a college out of town.

"GIVE ME FIVE MINUTES OF YOUR TIME"

After Kaisha Marshall dropped the charges of assault with a car against her boyfriend, she was given an order of protection by the judge, allowing him to see her because of their child but ordering him to refrain from abusive contact. Four days later, Darryl, remorseful, seemed willing to do whatever Kaisha wanted.

Although he was not a hands-on dad and contributed no child support, he agreed to baby-sit one night when Kaisha was waitressing part time. But he showed up unexpectedly at her restaurant and told the manager she had to leave because of a family problem. *What did I do now?* she asked herself.

With the baby in the backseat of his car, Darryl told her he had just heard from her neighbor that she had stayed out all night, the night before.

"I knew she never said that," says Kaisha. "But he began raging, calling me a bad mother, threatening me. I said, 'Let me out of the car,' and he punched me in the face, cut my cheekbone with his fist, and busted my lip and my eye. I was on the floor of the car. I tried to get up. I said, 'Give me the baby.' I didn't want my child to see him beating me up."

But he continued the night of terror in his apartment — stomping on her chest, scalding her in the shower, dragging her out by the hair, threatening to kill both her and the baby, who was screaming on the bed.

Since she could not physically escape with the baby, Kaisha instinctively used one of the techniques advised by Barrie Levy and other experts to defuse an explosive situation. She stopped fighting and yelling back — and gave him what she thought he needed to de-escalate the violence. Through her terror and fury, she counted to ten and tried to calm herself and soothe him. "I sat down and told him over and over what I knew he wanted to hear: 'Everything's okay, I do love you, I'm not seeing anybody else.'"

Reassured, he eventually relaxed. She had saved her life and the baby's. Later, he drove them to her mother's house.

By now, Kaisha knew that her dream of forming a family with him and their child was over. He was beyond therapy. All the love she had once felt for him had turned to rage. She would break up with him once and for all.

The next day, although she had her injuries treated by a doctor, she was still reluctant to report the crime. "In spite of everything, I didn't want to feel guilty about putting him in jail," she says in her soft, gentle voice. "And I was afraid he would get even madder if I did that to him. I only knew I never wanted to see him again."

During the next month, Darryl tried to get Kaisha to change her mind. "Let me come back," he would plead on the phone. "No," she insisted. He kept calling; she kept hanging up. He tried to get her neighbor to convince her to get back with him, that he still cared for her. But Kaisha believed that her neighbor had been intimidated by him.

At eleven o'clock one night, Darryl showed up outside Kaisha's house. "My mom and the baby were sleeping. I stayed inside behind the screen door."

"I'm your son's father; give me five minutes of your time," he pleaded. "I need to talk to you about our son." When Kaisha refused, he pushed open the door, pulled her out, and accused her of sleeping with someone else. (He had found her appointment book in her car, showing that she had recently had two dates with another man.)

"How could you do that to me?" he raged. "Do you love me or not?"

"I don't love you anymore," she said.

"I'm gonna kill you," he yelled, forcing her into his car. Nobody on the deserted suburban street heard her screams. He drove her to a nearby isolated park, where it was almost completely dark.

"He was yelling that he really loved me and that nobody would find me when he killed me," says Kaisha. "He picked me up over his shoulder, and when I started screaming again, he put his hand over my mouth. 'I just want us to be together,' he said. Then he started saying stuff about the guy I was seeing. He punched me over and over and bit me on the breast. I must have passed out. When I came to, he was on top of me. 'I just love you,' he said."

Dazed, Kaisha realized what had happened. "'You just raped me,' I told him. He said, 'No, that wasn't rape. You have had my son. I am the father of your child.' *As if it gave him the right to rape me.*"

Her nose was bleeding, she was bitten and bruised, her shirt was ripped, and she had to search for her underwear in the grass. "That was rape," Kaisha reiterated.

"I didn't mean to hurt you," he told her. "I just wanted us to be a family."

He insisted on driving Kaisha back. "'Are you gonna call the cops?' he asked me. I said no."

From home, Kaisha immediately called a friend, who took her to the police station and the hospital. This time, she did press charges against Darryl. The police arrested him for assault and rape.

Darryl was denied bail. Kaisha found out much later that he had been in jail for three years — when he was seventeen — for doing the same thing to another girl, whose dad was an assistant district attorney. Her father's position of power had evidently been no deterrent to Darryl.

Darryl would claim later that he was on drugs when he raped Kaisha. She is doubtful. He was sentenced to two to four years for first-degree rape.

I KNEW HE WOULD HURT HER

Several months after Helen Tarnares had banished her daughter's controlling boyfriend from her home — as she describes in chapter 2 — Vasso herself decided that she had had enough of Ray's jealousy and possessiveness. She asked her mom to drive her to his house to pick up the stuff she had left there. It was only then that Helen realized how physically violent Ray could become.

He screamed at Vasso, then pushed her. When Helen threatened to call a policeman and her husband, he barked: "You send your husband with the police, and I'll blow you away!"

"Breaking up with an abusive boyfriend is a sexual rejection of him. He's very fragile. Without the other, he collapses, he fragments, he doesn't feel manly," says Dr. Shelley Neiderbach. "He's like a two-year-old; he has entitlement narcissism. Once you've scraped his ego, you're going to pay for it."

"An abuser's biggest fear is abandonment," agrees Dr. Noelle Nelson. Twenty-year-old Raymond Purvis's mother had left home years earlier.

During the six months following Vasso's breakup with Ray, there were threats, stalking, and four incidents of burglary. A brick was thrown through the windshield of Vasso's dad's car. The stuffed animals that Ray had given Vasso disappeared from her room; he told Vasso that her mother must have thrown them away.

Ray could often be seen sitting in his car on their street. Vasso would say to Helen: "Take me to school. He's at the bus stop."

At four different times, Helen called the police. However, stalking was not yet against the law, and she could not give them evidence of "probable cause" to arrest him for burglarizing her home.

Although his hatred seemed to be centered on Helen, "for breaking us up," and although to her knowledge, he had never hit Vasso before — actually he *had* slapped her during arguments — Helen became more and more convinced that he would seriously hurt her daughter. But the police, her husband and friends, her fourteen-year-old daughter, Stacey, and Vasso herself believed that Helen was overreacting. Vasso had a different fear: she was afraid of what he would do to her *parents*. He had threatened to burn down her house with her parents in it.

Ray was jailed that December for burglarizing another home, as well as his own. His father brought the charges. But even from jail, his threats to Vasso's family did not stop.

Helen and her husband obtained an order of protection against him. It was dated February 10 — the very day he was released from jail.

"An order of protection makes an important statement," says Dr. Nelson, "but unfortunately sometimes it ignites his rage further." Predictably, Raymond Purvis, a sociopath with a criminal history, violated the order. But the police, who had an arrest warrant sworn out by Helen, were negligent in rearresting him.

Although the school had received a registered letter restricting

Ray from entering the premises, the security guards — who were his cronies — allowed him in. He grabbed Vasso's hand with so much force that her school ring came off her finger into his hand. On that February day, Vasso thought a school ring was not worth the trouble to get back. She wanted to be rid of Ray once and for all. And after he was removed from the school, she thought she was. But the ring would remain a temptation.

Still not rearrested for violating the February 10 order of protection, Raymond Purvis was due to appear in court on March 13 for the December burglary charges. On March 12, Purvis appeared at Vasso's door after she returned from school. She made the mistake of listening to what he had to say — what Gavin de Becker calls negotiation, allowing any contact to take place — and then answering him.

Ray told Vasso that all he wanted was the beautiful picture she had once drawn for him of Jimi Hendrix — and that he would return her school ring. Vasso asked him to wait outside.

This is the rest of the story, as Helen has pieced it together: The music from Vasso's CD was playing so loudly that she didn't realize Ray was right behind her as she went up the stairs. In her room, Ray choked her and stepped on her neck. (He later told a friend: "I would have fucked her, but she wet her pants.")

When Vasso's fourteen-year-old sister, Stacey, came in from school, she saw Vasso's boots and keys and heard the loud music playing. Wondering where Vasso was, she suddenly realized, as she was speaking to a friend on the phone, that Ray was sitting at the top of the stairs. She informed her friend of his presence.

"I had to use the bathroom," Ray explained.

"Where's Vasso?" Stacey asked him. He suggested they look in the basement, but Stacey tried to get into Vasso's room. "Don't go in," he said. She managed to pry the locked door open; she found Vasso in the closet, in the fetal position, blue. "What's wrong with her?" she asked Ray, never believing that he would cause such injury to Vasso. "Call 911," she screamed. Pretending to comply, Ray took the receiver off the hook. After a few minutes, Stacey herself reached 911.

The medics, believing there was no hope that she could survive, took Vasso to the local hospital rather than the trauma center.

Ray told the policeman who arrived with the medics: "I'm not supposed to be here because of a restraining order, but Vasso called me to help her." Believing Ray's story and voicing concern about vengeance from "those old Greeks" — meaning Vasso's dad — the policeman told his colleague to take Ray wherever he wanted to go. At his friend's house, Ray burned the gloves he had worn and said enough incriminating things to lead his friend's father to call the police, who arrested him. Held in jail on a million-dollar bond, 2½ years later he pleaded guilty to attempted murder. He was sentenced to 7⅓ to 22 years.

Vasso miraculously did survive. She was on a respirator for six weeks and in a coma for six months. Milk had to be squirted into her mouth; Helen had to feed her like a baby. For the next six months, she did not speak.

Vasso spent more than two and a half years in a rehabilitation facility, where she had to learn to read and write all over again. She has come a long way cognitively, her mother points out, but she is still undergoing physical therapy for her balance.

"I THOUGHT HE WOULD TAKE BULLETS FOR ME"

Unlike Raymond Purvis, Deirdre Weigert's controlling boyfriend, who had removed all her pictures of male friends — as she describes in chapter 2 — was completely law-abiding. "Ryan Lawrence never even got a parking ticket," says Deirdre. "He didn't do drugs; he played basketball."

Although her mother would hear her squabbling with him on the phone, Deirdre kept his abuse to herself. She didn't even confide her unhappiness to any of her girlfriends.

Three times they broke up and three times they made up. But after thirteen months, Deirdre decided to make the final break. She told him that she was coming to his house to get the things she had left there.

"He said okay, and he was sitting on the stoop when I got there, waiting for me — with all my stuff. That was the big day we both knew we were *really* breaking up." As she walked away with her possessions, he threw her down on the ground and pushed her face onto the concrete, hurting an old whiplash injury.

Deirdre was shocked. "I thought Ryan loved me so much, there was such a bond between us, he would never hurt me physically. For more than a year, he did anything you can possibly imagine for me. There was a good part to the relationship, and until that day, he never laid a hand on me." Before she left, he kicked in the door of her car, causing $600 in damage.

A month after their breakup, around Valentine's Day, when Ryan realized there was no hope for a reconciliation, his stalking began. Deirdre would receive voice mail: "I saw you going into the movies." He would call her at her job — "just to talk." Then came the threats: "If I can't have you, nobody's gonna have you." He said he would throw acid in her face. He told Deirdre and her friends that she was going to die. Deirdre's best friend thought he was joking. "Get a life, move on," she told him.

But Deirdre believed he would hurt her . . . especially on the day he showed up at her door with a bullet and said: "This one has your name on it." Deirdre was thinking of staying with relatives in the Bronx, but he threatened to kill her family if she moved away.

"Violence in dating is a form of terrorism," says Dr. Neiderbach, who is a certified trauma specialist. "You don't know when the next attack is coming. You live in terror. There's no way to head it off. Moving away can be lifesaving when you're dealing with an ex-boyfriend who is an obsessive sociopath."

On two separate occasions, Deirdre's parents complained to the police. On July 31, Ryan was arrested and charged with second-degree aggravated harassment. The judge released him on $200 bail and issued an order of protection, requiring him to stay away from the family and refrain from any contact with them.

On August 10, seven days after Deirdre's parents had obtained the order of protection, there was a knock on their door. When Deirdre's brother asked who it was and heard the name and voice of one of his friends, he opened the door.

Looking down from the upper level of the house, Deirdre saw Ryan with a gun pointed at her mother and brother. "Call 911," her mother screamed up at her. Deirdre ran into her brother's closet and shrieked to the 911 operator that there was a man downstairs with a gun pointed at her family. She gave the address, but had to put the phone down when she heard his footsteps coming up the stairs.

Deirdre knew he would find her hiding place. "I thought when he opened the closet door that he was gonna shoot me right there. . . ."

To Deirdre, the order of protection "was just a piece of paper. I couldn't grab it that night when he came at me with the gun and say stop. Not if a guy is determined to hurt you, like Ryan was. Everyone doubted him, but I knew he was gonna hurt me in some way."

Ryan dragged Deirdre by her hair out of the closet and down the steps, and pushed her into her car. With his gun to the side of her head, Deirdre, her legs shaking, had to drive several miles on a busy road. "He was telling me to go faster and calling me every name in the book, and saying he had lost his job, had no money, and it was our time to die together. He said: 'You thought I was joking.' I pleaded with him to throw the gun out the window. I lied and said I would tell my parents we had plans. But he kept telling me to go faster."

A policeman, who had arrived at her home two minutes after the initial call came in over his radio, was following Deirdre's car with his lights and siren off. As Deirdre spotted him, she flashed her car's hazard lights. Ryan grabbed the steering wheel and pulled the car over to the side of the road. By then, several police cars were closing in, with their lights flashing. With the car surrounded and policemen ordering him to surrender, Ryan grabbed Deirdre in a headlock with one hand, still pointing the gun at the side of her head with the other. "We were wrestling in the car. At one point, I had my hand over the whole barrel of the gun," she remembers. "I tried to push it away, but it went off and everything went black for a split second."

After they saw him pull the trigger at Deirdre's head, the police opened fire on him. Moments later, he was dead. Surprisingly,

Deirdre was conscious and able to walk out of the car as the police sat her on the side of the road to receive emergency medical aid.

The bullet that Ryan had meant for Deirdre's head had entered her neck. But one of the policeman's bullets, after going through Ryan's body, lodged a fraction of an inch from her spine, breaking her ribs. She spent thirteen days in the hospital and had to return later to have the bullet near her spine removed.

What drives a rejected boyfriend who has been a "solid citizen" like Ryan Lawrence to become a killer? He may lack a firm sense of identity and need to merge with the young woman, whom he doesn't regard as an individual, but as an extension of himself. As Dr. Martin Blinder, a California-based forensic psychiatrist who has interviewed hundreds of killers across the nation (including several who have killed their young girlfriends), states in his book *Lovers, Killers, Husbands and Wives:* "When he falls in love, he fuses completely with his lover. For him, quite literally, two hearts beat as one." However, when she leaves him, he experiences her loss as a destruction of a part of himself. "Murdering her makes real the death that for him has already occurred in his psyche."

Deirdre has fully recovered physically — but emotionally she says she will never get over the trauma. "I thought I was dying. I couldn't breathe. My lung was punctured."

For a long while after the shooting, her relationship with Ryan left her bewildered. "At one point, I thought he would take bullets for me, never mind be the one shooting me with them. You just don't think that the guy you loved for more than a year is gonna shoot you. You just don't think it."

FOURTEEN

AFTERMATH OF ABUSE
The Healing Journey

For a long time, I didn't want guys to latch onto me. I needed my space. I didn't even like hugging my father for a while. I didn't want a man who was bigger than me in my space.

Nina, now in her early 20s

A GIRL'S ABUSIVE RELATIONSHIP may be in the past, but the shards of it often turn up eerily in her present and future. Scar tissue on her body from beatings or bullets may be barely perceptible, but the marks on her soul go deeper and tend to flare up time and time again.

Weeks, months, even years later, survivors of abusive relationships often feel an irrational but overwhelming sense of shame. A sudden state of panic. A primal wave of rage. A loss of trust in the universe.

Flashbacks — reliving the feelings of the trauma — can be triggered by anything. A news report. A movie. The scent of a perfume. The sound of a song. Even a gift of roses or the make of a car. The clinical name for this condition is post-traumatic stress disorder (PTSD).

Says Barrie Levy: "Usually the active support of family ends before she's over the breakup (a period which can take many months). Forget about saying 'get over it.' Intense counseling may be needed to get her over the urge to call him again. If she has PTSD and her feelings are frozen, once those feelings thaw out, they implode."

"Imploded feelings are those that explode inside you," explains Dr. Shelley Neiderbach. "Victims — people of conscience — blame themselves and take out their rage on themselves.

"Years and years after the relationship has ended, a young woman may still need clinical intervention to desensitize her to the trauma of her victimization and to help her recover from its long-lasting effects," says Neiderbach, whose practice is almost exclusively devoted to patients with PTSD.

Among the common symptoms of PTSD after an abusive relationship are

- Sudden personality changes
- Drop in school performance
- Withdrawal from usual school or social activities
- Flagrant promiscuous behavior
- Sudden phobic behavior
- Sudden alienation from peers or family
- Self-destructive or risk-taking behavior
- Recurrent intrusive recollections
- Nightmares
- Sudden unexplainable feelings of terror or hostility
- Emotional numbness and feelings of estrangement from others
- Reduced involvement in the external world indicated by diminished interest in activities
- Hyperalertness
- Sleep problems
- Problems with memory or concentration
- Avoidance of activities
- Intensification of symptoms when exposed to stimuli related to the traumatic event

"I CAN'T DO A RELATIONSHIP AT THIS TIME"

Even a couple of years after her three-year relationship with Jack, Kristy Broome believes that the abuse she suffered has had long-term effects on her personality. "That's why I'm in therapy," she says. "I need to get a lot stronger — to deal with the whole injustice thing."

Shortly after Kristy broke up with Jack, she found a new love interest. "We just clicked, and I could tell Jared anything. But I was a little more timid than I used to be. I was indecisive, even about picking a movie.

"Our feelings for each other were strong, but I told him: 'I can't do a relationship at this time.' I was just not ready. I had never dated anyone before Jack."

Kristy tells me she is on a "quest to figure out what a good relationship is all about. I'm reading a lot of books. Counseling helps. One of my professors has a wonderful marriage; I go over to his house all the time. I watch their relationship; he adores her."

Kristy is also trying to restore the close relationship with her parents. "She's really fun again," says her mother, Gwyn. "She's made the click to adulthood. It's so much healthier."

But Gwyn confesses that she herself has had to get over the emptiness she felt for so long. "We missed so much. During her last two years in high school, none of the kids came over anymore. Before, the house was always noisy, kids running all over; they would even come into our bedroom to talk to us! We were really active in her life, and then it was gone. Kristy wasn't here anymore; the kids weren't here. When I would go up to her high school, these kids who used to hug me were acting like I was the evil mother, the enemy. Kristy realizes now how much she put us through."

"Jack actually kind of did us a favor," says Kristy's dad, Dan. "He was probably four bad boyfriends all wrapped up in one. Now she knows all the lines and the BS, and I think she is pretty well educated as to whom she wants to see, what she wants in a relationship. She is concentrating on her future career as an opera singer. Only recently has she begun to get interested in guys again.

"But Kristy and I are still working on fixing the aftermath of all this," he says. "Our relationship has been damaged."

And Gwyn and Dan still worry about Jack stalking their daughter during the summer, when both Jack and Kristy are in town.

Like Kristy, Julie, whose abusive boyfriend was sentenced to jail for assault and burglary, found counseling helpful.

"At first, Julie felt shame," says her mother, Sharon. "She didn't want to talk about it. She didn't feel it was anybody's business. The only girl Julie told was her roommate because she was being abused by her boyfriend. She said she had been with the guy a long time, but Julie still talked her into breaking it off with him."

Sharon and her husband also went into counseling. "We wondered what we should have done, but we just did not see the abuse. Maybe because we just couldn't imagine such a thing happening to our child."

Julie did not have a boyfriend for a long time after she broke up with Mike. "But in her sophomore year in college," says Sharon, "she met a wonderful guy, and he knows what happened." Julie, who was once shy, her mother tells me, is now much more self-confident and intense about her career ambition in the criminal justice field. The 5'1" petite blonde plans to become a homicide detective.

Mallory decided to continue Dr. Bob's counseling for a long time after she broke it off with her abusive basketball-star boyfriend. In her letter to me, her mom, Pat, writes: "Mallory had a rough time for several years. She had other boyfriends and soon broke up with them. She has found out that she's really a neat person and deserves someone special. And that someone special came along. She married him!"

RECAPTURING A SENSE OF TRUST

A happy marriage by itself does not cure the aftereffects of an abusive relationship. Although she has been married for many years, Rosalind Wiseman says: "Even in my marriage, I will have lots of dreams about [the abusive] relationship. I still try to get insights as to why it happened. It took me years and years to get over it. I didn't trust men for a very long time."

Rosalind went to counseling long after the abusive relationship ended. "Sometimes I still have flashbacks. I have to check out present time by looking at my watch."

One of the psychotherapy techniques that many experts find effective in treating PTSD is "flooding," a process in which survivors repeatedly relive the traumatic situations to unlearn the fear of both the memories and the abuse, along with their triggering cues.

In the anthology *Dating Violence: Young Women in Danger,* Johanna Gallers, Ph.D., founder of the Valley Trauma Center in Northridge, California, and Kathy J. Lawrence, a clinical psychologist, write: "Once survivors can reexperience the emotional content of a traumatic memory with someone who cares, someone who can listen to and validate their pain, the meaning of the outcome changes. This time they are not going to be hurt. This time they are not alone with their terror and rage. This time they can begin to integrate and master those feelings, which in turn lose their power to cause them to feel so intensely anxious and fearful. . . ."

Flooding is just one of a whole arsenal of techniques that Dr. Shelley Neiderbach uses to treat PTSD. "I do an assessment," she says, "and decide which ones would be right. I don't do too much flooding; most of my patients have had enough trauma." Instead, Neiderbach uses various desensitization, traumatic-incident-reduction, and cognitive therapy techniques. Some therapists use what they call "cognitive restructuring," helping the patient to reevaluate the dynamics of the situation she has been through and to place the blame where it belongs — on the abuser — while also pointing out how she herself might have been unwittingly complicit. It helps her to "rewrite" her story and rebuild her self-esteem.

"I teach them that you can use your brain to change your behavior," says Neiderbach. "A person can mediate with herself." Usually, Neiderbach treats PTSD in her Brooklyn, New York, office during a double session (two hours) once a week for as long as necessary.

STOLEN: A PERSONALITY

Clinicians Gallers and Lawrence maintain that the loss of wholeness that sufferers of PTSD experience after an abusive relationship is especially devastating to a teenage girl; the feeling that her sense of personal integrity has been violated comes at a time when she is still in the process of defining who she is. Her sense of self, or autonomy, has been eroded.

As a seventeen-year-old college freshman, Lisa thought she knew who she was before Bart entered her life and dominated it. During the years since they broke up, Bart has continued to exert a shadowy influence over her. "I was a very strong person before, no one would have thought he could control me, yet he was successful in taking a strong girl and completely changing her."

I challenge Lisa on this: "How can another person so profoundly affect and control you that he can take your personality away from you?" Lisa explains it this way: "It's like — maybe if my personality were the way he wanted it to be, then he wouldn't be so angry with me all the time. If I were what he wanted, he would be happier. Then none of the abuse would be going on."

"Many girls do experience a change in personality," says Barrie Levy. "These girls never make up for having missed their adolescence, for the loss of innocence. They can never recapture the social environment of school. They are dealing with trauma; they lose self-confidence. 'I have a mark on me; I will only attract the same kind of guy.' If they don't recover from the trauma, the possibility is that they could repeat it. It is frozen fear, and they can't do anything to help themselves."

I ask Lisa: "Did you ever think about why he was attracted to you, about the fact that he liked you the way you were in the beginning?"

"It never crossed my mind," she says. "I really didn't know. The only time he could talk about that was when he had a few drinks; the only time I heard 'I love you' was when he was drunk."

Lisa recalls that six months after they broke up, she tried to go back to school full time, "but I think that's when it finally hit about everything that had happened. I was just a basket case. I didn't want to leave the dorm because I thought if I did I would see Bart."

Lisa has difficulty continuing her story. "This is so embarrassing. I had to go to the Student Health Center and be treated for bed-sores because I never got out of bed. Looking back now, I know it was depression. At the time, I thought I was just being lazy and deserved to indulge myself after not being able to do what I wanted for so long."

Lisa still rails at the injustice of the situation: "The person who is committing all these acts can go on like nothing happened, and the person it is happening to doesn't talk about it because she is so ashamed or so afraid. Their lives can't go on as normal." She seems to shudder at a sudden image in her mind: "Lying in bed, getting bedsores, that person wasn't me, nothing close to who I am."

Although Lisa was totally unable to concentrate on courses, she was able to make and confide in new friends — her roommate and her boyfriend, and his study buddy, Tim — the man who would eventually become her husband.

"I asked Tim out for our first date, but I said, 'I have to tell you something: If you ever lay a hand on me, that will be our last date.'

"When Tim and I became romantically involved, he knew everything that had happened. I used to think we were together because he felt sorry for me. I didn't think anyone would want me after I had done so badly with my last relationship. I wondered: *Is everybody going to be like Bart if I do something wrong?*

"When I was really getting involved with Tim, I told his roommate: 'I'm afraid I'm going to start this whole thing all over again.' He said, 'Tim is not like that.' But I didn't think Bart was like that the first year I met him."

Even her happy marriage to Tim has not erased Bart's imprint. "For the first couple of years it was hard for both Tim and me, as I had to get past realizing I didn't have to ask him if I wanted to go somewhere; he thought he was making me feel like I had to. He kept saying: 'You don't have to ask my permission.'

"There's a bunch of little things I still do that are remnants of my relationship: like if Tim is in a bad mood, I automatically think I did something wrong, and I need to fix it right away. We have normal marriage squabbles, and I apologize for every little thing. He hates that. It's hard to get past doing that because I used to think everything was my fault. Bart had subtly convinced me that I was always wrong.

"One time, Tim set his alarm wrong and was late for class, and I apologized to him! I thought it was my fault that he had set his alarm wrong."

Lisa's mother, Joanne, tells me: "Some of her self-esteem has not come back. I just want Lisa to have a mind of her own again. She's afraid of making decisions because she made bad ones with Bart. She always checks with her husband. I asked her one year what she wanted for Christmas, and she said, 'I'll have to ask Tim.' When I said, 'I didn't ask you what Tim wanted,' she said: 'He is my husband. I need to check with him.' It's a shame that after Bart changed her, she couldn't change back to the way she was before."

For Lisa, the worst aftershocks of the relationship with Bart have been the nightmares. "They aren't as bad as they used to be. I used to have them every night. The same one over and over. About Bart coming after me, about him finding me. Him knocking down the door to my room, coming in, and taking me somewhere and just killing me."

Joanne still feels that the rupture Bart caused between her and Lisa has not completely closed. "It still seems like she is on one side, I am on the other. She wouldn't believe me for so long. I know she feels bad about it now, but she can't seem to get over it and say, 'I'm sorry.'"

Although Lisa will not share with her mother the extent of Bart's physical abuse, she became interested in her mom's high school student who had come in with bruises inflicted by her boyfriend but who refused to get help from her parents and a psychologist. "I wrote her a letter and explained what had happened to me. She got out of the relationship the next week. That made me feel good."

"I just want our relationship back," Joanne says plaintively to me. "Now it seems Lisa wants her family back too. I never gave up. I always thought she would come back." Joanne's voice softens at this recollection: "At her wedding, she called me up to the front to sing a duet with her, a song we had sung many times when she was a child. That made me so happy!"

DISCOVERED: A NEW SPIRIT

Unlike Lisa, Nina found that after she broke up with Ethan, she became more independent and assertive than ever before.

"I think it was an ego boost for Nina when she got out of the relationship herself," says her mother, Carly. "'My mom didn't do it, I stood up to the plate and figured out a way to get free.'"

But Nina did have to slowly relearn her sense of trust. "For a long time, I didn't want to be touched by men at all," Nina tells me. "I would flinch. Especially when people had their hands around my face . . . or even latching onto my arm in a friendly way. I can't stand to be backed up against a wall — just because Ethan's thing wasn't so much hitting but pushing, grabbing, holding, using his size. He was much bigger, and . . . when he wanted to latch onto you, he could and you weren't going to get away."

When Nina fell in love again during her second year in college and began living with her boyfriend, it was with an entirely new spirit. "One of the things I don't like is when guys tell me what to do. One day, he wanted me to go swimming — which is the biggest hassle in the world for me, with contact lenses and bad hair. He didn't ask me if *I* wanted to swim, just said guess what, this is what we're going to do tomorrow — go swimming. We got into the biggest fight over that.

"I was never independent before Ethan, so I changed completely. My mom is just amazed. I don't need anyone; I want someone, but I don't need them. I definitely don't want them controlling my life. I don't want a father figure, I want a partner."

Carly tells me she found new hope when in Nina's second year of college, she broke up with the boyfriend she was living with "because she knew he was going to ask her to marry him. The old Nina would have figured: a man at any cost, doesn't matter whether it will work or not. I want to be attached."

Nina and her mother are closer than ever now. "We have worked out a collaboration of ideas. Now we can talk about anything. When I finally told her how Ethan had given me bruises — long after it happened — she went ballistic. Blew her top. The fact that somebody hurt me, she takes very personally."

CREATIVITY AS A HEALING TOOL

For Maria Fedele, the entire year after the breakup of her relationship with her abusive boyfriend was a silent, painful standoff. "We were still going to the same private school, and I saw him constantly during our senior year — and we never spoke."

Even more difficult was attending the juvenile court hearing that took place eight months after the pivotal incident when they had both been arrested for shoplifting in a mall. "We had to stay in the same waiting room. We didn't speak. I was taking creative writing in school, and I was writing a great deal about the relationship as a way to heal myself. I had a letter and poem prepared for the judge." (As first-time offenders, Maria and her ex-boyfriend suffered no serious legal consequences.)

Another way to heal herself was to educate others: Maria became a coordinator, with the school's drug and alcohol counselor, for programs about dating abuse — a topic that had never been discussed at her school before. "Like the other girls, I had known everything relating to dating — drugs, drinking, driving, sex — all except dating violence.

"And I kept writing about my experience, all the raw emotions. The drug and alcohol counselor suggested I send my story 'Do Not Fret Over Evil Men,' in to the project that became the anthology *Ophelia Speaks*."

The act of writing down her scalding emotions helped Maria to vent them before they exploded around her and inside her. She found that putting her feelings into poetry had special therapeutic power:

Escape

If I only could escape
The mind he gave
The hate he dropped in my bleeding heart
There is no love
Who believes in that?
It's all a foreign term to me and my soul
The trust I had
I've been robbed of
The closest one to me
Lied, betrayed and hurt

Everyone is a distant stranger
So I say, no need to cry
There are no tears, left in this chapter
Maybe this independence, this distrust is better than
I do see
I'll never understand how I let him hurt me
He did a fine job if he did try
All the while I never thought
I'd end up like this
I'll never feel the same
Trust and love, I'm not sure if I'd like to regain
Maybe there is a sane reason
All this built up
Maybe there's no man in my dreams
Maybe he's a monster in a nightmare
I was fooled
Bewitched by promising words of love
Don't promise, I don't trust or love you
He cried, pleaded me to stay
Things would change
So you fooled me
Satisfied?
I stayed and again you fooled
Control freak
Anything for control
Anything to run the show, my show
I picked up the pieces and walked away
Who runs the show now?
Don't tell me of love or trust
I don't believe you
I think I never did
Fool someone else would you?

Once she started college, Maria decided to become an English education major. With her creativity, her love of words, and her beautifully articulated speech, she is looking forward to teaching English in a public school and, she adds, conducting classes about teen dating violence. If such a program is not in place in her school, Maria intends to initiate one.

Maria now looks back at her abusive relationship as a "learning experience. I have learned what I really want of people. I have become more assertive." Maria has also become quite selective about friends. Especially boyfriends.

In describing her present relationship, which has been thriving for the past two years, Maria sounds positively buoyant. The man in her life talks of how much he appreciates her sensitivity, her great listening skills, and her strong determination and will. "Our relationship is wonderful," she says, "because there is love *and* trust."

"GET OVER IT, KATE"

Unlike Maria, Kate Landis did not have to contend with the ubiquitous presence of her ex-boyfriend during her senior year in high school. He had already gone on to college and was no longer getting in touch with her.

As she has already described, after their breakup the year before, his harassment had caused her to go through a period of depression. She sums up the little therapy she received, from a guidance counselor in school, as a basic four-word sentence: "Get over it, Kate." Afterward, Kate had one session with a women's issues counselor — the wrong one, she feels — whose only suggestion was that she take a self-defense course.

Like Maria, Kate found it healing to educate other girls about the issue. In college, Kate helped some of her friends recognize that they were being abused emotionally. "And worse," says Kate. "One guy tried to run my friend over with his car. It happens all the time."

Back to her outgoing, sociable self and concerned with public policy and feminist issues, Kate became politically active. She also began speaking at high schools and conferences about her experience.

After a speech that she gave on teen dating violence at a conference of the National Council of Jewish Women, which she attended with her mother, "a roomful of Jewish mothers started blaming my mother for not seeing the abuse. But how could she? How could I? When you are in such a close relationship, you never see it. If someone had told us about dating abuse in the eighth grade, I would have known to break up with him sooner, and my mother would have been able to help me."

Kate was wary about settling down to one relationship in college. But as a sophomore, she allowed herself to fall in love again, and her relationship has continued to flourish. After graduation, Kate put her political ambitions on hold — she had worked summers for a congressman in Washington, D.C. — and moved to Manhattan with her boyfriend. She is developing a wine-education program for a magazine, but she has not given up her interest in teen dating violence education. She still speaks occasionally to New Jersey high school audiences of wide-ranging socioeconomic and ethnic backgrounds.

"It was very cathartic to speak to audiences for a couple of years after I came out of the abusive relationship. I don't *need* to talk about it anymore. I am now interested in working on policies for prevention."

"AT LEAST YOU DIDN'T LOSE HER"

Vasso Tarnares, whose boyfriend's attack put her into a six-month coma, has had the longest-lasting and most traumatic aftermath. And so has her family.

Two months after the attack on his daughter, Vasso's dad, a baker, went into cardiac arrest at the sight of his daughter and has been on disability ever since.

Vasso's mother, Helen, has had to give up her career as an advertising sales executive to take full-time care of her child. "When Vasso was in rehab, the therapists told me: 'Your life will be more difficult than if you had lost her,'" she says.

Although Vasso's speech has finally become clear, her voice has not regained its full strength. Her face has gone back to normal, but she has gained some weight and she needs to wear glasses for the computer and for distance. Vasso spends much of her day on the computer, which she can operate with only one finger. And she is a voracious reader.

"Vasso is a miracle — she is alive, and mentally she is totally cognitive now," says Helen, "but she will never be able to live alone. Her fine motor skills are gone; she can't even heat food for herself in the microwave. She will never be able to drive, or even go to college without an aide." Yet Vasso still hopes to follow her original plan to be an artist. Her art too has changed; she recently drew a face, not recognizable, says her mother, yet it has a haunting quality showing all the emotions she's been through, the fear and the sadness.

Vasso has also expressed her feelings in a poem, which appeared on poetry.com:

4:03 A.M.

I'm finding it more difficult
    To sleep at night
My mind is constantly thinking
I've noticed my headaches reoccurring
    Is it the stress?
Or the inability to just stop thinking?

Today felt as though I snapped
As though there was no salvation of my sanity, my life.

The day is usually bearable with thought of the near
        future.
But today, I couldn't see anything.
    Just misery and sadness.

I have few outlets to release this feeling on.
Of course there's my art, which is probably my best
        escape,
But I have little if any desire to surrender myself
    To my art.

Vasso's girlfriends from her high school class contact her now only to tell her about their new relationships, their coming engagements and marriages. "They never take her out," says Helen bitterly. Vasso and Helen have both been treated for depression.

Not only have Vasso and Helen been in long-term counseling, but so has her sister, Stacey, who at fourteen found Vasso and saved her life. "Because of Vasso's consuming physical rehab regime, Stacey felt neglected a lot of the time," says Helen. "She is still very angry. She has difficulties with her relationships with boyfriends; she becomes verbally abusive to them."

Vasso and Stacey are very close now. Along with their mother, they recently visited Paris, but Vasso could only tour the city using a wheelchair.

Well-meaning people have tried to comfort Helen by saying: "At least you didn't lose her." Helen reflects: "I didn't lose my daughter, but I don't have my daughter. She's not the same person. But I still love her very much."

I often think of Vasso and her family. She and my daughter Jenny had many things in common: love of learning, lots of friends, sweet nature, even their passion for dance. When I consider the condition that Vasso is in now, sometimes I wonder: *Was Jenny the luckier one?* Maybe it was easier for our family to recover from the shock and reality of her death because there was nothing we could do to change it. I can imagine how her mother and father were praying so desperately for her to make it, at the time thinking, *Lord, I don't care, any condition, just let her live.* Now I wonder what it is like to live with a child who has been so permanently changed and to watch her struggle and go through this process of learning all over again, to see it every day. As Helen describes it: "You are looking at your child for signs of the way she used to be." Yet you know that she can never do so many things she once loved. I think the pain must be overwhelming. For me the rawness ended; for them it goes on forever.

The family's relationships with the medical world and the criminal justice system continue. Helen and Vasso have just won their civil case against the county for neglecting to rearrest Raymond Purvis for violating the order of protection they had against him. With the money from the settlement, they have finally been able to move from the house where the crime took place — "There's a lot of negative energy there," says Helen — to a larger home with a swimming pool, so that Vasso can keep improving by doing therapy in the water.

Every two years, Raymond Purvis comes up for parole. Before she had to attend his most recent parole hearing, Vasso wrote to New York's Governor Pataki. "It's insulting that we have to keep coming here, that he was allowed to plead guilty to a lesser sentence. Where is my lesser sentence? He may be a prisoner in a building for a certain number of years, but I will be a prisoner of my body forever."

So far, parole has been denied. But Raymond Purvis will eventually be free. And Helen is still terrified of him.

Yet Helen remains hopeful. "I know in my heart that Vasso is here for a reason," she says, "that she will do good work; she wants to volunteer in a literacy program to help children and adults learn to read, and to participate in dating violence education. And someday, I believe she will get married."

As I consider Vasso's indomitable spirit and ambitions, I can see that had Jenny survived in that condition, I would have eventually come to Helen's belief — she was meant to be here; her life is valuable, and she has much to contribute.

A NEW LIFE

Like Vasso and her family, Kaisha has had to cope with the criminal justice system. She testified against her abusive boyfriend, who was sentenced to prison for two to four years for first-degree rape. His aunt scolded her for having him arrested — "He didn't do anything to the baby."

Kaisha has had a great deal of support and therapy, both individual and group, from her local domestic violence coalition. In addition to dealing with her own shattered emotions, she has had to contend with Darryl and his family. Right after his arrest, he sent letters to her, ordering her to "bring [his] son around." After his sentencing, his family continued to send letters asking to see the child. But Kaisha remains firm. "I don't let them see the boy."

After he went to jail, Kaisha and her son moved out of her mother's house and into a small apartment, where she has an unlisted phone number and a PO box for receiving mail.

Newly confident about her abilities, Kaisha has reconstructed her life. "I'm very proud of myself," she says. "I know what I want, and I'm determined to succeed." Kaisha, who loves art and painting, is now working as an assistant to a Cablevision executive and studying graphic design.

"My son is doing very well," she says. "I have lots of friends, and I have been in a healthy relationship for the past few years. My boyfriend and I hardly fight. When we do, it's just an argument."

Recently, Darryl was released from prison. Kaisha has an order of protection stating that he is not to contact her in any way for three years. Not trusting an order of protection alone, Kaisha takes all security precautions. So far she has not heard anything from Darryl, but she keeps in touch with his parole officer, who tells her that all Darryl seems to be worried about is whether he can get into trouble for not paying child support. "That would be the last thing I'd ever want from him," says Kaisha.

IS IT SEX OR VIOLATION?

Like many survivors, Kaisha has had flashbacks of her trauma — especially at first, when she was having sex with her current boyfriend. It took time and intense therapy to allow her to find sex pleasurable.

Experts agree that an abusive relationship often damages a girl's emerging sexuality because of her lack of ability and experience to clearly distinguish between rape and consensual sex; relationships that follow may be tinged with a feeling of violation.

A CAREER OF HEALING

Many survivors of abusive relationships have healed themselves even more by incorporating their hard-earned wisdom into their life's work to help other girls avoid their mistakes or remedy them. Some become professionals; others become dedicated volunteers.

Kaisha has revealed her story at many teen "speak-out" conferences, but now that Darryl is out on parole, she is keeping a low profile.

Kristy, angry that abuse is still happening to other girls and that they are not being taught better skills, is adamant that she will help them. She has volunteered to work with a sexual assault/domestic violence coalition on her campus. Recently, she accompanied me to a presentation that I gave to a group of university therapists. After my speech, Kristy told her own story in a compelling and moving way.

Vasso has found the presentations she has given at many New York high schools truly meaningful. "Mommy, I feel I've saved a life this morning," she told Helen. "A girl from the inner city came up crying. She was a victim of dating abuse and home violence, and something is being done."

Deirdre Weigert, whose boyfriend kidnapped her and shot her in the head, has made a complete physical recovery and has found that her experience propelled her into a healing profession. Dealing with her emotional trauma in a dynamic way, she majored in sociology in college, researching all the journals and literature on the subject of dating abuse and violence against women, and writing papers on the subject. Deirdre is now getting her master's degree in sociology and hopes to become a counselor in the field.

In college, Meredith Blake volunteered in domestic abuse shelters, and as soon as she received her law degree, she founded Break the Cycle. She has a charmingly girlish voice, but you would not want to be her opposing counsel.

When she was twenty-two, Rosalind Wiseman cofounded Empower with her husband. Now the mother of a young son, Rosalind is still actively codirecting the organization. She radiates confidence and competence.

Whenever I meet attractive, vibrant young women like Rosalind and Meredith — of the age my daughter Jenny would now be, entering her thirties — it always starts my train of "what if" thinking. What if Jenny had lived? What would she look like? What would she be doing today? Would she be as fine and accomplished a young woman as Rosalind and Meredith are? Would she be married? Would she be like Rosalind and Meredith, who have taken their painful experiences from their past and started non-profit organizations trying to protect other young women? Her ambition had been to use her gift for foreign languages in an international career. Would she too have combined it with a career of healing?

FIFTEEN

IF YOUR CHILD IS A WITNESS TO ABUSE

ACCORDING TO VARIOUS SURVEYS, 40 to 55 percent of girls ages fourteen to seventeen report knowing someone their own age who has been hit or beaten by a boyfriend. Whatever the exact percentage, young people are deeply affected when their friends are involved in an abusive situation.

Your child, now aware of the dynamics of dating violence, may know how to avoid being a target, but a friend may not. Your child's friend may be a victim. Or even worse, a perpetrator.

A mantra of the Los Angeles Commission on Assaults Against Women is "silence is violence." But what to do? To say? The wrong kind of intervention could be dangerous to your child. But no intervention can also be traumatic.

IF ONLY, IF ONLY . . .

After I had told Jenny's story at a National Lutheran Women's Conference, Melanie Foster* and her mother came up to me during the lunch break. As we ate our chicken-salad wraps and drank our coffee, they too had a story to tell.

Three years earlier, when Melanie was fifteen, she felt as if she herself had been assaulted — and at the same time responsible —

when her best friend, Bridget,* was raped and left unconscious with a broken jaw by her ex-boyfriend "who wouldn't go away."

Looking back with laser-sharp hindsight, Melanie, a small, delicate-looking girl with permed brown waves cascading along her porcelain face, realized that she could have done something to prevent the crime. *If only she had spoken to Melanie's mom — or her own — at the time that Todd was stalking and threatening Bridget!*

Melanie's voice was tremulous, and she seemed on the verge of tears as she told me that she never dreamed that Todd would be capable of that degree of violence. He seemed to be so basically decent. Everyone thought how lucky Bridget was when she started going with him at fifteen. Melanie recalled:

> *Todd was a Matt Damon double. After he graduated high school, he said he was gonna look into a modeling career instead of going to college. He worked out a lot, and he was getting more glossies made up. And we were sure he was gonna make it.*
>
> *But he was more than drop-dead gorgeous. He was a real cool guy. And fun. He could be kinda goofy. Me and all Bridget's friends, we loved Todd. He was always interested in us and our problems. Todd was our buddy, our friend too. We trusted him.*

Melanie also knew about Todd's downside — that he was extremely jealous and had a bad temper.

> *That was why Bridge broke up with him a couple of times. But then he would send her flowers and nice notes saying how sorry he was. And for weeks afterward, he would do anything for her; he was scared she would never see him again.*
>
> *The only time I saw him really hit her was at the teen club. She was there with her friends. He wasn't supposed to be there, and all of a sudden, he showed up. And that's when she told him to quit following her around. That's when he punched her. And this time the notes and flowers didn't work.*

Melanie remembered the weeks when Bridget was trying to convince Todd that "it was over."

The next note he sent her wasn't so nice. She showed it to me: he loved her so much, he wanted her back no matter what, he wouldn't let anybody stand in their way. If he couldn't have her, no one would. I think all of Bridget's friends knew about the note. I think she wanted all of us to know that he had threatened her.

The day of the rape, we had gym class together, and she told me he had called her that morning. He said, "Don't do this to me, you little bitch. If you don't go back with me, I'm gonna get you." He was just very, very hateful. That's when she told me she was scared. She said: "I don't know what to do, I've tried everything. I've tried telling him we can still be friends. I've tried telling him to leave me completely alone, don't come around, don't call me. I've tried everything. What he said to me today really scared me."

And I said: "Don't worry, Todd's just mouthing off. He won't really hurt you, he loves you."

"And I really believed he did," said Melanie, a quaver in her voice. "Deep down, I trusted Todd. We all trusted Todd."

Her words to Bridget, "He won't really hurt you, he loves you," would continue to stab Melanie for years after Bridget's jaw had healed (though her face would remain asymmetrical) and Todd was sent to a maximum-security prison.

Melanie took the first unenthusiastic bite of her wrap, while her mother, small, blond, and drawn-looking, continued the story in an edgy staccato: "Right after the rape, we had to take Melanie to a motel. She didn't want to go back to our house — because Todd used to drop in. We had to stay there for two weeks. Melanie went on sleeping in our bed for a whole year. She was hysterical at the thought of testifying at the pretrial hearing before Todd pleaded guilty. She could never look at Bridget and her mom without crying."

A year later, Melanie's father decided on a "career move," a return to their hometown, so that Melanie could live in a setting far from the scene of the trauma. And like Bridget, Melanie had to have intensive counseling.

STEPS A GOOD FRIEND CAN TAKE

This is what you can advise your child to do if she has witnessed a friend being abused or if her friend confides in her about abuse:

- Tell her you care about her.
- Express your concerns. Rather than demonizing her boyfriend, point out specific incidents that worry you — even if they are "only" verbal put-downs.
- Help her recognize that abuse can be more than getting shoved against a locker, hit, or slapped.
- Tell her you are worried about her self-esteem and her safety.
- Help her to see that changing her behavior will not change his — that abusers *choose* how they behave — and their abuse only gets worse over time.
- Tell her he's not the clasp on her gold chain — she can't "fix" him.
- Encourage her to reach out to adults for help. Some suggestions: a domestic violence/sexual assault program, school counselor, teacher, clergy member, or relative. Crisis lines are answered twenty-four hours a day, and she doesn't have to give her name. Offer to go with her or make the first call for her.
- If she won't talk to an adult, then you must find an adult you trust to talk to about it.
- When she breaks up with her boyfriend, keep up the support — invite her to take part in activities with you.

According to the National Coalition Against Domestic Violence, your teen can never say these things too much to a friend who is in an abusive relationship:

I'm worried about you.
What he's doing to you is not your fault.
I'm glad you told me about what you're going through.
You deserve better.
I'm here for you.

YOUR CHILD'S SAFETY

Warn your child not to try to talk to the girl's boyfriend about the problem . . . or to try to be a mediator. That may only cause more trouble for her friend — and for her. *She should never put herself in a dangerous situation with the victim's boyfriend.*

Make your daughter aware of safety plans discussed in previous chapters. Even if her friend dismisses her boyfriend's threats ("Oh, it's nothing, he's all talk"), your child should take them seriously and report them to you. Together, you can discuss the best way to inform the friend's parents. Never assume that they know their daughter is being abused. Betraying a friend is not the issue; saving her life is.

If, after all your daughter has tried to do to help, her friend goes back to her boyfriend, explain to her how difficult it is to rescue someone who is not ready to be helped. And while she can support her friend through the ups and downs of the relationship, she cannot neglect her own life.

SHE'LL KILL ME IF I TELL MOM AND DAD

Siblings have an especially difficult time knowing, yet not telling, that their sister is in danger. They worry but have often been sworn to secrecy.

"Siblings do reach out to counselors," says Karen Harker. "They'll say: 'My sister's getting beaten up. I had to take her to the emergency room; Mom and Dad were out of town. But my sister will kill me if I tell them. How do I help her?'" Harker often urges the sibling to bring in the victim for counseling, promising strict confidentiality. "Sometimes the child feels she is in more danger from the parents than from the boyfriend. And you want them to have a safe harbor. In cases like these, the counselors will only tell the parents if the girl is in immediate danger."

ALL HE DID WAS A LITTLE SHOVING

Bailey, the "nosy little sister" you read about in chapter 8, had a similar should-I-keep-this-quiet problem after she stood up to her sister Julie's abusive boyfriend. Bailey's immediate instinct had been to tell their mom and dad, but Julie convinced her that Mike had promised the abuse would never happen again.

But Mike did not keep his promise . . . and Bailey is sorry she kept hers. "I should have followed my gut instinct," she says, "but I didn't know he was still hurting her."

After Mike's arrest, her mom, Sharon, confronted Julie's close friends and said, "You guys had to have known."

"We didn't think he would hurt her," they said. "All he did was a little shoving."

"Shoving can do a lot of damage," she told them. "People have fallen on their head and gotten serious brain trauma."

As a result of her sister's experience, Bailey, a cheerleader with a tall, reed-slender model's figure and an outgoing Oprah personality, has been wary throughout high school about entering a serious relationship herself. She finds that most of her friends who do have boyfriends are being emotionally abused by them. "They put up with a lot of crap," she says, "and I tell them they're nuts to take it." She often defuses a situation between a friend and her boyfriend by snapping at him so vehemently, "Don't talk to her like that," that he will — at least for the time being — stop his verbal abuse. She has written about her confrontation with her sister's boyfriend for *Teen Ink* magazine.

ANOTHER TATTLETALE WITNESS DILEMMA

Sometimes a girl can lose more than a friend. Sarah Buel tells of an all-too-frequent experience: "A friend of the abused girl says, 'If I tell on her boyfriend, no other guy will go out with me.' Being popular means not being seen as a tattletale."

To tattletale or not to tattletale? It's sometimes more than just a question of popularity. Last year, I was making a presentation at a conference about dating violence in a high school in a Chicago suburb. As the students started filing into the room, I noticed three girls dressed almost alike — lots of bracelets and rings, nails polished dark blue, skimpy little tops, baggy jeans, their hair pulled back into teased ponytails. They went to the far side of the room and sat one behind the other, each alone in her row. During the speech, I saw them move off the chairs and sit on the floor, huddled together, whispering and giving each other the "look" that I have come to know so well, the look that tells me I am describing one of their lives. They seemed to react to every warning sign I mentioned.

When the presentation and the question-and-answer period were over, all three were eager to talk to me privately. The story they related was not about themselves, they claimed, but about their friend Zoey,* who was in a dangerous relationship. They had asked her to come with them to the conference, but she had refused. (The conference was voluntary.) I wondered, was it Zoey they were worried about or one of themselves?

Zoey, they told me, was constantly being put down and occasionally punched around by her boyfriend. "We've tried to tell her how bad Craig's* been, but she won't listen," said the girl with the blond ponytail, pulled so high it was almost a topknot. Her name was Sari.*

"Do you think we should tell Zoey's mom?" Arlette,* the girl with the red, spiky hair, asked anxiously.

"Zoey would hate us for that," said Lacey,* pulling back one of her dark brown strands, which had fallen across her face.

Sari shrugged. "What's the difference? She's hardly talking to us now anyway." There really did seem to be a girl named Zoey with a problem boyfriend, I decided. I, of course, urged them to tell Zoey's mother about the abuse.

"But what about Craig?" said Lacey. "He hates us because he knows we talked to Zoey."

"I'm not afraid of Craig," Sari said, with a defiant shrug, but I could see she was. All their pretty faces were scrunched up in fear — and suddenly I was afraid for them too. Was Craig threatening them? I gave them my card and told them to get in touch with me if they had more questions. And I suggested they discuss the problem with a school official. As I left them, I was not at all sure that they would take my advice.

None of the girls called me, but six months later, when I was participating in another conference at their school, Sari, flushed with excitement, ran up to me when she saw me in the halls and related what had happened.

The very day we had spoken, the girls were walking home from school discussing their options when Zoey's boyfriend, Craig, jumped out of his red Corvette, blocked their way on the quiet shortcut street they were taking, and began his diatribe. *What right had they to try to get his girl away from him?* To make his point, he pulled out a knife and made poking motions with it at Lacey. When Arlette yelled: "Quit it, Craig," he put the knife to her throat, then turned back to Lacey and held it to her stomach.

"I lost it. I started to scream and began punching his back," says Sari. "He threw the knife into the car and started laughing: 'You guys can't even take a joke.' 'It's not funny, Craig,' I told him. 'No, it's not,' he said, and put his hands around my neck. 'I don't want you butting in with me and Zoey again. Get it?' I could hardly breathe; he was trying to strangle me. I pulled away; Lacey and Arlette were screaming, and he jumped into his Corvette and took off."

They all decided to keep what happened just between them — they were scared about what he would do to them if they told anyone else — but Sari admits she was thoroughly shaken. "I wasn't eating. Every time I tried to speak, I was stuttering, and I actually started to hyperventilate when I thought about what he did. My mom always knows when something's wrong with me. This time it was written all over me in neon. I had to tell her what happened. I begged her not to — but she called the police right away."

Sari told me that emergency protective orders were issued by the court for all three girls — Craig had to stay away from their school and their homes. And they were given a safety plan. "We weren't taking any more shortcuts home." From that time on, Craig followed the orders; he wasn't taking any more chances with the law.

Although Zoey's mother, once aware of her daughter's unhealthy relationship, wanted the same intervention, Zoey refused to cooperate. She loved Craig. She would help him get better. But Craig, knowing there *could* be consequences if he hurt *anyone*, moved on to a new girlfriend in a new neighborhood. "Zoey finally forgave us for messing up her relationship," says Sari.

"Does she know you saved her from being really messed up by Craig?" I said. Sari lifted her shoulders, not quite sure. She smiled, and we hugged.

BOYS — TOO OFTEN THE SILENT WITNESSES

"Boys hate to see other boys abuse girls," says Rosalind Wiseman, "but they are afraid to step in. Most boys don't want to be perpetrators; it's so difficult for them to confront their friends who are."

Part of the Empower program is the belief that "while relatively few boys and men actually perpetrate violence, the vast majority of boys and men *witness* violence but have no idea how to stop it."

Wiseman points out that boys and men are often the "silent witnesses of violence. They see a friend get into a fight or bully a smaller, younger boy or girl; they hear a friend brag about a girl he raped, but they don't know what to do about it. We need to change the definition of masculinity, so that it is not based on expressing control, power, and domination over others, but on standing up for what is right."

Cambridge counselor Jacey Buel agrees: "Guys regulate one another's behavior. More guys must change and teach others that it is wrong to batter. They must do something, say something, not watch passively."

Or disappear forever from their friend's world, as did an old boyhood friend of Bart's, Lisa's abusive boyfriend. She recalls: "When we got back to college a week after Bart had pushed me off the balcony, one of his oldest friends asked me why my arm was in a cast. I told him I had fallen at Bart's house. He just said: 'Oh, okay.' Bart never heard from him again."

"If a boy is witness to a friend's abuse, it's important to be an active bystander," says Chad Roehner, the coordinator of a men's nonviolence program in the Midwest. "We can't say: 'Oh, they'll work it out.' We need to butt in; this is not just *their* issue. Safety and nonviolence are *our* issues."

These issues are exactly what Antoine Jeter emphasizes to his Empower training classes of boys ages fourteen to twenty. "The key thing is," he says, "only ten percent of boys are abusers. The majority are bystanders. We train them to speak up, *how* to speak up, how they can protect someone.

"It's a difficult challenge to talk to a friend about his abuse. It's tricky. His masculinity is at stake. We tell them not to physically intervene, but to challenge his behavior." Jeter also suggests that he challenge his friend's ideas, the macho messages that are all around him:

You gotta be tough to keep the girl.
Men need to be strong.
Men should have power over women.
Men are supposed to be the dominant sex.
A real man doesn't get pushed around by a girl.

"A boy's intervention in his friend's abusive behavior is sometimes successful," says Jeter. "More often than not, the friend will listen."

At that time, perhaps. But how to change his pattern of behavior? It takes more than one-by-one, incident-by-incident, on-scene interventions. The experts suggest you advise your son to do the following if his friend is an abuser:

- Avoid direct interventions that may endanger your own safety.
- Approach the abusive guy in a group when speaking to him — for safety's sake.
- Advise him to get help for his behavior. Offer to go with him. (If the police are called during an assault, in many cases the abuser can be required to get counseling.)
- Help him focus on how his behavior makes other people feel.
- Talk to him about the serious effects of abuse for both the victim and the perpetrator.
- Make it clear to him that he and no one else is responsible for his behavior.

One of the best things your child can do is to be a role model — demonstrating respect with his friends, treating his girlfriend with respect — and to pick more evolved friends.

WHEN YOU SUSPECT YOUR CHILD MAY BE AN ABUSER

DARA GAUDETTE* WAS IN a state of shock when she got the call from her seventeen-year-old son's school counselor. It was an emergency — a murder / suicide alert. Zach* was thinking of killing his girlfriend and himself.

From the time Zach was thirteen and started going out with girls, Dara knew he could be abusive. Verbally mostly. Nothing physical other than a little shoving. She blamed his attitude on the kids he was hanging out with in the neighborhood — minor-league gang kids who drank, committed petty thefts, and talked tough — repeating and acting out with their girlfriends some of the rap lyrics that were the only poetry of their lives.

It was difficult for Dara to believe that her son had become a gang wannabe in the first place. Zach and his older sister attended a fine private middle school and high school, where they both got good grades. But the school was an hour away from home — and Zach mixed in two circles of friends, one from his school in the upscale California area, the other from their own outlying "small-ish town," a working-class community of modest houses.

A single mom, Dara had risen to assistant director of a marketing company, but she could not afford the dot-com-inflated home prices near the private school. And sometimes she had to work extra hours.

After the bus dropped him home from school, Zach would hang out with the kids in the neighborhood, whom he had known from elementary school. Little by little, their anti–intellectual values began to seep into his consciousness — even when it came to his academic work in his own school, towns away. "He got very high grades," said Dara, "but he'd get embarrassed when he was called up to receive an award in an honor-roll assembly." As a compromise, the assistant principal encouraged Zach to keep up his good work and promised not to call him up to the stage again.

"The girls he started to hang out with were all gang girls," says Dara. "To them it was a given that they had to be controlled by boys. I would overhear the way Zach talked to a girl on the telephone and get very upset. My personal point of view is that verbal abuse is the gateway to physical violence." Dara was speaking from her own experience: years earlier, she had divorced her husband after his constant put-downs culminated in a black eye.

"I would get on my soapbox about the issues — not only to Zach, but to the girls he would see. What bothered me most was that the girls accepted all the verbal cruelty and belittling, the control. These girls had a lot of insecurities; if they didn't comply, they knew they wouldn't have a Saturday-night date."

Zach was popular in his school, and Dara tried everything she could think of to wean him away from his gang friends: encouraging him to get involved in extracurricular activities around the school and to invite school friends home, as his older sister, now in college, had done.

"Zach and I have always been close," says Dara. "His dad hasn't been around in years. I always encouraged him to speak freely to me about his problems. And he did — until he reached his teens. Then I tried to get him into therapy, but he would go only a few times. One of my male friends tried inviting him to ball games, tried to mentor him a bit, but Zach would have none of it. I even tried bribery, buying him more stuff, but that didn't work. He would still see the friends he wanted to see. He would go out when he wanted. I couldn't stop him. He was more than six feet tall, very articulate, and assertive."

"Some single moms," says Barrie Levy, "are afraid of their sons when they challenge her authority." But even after her daughter went away to college, Dara never feared that Zach would attack her physically. "I would have dialed 911 if I had been afraid of him," she says. "I don't cover for him."

Why did he want to adopt a thuggish pose? "One therapist told me it was his rebellion against growing up in a household of women — with just a mother and an older sister . . . a conflict within himself about being more tender than tough," Dara reflects. "I think I might have been a little overprotective because Zach has juvenile onset diabetes. After being so close to me, I think when he got into his teens and was more independent, he became fascinated with the freedom of the devil-may-care male world and the excitement of seeing what he could get away with."

Dara is not sure how much Zach did get away with, but he was eventually caught stealing a sweater in a department store. And he no longer had to be embarrassed about making honor roll in high school; his grades were on the downslide as he continued seeing his gang.

At seventeen, he fell in love with a girl his age who also had a lot of problems. "She was a rebellious young lady, whose parents couldn't do anything with her," says Dara, who had contacted them. "She moved out of her home and was in the process of getting emancipated. She would sleep at different friends' houses when she could. Although there was lots of verbal abuse in the relationship — she and Zach would break up, then go back — I knew they loved each other. But for him there was a false sense of responsibility: he felt he had to protect her; she was virtually homeless.

"I felt bad for her. He'd say: 'Mom, she has no place to sleep tonight' — but I wouldn't let her stay with us. Either she had to sleep at other friends' houses or go home. I was afraid if I let her stay for one or two nights, it would have become a permanent arrangement. At first, Zach was upset — but he got to see the bigger picture — that I was right, we wouldn't have been able to get her out of our house."

Nevertheless, during their time away from each other, Zach had insecurities: *Who is she with? What is she doing?* His mistrust was fueled by his gang "friends," who didn't want him to have a special girlfriend because it took too much time away from their activities. "They would feed him information," says Dara. "Probably a lot of it was false, but he was hearing stories about her that enraged him."

As a diabetic, Zach was usually very conscientious about his diet, "but he started taking marijuana, and he was very good at hiding it from me. It threw his sugars way off, and his mood became completely disordered."

It was at that time that Zach spoke to his counselor at school. "He told him," says Dara, "of his horrible feelings about his girlfriend. He said: 'I have gone through a very dark place, and I've come up with three options: killing her and myself; killing her and spending the rest of my life in jail; or coming to you for help.'

"Zach is basically intelligent and spiritual; thank God he knew he had to do something constructive about his feelings."

Court action was immediate. They notified Zach's girlfriend about the threat to her life and the safety steps to take, and he was ordered to have no contact with her for three years. Zach was remanded to a behavioral center for four days, given off-site counseling, and sent for four months to a ranch run by Santa Clara County in California for the rehabilitation of youthful offenders. There, in a group setting, he received behavioral therapy and counseling about dating violence.

"The ranch was almost like another rite of passage for him," says Dara. "He saw people he knew there . . . some of his gang friends. A few reported news of his girlfriend: 'Oh, she's saying that you went crazy.'"

But Zach obeyed the order of protection and never contacted the girl again.

THE FIRST COURT OF ITS KIND

Eugene Hyman is the judge who sentences youthful offenders to the Santa Clara County ranch. Judge Hyman, who used to adjudicate adult domestic violence cases, now presides one afternoon per week over the first and only domestic violence juvenile court in the country. (The rest of the week he presides over the general delinquency court.)

Launched in April 1999, the court deals with perpetrators ages sixteen to eighteen (the typical age is seventeen). Judge Hyman finds that some parents are in denial — but a woman who doesn't want her son to be an abuser will be very cooperative. The average age of the victims is fifteen. One-third of the victims have children with the perpetrators.

"If the perpetrator is under eighteen, we require a complete twenty-six-week intervention by having him go to batterers' classes," he says. "If he reaches his eighteenth birthday in the middle of the sentence, then he has to attend fifty-two weeks of sessions, as adult men do."

Judge Hyman finds that protective orders are very effective, although he stresses that safety planning must go along with them. "Perpetrators are told that if they violate the order of protection, there will be a new, more serious offense charge; there will be more criminal sanctions, and they will be taken into custody."

The intervention of the judge, as well as the batterers' classes, contributes to the program's effectiveness: "We're more on top of them at the time of the intervention program," says Judge Hyman, "and there is more victim safety during the program. But after they complete it, we find that they're still using control over their girlfriends." And in the years that follow, Judge Hyman admits there is a high incidence of reoffending with violence. But the level of juvenile domestic violence has not reached the level of adult violence, probably, he believes, because of this program.

There are two probation officers assigned to Judge Hyman's juvenile domestic violence court, each with a caseload of thirty to thirty-five offenders. "I also do prehearing reports and pretrial reports," says Suzanne Stephens, one of the probation officers. "I never view the kid separately from the family. I delve into the family background. Sometimes the mothers don't want to tell the court that the father has ever been violent to them. If things are okay between them now, I just go into the judge's chamber to give him the history."

Officer Stephens explains how the retention system works in Judge Hyman's court:

> *The minimum stay at the county ranch is four months; the usual time done is up to twelve months. Offenders can earn passes to go home — some with an electronic ankle monitor. And I always let the victim know when he's getting out of custody.*
>
> *When he goes home, he must continue his batterers' group sessions. He has to take responsibility for his actions. If after twenty-six weeks he's still in denial, if he's still victim-blaming, if he can't show nonviolent alternatives, he has to take more sessions.*

How effective does she find the program? Not as effective as she would hope for. "The young men may stop being violent, but they will still be using power and control."

Dara too felt that the program did not bring all the changes she was hoping for in Zach. "He stayed at the ranch about four months. There was gang activity there. His behavior didn't change immediately because of the dating violence group therapy."

Having dropped out of high school, Zach got his GED and eventually began working full time and taking courses at a community college. "It took about two years for the behavioral therapy to kick in. He has a new girlfriend, who lives about thirty miles away, and it's a much better relationship. He can still be abusive verbally if she lets him," Dara admits, "but he would never do anything physically abusive."

Of the fifty to sixty cases Suzanne Stephens supervised during a recent year, only three reoffended with the use of violence. A few of the others violated their restraining orders by phoning their girlfriends.

Sometimes the victim still wants to have contact with her abuser, but she is not allowed to do so. (This jurisdiction seems to be the exception to those in the rest of the nation; it monitors the victims as well as the perpetrators.) "We do surveillance," says Stephens. "Are both perpetrator *and* victim obeying the restraining order? The perpetrator could seem completely well and then reoffend by breaking the restraining order and calling his girlfriend."

SUSPECTING ABUSIVE BEHAVIOR BY YOUR CHILD

Experts agree that parents should be alert to these warning signs, which they may see or hear:

- He's checking up on his girlfriend constantly on the phone and interrogating her.
- He's telling her what to wear, whom to see, what to do.
- He is verbally abusive to her, pouring forth a cascade of demeaning names.
- He seems obsessive about her, unable to focus on his normal activities and interests.
- He talks about her in a degrading way.
- He is *always* blaming her for their conflicts.
- He has an explosive temper and breaks objects.
- He is prone to sudden mood changes.
- Neighbors and friends report abusive incidents.

EMOTIONAL REACTIONS, INTERVENING ACTIONS

Recognize the danger of denial. Probation officer Suzanne Stephens says that most parents of abusers are dealing with denial issues. As we have seen in previous chapters, the parents of the boys tend to turn the tables; when they hear the girl's parents complaining about the abuse, they blame her instead.

Confront the situation. As difficult as it may be for you to believe that your child could abuse his girlfriend, it's vital that you learn the truth. Be clear when you tell him what you've seen or heard. He may not be fully aware that he is behaving abusively. Discuss with him the Power and Control Spiral outlined in the early chapters of this book, and the Cycle of Violence. Rather than labeling him a batterer or abuser, question him about specific behaviors.

Barrie Levy emphasizes the importance of intervening early — in the teen years, before his "machismo" gets worse. "Who is 'picking up' on these boys when they exhibit these behaviors?

There is a need for parents to parent, to teach, to provide social support for their children."

Even if parents recognize their son's tendency toward abuse, they often hope that his girlfriend will be "a good influence" on him. Or, if he's overtly violent in the home, Levy often hears parents say, "I can't do anything about him." She advises parents to "do everything you can do. It is not the same as if you do nothing. *Don't do nothing!*"

Leah Aldridge agrees: "If you believe that your child is a perpetrator, you must be proactive. Identify his anger and get him into services early. And love him!"

"Parents of abusive boys are desperate," says Sarah Buel. "They are afraid of him themselves; yet they don't want him to go to jail. They're afraid of what will happen to him in jail."

One family that Suzanne Stephens worked with actually asked the police to take their son into custody. After an incident that took place on the way home from school, in which he had been blocking and pushing his girlfriend, the family asked the officer to bump up the charge to a felony — because they were afraid he might do something worse to her or to himself. This was the only way they could get him into the counseling program at the county ranch.

Overcoming guilt and shame. Dara, like many parents of perpetrators, needed a great deal of emotional support herself and went for several counseling sessions. "I felt terrible shame and embarrassment. You take it personally, and it took me a long time to realize it wasn't anything I did. At least not consciously."

Donald Dutton points out that boys like Zach, without father figures, lack a "secure attachment" and are "most susceptible to cast about for aggressive aspects of the culture to emulate. The teenage years are notable for identity issues."

Dara realizes too how confusing it must have been for Zach to reconcile the cultural imperative on the street "to be a man" with her own feminist urgings to be sensitive and open. "He was receiving mixed messages. We want boys to share their vulnerable feelings *and* cover their vulnerable need for dependency *and* hide their feelings of love. Impossible!"

CAN ABUSERS EVER CHANGE?

In spite of some disappointing statistics, there are some school classes and groups that are helping abusers change their behavior. One of them is the dating violence course called "When Relationships Go Bad" in Antoine Jeter's Empower training program for boys ages fourteen to twenty.

Jeter explains: "We teach them how to recognize if they are being an abusive partner. The key thing to remember is that these kids are deeply involved even if the relationship is only three months long. It is often intense — depending on how the relationship is set up. In our class, boys will ask: 'Guys, I did this, is that considered abuse?' Many of them are now rethinking abuse."

HOW TO HAVE A HEALTHY RELATIONSHIP

"We never call it the perpetrators' group," says Barri Rosenbluth, director of Expect Respect. "It's the 'boys' program' or the 'men's group.' We do initial screening and intake of each child referred. They have to have some experience of abuse. We also do a bunch of questionnaires.

"The groups help boys who feel they're having trouble with jealousy in relationships, who know they have a bad temper and are afraid they will hurt someone they care about. We tell them, 'You are *not* going to get what you want if you are abusive.'" She finds middle and high school groups are much more successful in changing behavior than court-ordered group therapy for batterers is. "There are waiting lists to get in," she says.

Emiliano de Leon was one of the boys helped by the Expect Respect program. After he had slapped his girlfriend at the mall — an incident he describes in chapter 6 — he asked for help from a counselor at school.

"SafePlace programs were just coming to the schools," says Emiliano. "I told my counselor that I was experiencing domestic violence at home and what I had done to my girlfriend. It was scary for me. I was fifteen. I wanted a place to talk about it; I wanted to figure it out.

"I was in the boys' group of Expect Respect for three years. It takes all that time to be able to register the information better, to connect it with relating to others, to be able to use the tools of anger management that they were teaching us. I learned other ways of expressing my feelings; listening skills — to be able to really listen to the other person. I learned empathy.

"And I was resolving my own feeling of being a victim. I had no power as a child. Violence was a way of assuming power. Being small and skinny, I couldn't have power over my guy friends, but it was easy to control girls."

Emiliano began to see men who were modeling healthy relationships, as opposed to his stepfathers and the boys in the neighborhood. He has had men as mentors in the Expect Respect program. He met other nonviolent men whom he respected at Our Lady Family Center, the after-school community center he attended.

The groups provided no sudden fix for old habits. "There were elements of abuse in my relationships with girls after that, verbal and emotional, little things I was able to realize I was doing. It is an ongoing process."

Emiliano, who comes from a family of social workers, decided to make social work his profession. After attending community college in Austin for two years and learning from being in the field, he began working in the shelter for battered women and their children at SafePlace, giving public presentations and facilitating parenting groups — serving himself as a male role model.

After having a healthy relationship for four years, Emiliano got married at twenty-five. But modeling a healthy relationship with his wife is not appreciated in every segment of his world. "At family reunions, I still feel separate from the rest of my Latino family," he says. "These are my uncles and my aunts and my grandfather. My male cousins think my attitude about equality in relationships is completely off."

"VIOLENT BEHAVIOR CAN STOP — IF YOU WANT IT TO"

I've come a long way dealing with my anger. She wanted to go out — but I was too tired. Then she pushed me away. I was mad, awful

mad. The old me would have decked her . . . but this time I just
walked away.

Eric, age 19

As he recounted in chapter 6, at the age of nineteen, Chad Roehner, having been arrested for hitting his girlfriend, was ordered by the court to attend an abuse intervention program.

"It dramatically changed my way of thinking," he says. "I have taken on some new beliefs. Violent behavior can stop — if you want it to. We learn to be violent, just like we learn to love and to negotiate.

"I have been turning the magnifying glass on my behavior. It takes years of traveling the path. It's been a long process, but we can start to benefit from the rewards almost immediately, to change our relationship relatively soon.

"I promised myself that my kids would never see the Cycle of Violence. I have two stepdaughters. I have been married for more than ten years and have a healthy relationship. We've had our struggles, but we keep getting closer all the time."

As he was earning a bachelor's degree in psychology and taking intensive training courses at the domestic abuse intervention project, Chad began to facilitate boys' groups. For many years, he ran a teen violence prevention class for boys on probation for committing violence against other boys, mothers, or girlfriends. "There are some positive results, a reduction in recidivism," says Roehner, who now coordinates all the men's groups for a domestic violence program in the Midwest. "I teach kids and adults how to control their aggression. I hear a lot of confusion about relations between men and women and the role that male privilege plays.

"In the group, we talk about who we are as guys, who we want to be. We teach communication skills, anger management. The boys have learned that violence gets them some things, that is, it's a means to achieve power. They have to look for *positive* ways to achieve power.

"The groups are participatory. After a while, some boys can take a leadership role. The boys challenge each other and offer support and encouragement."

Judge Eugene Hyman believes that his court-ordered batterers' classes are truly effective when the boys "make a lifetime commitment to live a violence-free life." Like Chad Roehner, a few young men in his groups have said that they wanted to continue being in the group after they had finished their court-mandated sessions. "Eventually they lead the group," says Hyman, "and this helps them to keep their commitment." As Emiliano de Leon puts it: "Violence remains an ongoing issue, an uphill battle."

BIG BOYS DON'T CRY ABOUT *HER* ABUSE

Although statistics show that only 5 percent of abusers are women, the figures may not be totally accurate. "Men are reluctant to complain," says Westchester County district attorney Jeanine Pirro. "We don't hear about them unless they get to the hospital."

"In my twelve years of experience handling domestic incidents on Long Island," says Sergeant Lori McIntyre, "I have never met a boy in fear for his physical safety."

Or at least one who will admit it. Sarah Buel agrees that men often feel embarrassed about bringing charges. She relates one incident in which a girl hit her boyfriend over the head with a beer bottle. "He would not have brought charges, but there were witnesses, and he was bleeding."

"Some girls think it's okay for them to hit the guy," says Antoine Jeter. "A lot of guys take it, but when they finally defend themselves, girls can get hurt."

But most experts agree that the abuse a girl heaps on her boyfriend tends to be mainly the emotional and verbal kind. Nevertheless, it can be a strong display of power and control. And sometimes they find themselves in Judge Eugene Hyman's court. In fact, he has initiated a girls' teen dating abusers' class, which they must attend whether or not they are sent to the county ranch for rehabilitation.

"In the group, they learn about the same power and control issues that the guys do," says Suzanne Stephens. Of her recent caseload of thirty teenage abusers, two were girls; her coprobation officer has three girls out of a caseload of thirty. Their abused boyfriends don't bring charges, but their boyfriends' moms do. And they demand action!

Gia Thorsen* seemed to be the child that every American mother would covet. At sixteen, Gia was endowed with a model's figure, thick blond hair, and enormous blue eyes. "Born with a nose job," her mother, Laura,* used to say, thinking of the rhinoplasty she herself had to have at age twenty-one. In Gia, her own genes and her husband's had merged to their consummate expression: his high cheekbones and carb-proof metabolism and her verbal and mathematical ability.

Gia sailed through her studies with a 4.0 average. And she was not a rebellious kid. She obeyed the rules that Laura had established with her. Her dates didn't seem to question them either.

In fact, Gia's looks and achievements might have been a bit intimidating to them. Sometimes Laura wondered if that kept guys away. But never for long. Gia's affected "don't hate me because I'm beautiful" modesty seemed to work. At first. Although she is sometimes loath to admit it, Laura, remembering how guys had treated her during high school, almost took pride in the way Gia spoke to her boyfriends, bawling them out if they hadn't called on time, criticizing their clothes, correcting their speech, nagging them to diet and work out, demanding that they take her to expensive places, listen to the music she liked, read the books she suggested. If they didn't comply, she'd threaten to see someone else.

Gia's relationships never lasted for more than a few months. Then she'd get bored, break up, take some time off, and find a new "project" to work on. Until Jason — a "genius" in science — who was not as malleable as the others, came along. He had too many of his own interests, which he refused to give up for Gia, as well as his job in a grocery. "You're too needy," he told her. Gia made no immediate response, used no manipulative tears, but started a repetitive tape in her head: *Nobody breaks up with me, I do the breaking up.*

The next day, she pulled alongside him when he was going to work and forced him off the road. She began screaming at him on the shoulder of the road. When he pulled away, she followed him to the specialty grocery shop where he worked. In front of the manager and the customers, she began another rant at top decibel, enumerating his many faults and inventing others. To cap off the public humiliation, she spit in his face — a misdemeanor.

Her timing was bad; a policeman was in the store.

When Jason's mother heard that the incident caused him to lose his job, she demanded action. Gia's mom defended her daughter, saying Jason was the one who had been harassing her. But Jason had witnesses. Gia was ordered by the court to attend the class for female abusers.

Another member of the class was fourteen-year-old Elena,* a star soccer player. Although she had never used power and control on her seventeen-year-old boyfriend, like Gia she could not handle rejection.

After her boyfriend told her he wanted to break it off, she invited him to her home in an affluent area "just to talk about it." He brought a friend with him, who was standing in the kitchen while the couple went into the library. There, she slapped her boyfriend's face — and spitting out the words, "I want you to know what it feels like to cry," she sprayed him with pepper Mace.

As he was rinsing and rerinsing his eyes at home, his parents insisted he call the police, who charged Elena with a felony. At the juvenile hall detention facility and on probation, Elena learned to recognize that she had committed a crime and was forced to deal with the consequences of her actions. She had to attend twenty-six weeks of the girl abusers' class with the knowledge that she could serve a stint at the county ranch if she ever violated the court order and contacted her ex-boyfriend during the next three years.

So far she has not. As Sarah Buel says: "The younger we get them under the control of the court, the more successful batterers' treatment programs are."

SEVENTEEN

A POUND OF PREVENTION
How to Bring Up Girls and Boys to Have Relationships of Trust and Respect

INOCULATING OUR CHILDREN against abusive relationships begins in early childhood — at home — long *before* they go on a first date. "Parents have to start way before their kids are in their teens to prepare them for healthy relationships," says Dr. Edna Rawlings.

SETTING A GOOD EXAMPLE IN OUR OWN RELATIONSHIPS

"The couple must come to grips with how they will each control anger and conflict in their own relationship," says Dr. David Sugarman. "Communication between them should take place in a positive light. Too many couples go through a negative, sick cycle — harping only on each other's faults."

But parents should not avoid all conflict in front of their children. Disagreements are a normal and healthy part of any relationship. Kristy Broome wishes her parents had felt free to disagree in front of her, so that she might have had a proper role model when her abusive boyfriend began to rage.

Parents should try to model effective conflict-resolution skills — problem solving with honest communication, willingness to listen to each other, an appropriate amount of assertiveness, and a spirit of compromise and sharing of power.

AVOIDING PHYSICAL PUNISHMENT

"We must teach children when they are very young to be nonviolent — by never using physical punishment to discipline them when they misbehave and make us angry," says Dr. Sugarman. Like most experts, he believes that corporal punishment of children is always wrong because "they may see violence as anger management." The experts also tell us to discourage hitting between siblings so they don't get the message that violence is okay.

Counselor Mary Ann Fremgen stresses that not only should external violence in the family be absent, but so should *subtle* violence, emotional and spiritual, and disregard for the child's feelings and thoughts.

NURTURING OUR CHILDREN'S SENSE OF SELF-ESTEEM

Give the kids *sincere* praise as much as possible. This is a mantra that we as parents often have to rechant to ourselves.

"Parents get distracted," says Fremgen. "They have busy lives, and they have personal issues that get in the way of good parenting — of consistency, structure, setting limits, nurturing, and listening to the child."

"Parents have to make sure that the girl's sense of self is strong, so that she doesn't need a boyfriend who is abusive, and that the boy's sense of self is strong, so that he doesn't need to abuse anyone," says Dr. Rawlings. One of the best means to accomplish this is to actively seek extracurricular and skill-building activities for your children. This is more important when they reach their teens.

"In this way," says Dr. Carol Eagle, "parents will be giving the girl or boy a sense of power in terms of his or her talents and skills."

Rosalind Wiseman agrees: "Stress self-confidence by competence. Let her have images of herself as competent in athletics or drama. By helping her to stand outside the social hierarchy — to see herself as other than someone's girlfriend — parents can counter the need girls feel for the social status of having a boyfriend, even one who is controlling."

TEACHING OUR CHILDREN EMPATHY
AND RESPECT FOR OTHERS

"Violence doesn't start when you bring a gun to school," says Wiseman. "It starts when a kid opens his or her mouth. Words like 'slut,' 'loser,' 'fag,' and 'bitch' are part of the venom that kids spit at one another every day." Venom that often escalates into violence expressed with fists and weapons.

Wiseman points out that elementary school bullying is part of the continuum that includes sexual harassment, gay-bashing, and dating abuse — all in the arms race for power and privilege and who gets to control. Helping kids to understand what might be motivating the behavior of others will give them the ability to empathize. "Empathy reduces the likelihood of their engaging in violent or abusive behaviors," says Wiseman.

KEEPING COMMUNICATION LINES CONSTANTLY OPEN

Parenting experts — Dr. Richard Gallagher of New York University and Dr. Carol Eagle of Einstein College among them — offer suggestions on how to have meaningful dialogues with our children throughout their child and teen years.

• Be in continual touch with your child through small talk — which may reveal, as an incidental "throwaway," a troubling issue that needs to be dealt with.

• Ask questions and show your interest in every aspect of your child's life — not in an overly prying way, but with gentle encouragement to share his or her experiences — even those that have been humiliating. Assure your son or daughter that you are strong enough to hear anything, no matter how terrible.

• Give your undivided attention to your child when you see or believe he or she needs to talk about something compelling.

• If necessary, be the first to bring up what might be a troubling topic.

• Use TV or movies as openers to talk to your child about what he or she would be doing in a similar situation. Current events or experiences that you yourself, or a friend or family member, had may provide the chance to pass along important values without being preachy.

• Make your child media literate. Critique with your child what he or she sees and hears on TV, albums, and videos, pointing out when and how they romanticize crime and violence against women.

Kristy Broome stresses the importance of parent–child communication. "When I was fifteen and my boyfriend was coercing me to have sex," she says, "my parents were in the next room, yet they were worlds away."

In addition to open communication, Dr. Rawlings and Dr. Eagle strongly encourage open homes, where parents can observe their children's friends.

TEACHING THEM TO AVOID QUAGMIRES

How do you prevent a relationship with a controlling, potentially dangerous boyfriend from ever taking root?

The experts agree that intense dating of only one boy in high school should be discouraged. And, before your child ever has her first date, she should be instructed about unacceptable dating behavior.

Help her identify *all* forms of abuse that can occur in a relationship. Acquaint her with the Power and Control Spiral. Familiarize her with the hallmarks of a healthy relationship. (See chart on page 231.)

PROTECTING THEM FROM "THE MOST LIKELY DELIVERY SYSTEM OF VIOLENCE"

"The danger posed by guns must be considered . . . when your kids visit or sleep over at someone else's house," writes Gavin de Becker in *Protecting the Gift*. "The larger solutions to the firearms-injury epidemic aside, each family can educate their kids about guns. Teens need the information even more than adults do." Emil-

A healthy relationship is built around . . . respect, honesty,

fun, a sense of humor, trust, love, space, compatibility, compromise, caring, listening,

growth, learning from each other, sharing, friendship, being faithful, and commitment.

Your Relationship Is Healthy If . . .

❧ You trust your partner.

❧ Your partner likes your friends and encourages you to spend time with them and wants to include them in his/her life as well as yours.

❧ You make important decisions together.

❧ Your partner understands when you spend time away from him or her.

❧ You don't have to lie to protect your partner's reputation or cover for his/her mistakes.

❧ Your partner encourages you to enjoy different activities (like joining the volleyball team or football team, running for student government, or being in a play) and helps you reach your goals.

❧ Your partner likes you for who you are—not just for what you look like.

❧ You are not afraid to say what you think and why you think that way. You like to hear how your partner thinks, and don't always have to agree.

❧ You have both a friendship and a physical attraction.

❧ You don't have to be with your partner 24/7.

maturity, forgiveness, understanding, empathy, change,

From *Reaching and Teaching Teens to Stop Violence*. Used by permission from the Nebraska Domestic Violence Sexual Assault Coalition.

iano de Leon of SafePlace agrees: "Parents should talk to their children prior to dating age about the danger of going with people with guns."

"When this question is asked in Los Angeles schools — Have you thought about what you won't tolerate in a relationship? — the answer is always cheating," says Leah Aldridge, "never how much tolerance they'd have for guys with guns. Or how much their parents would have. A very important preventive action is to screen for guns when your child is ready to date."

DISCUSSING DRESS CODE

Domestic violence expert Sarah Buel recommends that we talk candidly to our child about her style of dress. Tell her: "'I want you to think about how you dress; it's not about what you're wearing, it's how it's *perceived*.'

"'I know I look like a slut,' girls often say, 'but it's the only way I can get the boy.' There's tremendous pressure to dress like that by the media. Once she's got the boy, he complains that she's dressing like a slut."

In *Sex and Power,* feminist law school professor Susan Estrich notes: "My generation put on blouses with bow ties at the neck in an effort to eliminate sex as an issue; the Ally McBeal–ites take theirs off altogether in an effort to use it as a draw."

"MY MOTHER MADE ME AWARE"

Lorre Taylor, a single mom working in Washington, D.C., has developed a wonderfully open relationship with her teenage daughter, Nikki.

"I guess it really starts when they're young," says Lorre, an attractive Afro-American woman, who has a master's degree in social work and works for DC Action for Children. "You listen to your children, let them know they can trust you regardless of what it is. I usually talk in terms that Nikki can understand. She knows I can be her friend, but also I have to be her mother. My primary focus

is Nikki. I never brush her off; I have always made her my immediate concern. It's even more important to pay attention to them
when they are in their teens."

How does Lorre handle disagreements with her daughter? "The
more you fight with them, the more they do the opposite. I present
Nikki with the pros and cons of a situation: Is this person treating
you with respect? Is this person speaking highly of you when
you're not around? Does this person have integrity, honesty?"

Lorre admits that Nikki listens a lot to her peers. "She'll say:
'But Mom, they're closer to my age.' But she integrates my advice
with theirs. She often finds out that things don't work out the way
her peers say."

At fourteen, Nikki, pretty, petite, and vivacious, had a date for
homecoming. "I'm not old-fashioned, but I have to meet Nikki's
boyfriend and his parents. Otherwise, she can't go out with him. I
give her explanations: when you meet the parents, you can discuss
the parameters of dating with them, see if your values match theirs.

"Nikki and I talk about sex," says Lorre. "She would let me
know if she were sexually active because she would want to be protected against AIDS."

Nikki, an honor student, agrees: "I talk to my mother about
everything . . . like you can have confidence about yourself, yet be
insecure about your looks."

Lorre uses her own life experience as a teaching lesson for
Nikki. She herself had been in an abusive relationship for three
months when she was in graduate school. "Nikki, age nine at the
time, realized this person was being emotionally abusive to me. He
would take command, even order food for me."

Jealous of the time Lorre spent on her studies, he accused her of
being unfaithful and began stalking her, threatening to hurt her and
Nikki. "I had to call the police and get a domestic violence warrant
for his arrest; Nikki and I had to spend a night in a shelter."

After the arrest, he immediately stopped harassing them. Having
had no criminal record, he did not find the possibility of jail time
attractive.

"I would never let myself get into an abusive relationship," says
Nikki, "because my mother has been in one. She made me aware."

"MY FATHER MADE ME AWARE"

Fifteen-year-old Zeina Kinkel, Nikki's friend and comember on the Girls' Advisory Board of Empower, began learning important life lessons at an early age. "My parents started talking to me about things when I was three — like smoking. When I was in fifth grade, my father told me about abusive boys. I was aware of abuse because my father made me aware. He told me he'd always be there for me. Parents must talk to you."

Zeina, who displays great flair for drama when she role-plays an abusive boyfriend in one of Empower's training skits, is particularly sensitive to the nuances of discord. "When I got into a relationship with my boyfriend, and we had our first fight, I started thinking about violence. *Was this abuse?* I asked myself. *Or was it normal anger, normal fighting?* I know now that fights and abuse are two different things."

Zeina's dad, who is the librarian at the National Crime Prevention Council in Washington, D.C., learned about Empower and suggested she apply to be on the Girls' Advisory Board.

"I have always felt comfortable discussing issues with her," says Brien Kinkel. "She's a person of real substance; she's always been able to handle the things she has to be aware of. We made her aware of molestation as a preschooler, touching by adults, and so forth. We have always accepted that she had a capacity to understand that if things don't feel right, they probably aren't right. She knows she can always trust us."

Zeina's dad finds that children in kindergarten through eighth grade are very receptive to information from their parents. It was he who brought up the subject of boyfriends. "I took the initiative," he says. "Fathers should take a proactive role in their daughters' lives and not hesitate to do it.

"A father–daughter relationship should be a more substantive one than the 'daddy's little girl' cliché role shown in the media; I believe it has the potential of being meaningful. Zeina is as comfortable in confiding in me as in her mother."

In college, Brien read a great deal about feminism, a subject he believes is vital to parenting. "I don't want my daughter to be fearful of boys, but I don't want her to be naive. I want her to be aware of the potential for problems and be able to deal with them. I am happy to have that role in her life. I do what mothers do in most families. My wife thinks it's just fine."

SPECIAL LESSONS FOR BOYS

Although Zeina is his only child, Brien Kinkel, through his work at the National Crime Prevention Council, has definite suggestions for fathers of sons:

"I encourage them also to play a proactive role, to realize the potential of their sons may be wonderful — or not so wonderful. While you can tell young women about the prevalence of date rape, young men often don't appreciate what they're doing. They say, 'I got a little rough with my babe.' They don't think of themselves as rapists or as abusers."

What do teenage boys need? The answer lies in giving them *more of the very thing they think they don't need: nurturing.* As William Pollack points out, when fathers are actively involved in a son's life and refrain from heavy-handed disciplining, the boys are less aggressive, less competitive, less rebellious, and better able to express feelings. We should let our sons know that as much as we respect their need for independence, they always have a home where they don't have to act cool.

In *Real Boys,* William Pollack urges parents of sons to give them — at least once a day — their undivided attention, to let them feel their "regular loving presence." He assures us that a son who is given the space he needs cannot be spoiled by too much parental love. A boy should be encouraged to express all his emotions, even the sad and angry ones, and to cry if he feels like it. "Let your son know he does not always have to be strong," Pollack advises. "Let him know (or let him see) that men do cry." Pollack believes that when we don't allow boys to cry real tears, some of them "cry bullets." "When he is hurting, ask him if he would like to talk," suggests Pollack. But he warns against shaming the boy if he refuses to talk — and against ever using shaming language with him.

"The way parents care for their sons has a more powerful effect on their behavior than biology and testosterone," says Pollack. "A boy is as much a product of nurturing as of nature."

REACHING OUT INTO THE COMMUNITY

As a result of his daughter's disastrous relationship, Dan Broome has gained a new perspective on community involvement: "All kids need adults to tell them: 'I love you.' We all have to take care of each other's kids."

Brien Kinkel is a strong believer in mentoring other people's sons. "If there is no male presence in the household, it behooves club leaders, teachers, concerned citizens, to speak to young men about being aware of their actions and the consequences of their behavior."

Says Barrie Levy: "There is a trickle-down effect between the attitude of adults and that of the kids. If a school has a coach who won't tolerate women-bashing, then the whole school won't tolerate it. If a coach motivates his athletes by saying, 'You are not girls,' then that attitude permeates the whole school."

Sarah Buel is noticing a trend: "Parents are helping schools put together programs on healthy relationships. Many schools still resist," she admits. "They say: 'This can't be a big problem, I don't see black eyes.' They don't know that black eyes are covered by makeup — or that the girl is staying home."

Barri Rosenbluth's Expect Respect programs actively involve students, parent groups, and school staff, from kindergarten through high school, in banishing all unhealthy behaviors, from bullying to battering.

Jacey Buel, working with the Dating Violence Intervention Project in Cambridge, Massachusetts, believes that dating violence prevention should be part of the curriculum of every school — starting in the fifth grade, then seventh, ninth, and eleventh.

Community and religious organizations often sponsor dating violence prevention programs that go into the schools. The National Coalition Against Domestic Violence makes available thirty-five curricula from programs throughout the nation, as well as strategies for getting programs into schools. (See Help-Giving Resources in the Appendix.)

In addition to presentations, all the programs use role-playing of controlling relationships and healthy ones, interactive discussions, video guides, handouts, questionnaires, and evaluations. Therapist Karen Harker says of the *Reaching and Teaching Teens to Stop Violence* curriculum presented during the past few years in the Nebraska schools: "I have seen a big difference in the attitude once boys and girls become aware of the issue on an educational level. But we still have a long way to go."

MAKING SWEEPING CHANGES

"We need a larger societal change," says Mark Green of EMERGE in Cambridge, Massachusetts. "We need more prosecution of adults so that youth will see that violence is not acceptable. We should have strict sanctions on what we teach our boys about power. We must try to encourage men's organizations to counter violence. We need a campaign similar to MADD or the antismoking strategies."

Mark Smith, who murdered my daughter Jenny, wishes he could deliver the message himself: "I'd go out there with shackles on, with a couple of guards, if I could tell other kids. . . ."

I CONFRONT JENNY'S
MURDERER IN PRISON

"HI-I — VICKI, Greg — nice to see you." Prisoner number 803215 jumps up to greet us as we enter the small spare office at the Iowa State Men's Reformatory at Anamosa on November 10, 1994.

It has been two hours since Greg and I were ushered into the main gate of the Gothic-style building looming over the tiny farming town, its ornate gables and gargoyles giving it more the look of a European castle — possibly haunted — rather than a maximum-security prison.

The weather is bleak, but the warden has been warm and welcoming. "You need to come in the spring and see us when all the flowers are blooming," he says. My stomach is churning.

Yet this is the meeting I lobbied for, the promise of catharsis and closure I feel I need. And now we are about to have an in-person, in-prison "reconciliation" session with Mark Alan Smith at Anamosa — as part of the new Victim–Offender Reconciliation Program.

Greg and I are searched twice before we are allowed to go through a series of locked doors. Betty Brown, a social worker on the staff of Iowa Victim Services will mediate the session. Days before, she had premeeting interviews with us and with Mark, giving him the questions we wrote down. She tells us Mark is eager to meet with us — *to break up the boredom of prison?* I wonder — yet he is "terrified."

As we enter the small office, however, Mark's boyish features reveal no traces of fear. My stomach is still churning, my mouth dry, but when he jumps up to greet us and says: "Hi-i — Vicki, Greg — nice to see you," I do something unaccountable. I extend my hand. He eagerly accepts it. My action startles me. I am shaking his hand by instinct as if my humanity, reflexively, is trying to connect with whatever glimmer of his remains. My husband follows my lead.

Even under the fluorescent lights, twenty-seven-year-old Mark Smith, tall, golden-haired, and macromuscled, appears more handsome than he did eight years ago, when he was my daughter's boyfriend. I remember how Jenny adored his looks. "I've brought you pictures of Jennifer," I say, as I hand him a snapshot — of him and Jenny sitting on our fireplace hearth in 1986, when he was a high school senior. Jenny, a freshman, is leaning into his shoulder; they both seem like happy, innocent children. Mark studies the photo, shows it to Betty Brown, then clings to it. "We were so much in love," he says. He talks on and on about the great times he and Jenny had, eating lunch together every day at school, sharing a locker, going to games and dances — regarded as the "perfect couple" by their schoolmates. Betty Brown nods at his nostalgic smile. I know she is trying to put him — as well as us — at ease.

But I am becoming impatient. I slam two other pictures onto the table; they are eight-by-ten blowups of Jenny at fifteen on the autopsy table. "Then tell me, how did my daughter get from that picture to these?" Mark jerks his head away from the photos, and I wait to hear his words — lies though I believe they will be.

He looks to Betty Brown. She nods encouragement. He looks straight ahead and speaks with unaccustomed articulateness. *Has he memorized the lines?* "Vicki and Greg, I want to take this opportunity to tell you that I am truly sorry for what I did."

I take a deep breath and return to the question obsessing me: "Why did you murder Jennifer?"

"I didn't mean to hurt her," he says. "I just wanted to talk. I had to get control of the situation." "Control" — a word Mark likes to use. His relationship with Jenny had been all about his need to control her and every aspect of her life.

He recounts their frequent breakups, how Jenny would sometimes seem interested in getting back together again. "She'd lead me on, then she'd blow me off. . . ." *Yes, in her innocence, Jenny was waffling back and forth in the relationship — and I, in my innocence, had told her she could still be friends with him.*

He describes their last encounter, the day she came home from school, how they came into the house together. . . . *Came into the house together? Not according to the police's theory that Mark, using a copy of our spare key, let himself in . . . to lie in wait for Jenny.*

"I just went over there to talk, to make a point. I wanted to straighten things out between us . . . but then she told me to leave and turned her back on me. And I got real mad. And so did she. All of a sudden, she went in the kitchen and came back with a knife. I told her I was bigger than her and she should give me the knife . . . and the next thing I know . . . I grabbed the knife and I stabbed her in the chest. . . ."

Is he going to dare tell me it was self-defense . . . a six foot, 200-pound man against five-foot-four, 110-pound Jenny?

"And you kept on doing it, didn't you?" He looks down and nods.

"Over and over." I spit out the words. "Sixty-six times. Why?"

He turns away. He pauses . . . and the standard reasons repeat in my brain: *personality disorder, obsessive boyfriend syndrome, flawed brain metabolism.* But again I cry out: "Why, Mark, why?"

He opens his palms as if begging me to understand: "I was filled with uncontrollable rage — like a rush — I was all pumped up." *Not on drugs — just adrenaline — the thrill of the kill, the high of "I have the power to make you die." A high that lasted through the evening . . . when he showed up grinning at the homecoming football game with his date.*

"I was immature. I made a mistake. A terrible mistake."

"No. A mistake is something you can fix."

"I am really sorry," he says. "Vicki, I didn't mean for her to die."

The bitch deserved to die — his words to his cellmate, reported at his trial — resound in my ears.

"What were Jenny's last words? Was she in pain? Did she call for me?" *Why am I asking him? Would he know, would he care? Sociopaths have no empathy. He was too involved with his own rage.* Yet I must ask. He was the last one to see her alive.

He tells me he doesn't remember if she cried out; he can't remember her saying anything. "She didn't suffer," he says.

"She just died — instantly?"

He nods.

"Then why did she have defensive wounds?"

His blue-marble eyes give me a blank stare.

"Do you know how many lives you have ruined?" I say grimly. I take out a paper from my purse and wave it in front of him. Betty Brown, the mediator, makes no effort to calm me down. "Perpetrators need to see the victims' anger, they want to see it," she had told us. Well, here it is . . . I put the paper up to his face: "A letter to you from my daughter Kate. . . ."

"Little Katie, oh yeah . . ." He is smiling nostalgically again. *Little Katie — ten years old when he knew her — is eighteen now, almost as tall as he is. Because of him, her teenage years have been scarred with fear, guilt, and agitated depression. "Little Katie," who became vulnerable herself to controlling and manipulating men as she grew up.*

"When I told her we were going to see you, she started screaming and ran out of the room. Then she wrote you this letter." I read her words: "Mark, as long as I am alive, I will fight to keep you in prison because the prison where my emotions have been is far worse. For three years, my brother and I did not know my mother, my children will never know their aunt, and I lost my best friend, my sister, the only one who went through everything that I went through."

"Tell Katie I'm sorry." His mouth curls, and he pauses, as if deciding whether to say more. "You know, I never see my sister. . . . My family hardly ever comes to visit me."

I think about how supportive his family had been at first . . . visiting him every week. My throat constricts; he looks so forlorn. *What is this bizarre emotion I'm suddenly feeling — pity for Mark Smith?* I clench my jaw. I will not allow myself a sense of pity.

"My family's all involved in the wedding," he says without emotion. "My sister's getting married in two weeks."

His sister's name is Jennifer too. She's a year older than my Jenny would have been. My hands ball into fists. I feel a mixture of hatred and envy for his mom — mother-of-Jennifer-the-bride. I will never see *my* Jenny in a bridal dress.

"Vicki — Greg — I didn't have a family like yours." His voice still retains traces of the innocent boyish charm, the charm that captivated Jenny. "I had a lot of trouble at home. My parents were yelling all the time. Now I see where my rage came from." *Oh, no, the dysfunctional family excuse!* Mark whines on about how unloving and inattentive his parents were.

Until now, Greg has not said anything. He reaches out to Mark, spreading his hands as widely apart as possible. "Here, buddy, here's the box of pain and grief I've been carrying. I'm handing this over to you."

My laid-back husband, who had always been so polite to Mark during his seesaw romance with Jenny, has in his voice a coiled fury I seldom hear. "I want you to know what a terrible feeling it is to walk into your own house and see a child you love lying in a pool of blood." Greg's voice cracks. "All that blood and me feeling so helpless. I couldn't save her . . . I couldn't save our little Jenny. . . ." He lets the tears flow. I put my arm around him, and Betty Brown gives him some tissues. Strangely, I have not needed any. My eyes have been dry throughout this meeting.

The angry edge returns to Greg's voice: "How can I ever forget a sight like that? And then to be blamed for it — for what you did?" Greg recounts bitterly to Mark how the police took him in for questioning because he had found her and he was the stepfather. How they read him his Miranda rights and held him for three hours. How he had to call from headquarters to find out where Jenny was and if they were able to revive her.

Greg stares hard at Mark. "Do you know how you ripped our family apart? You killed Jenny, and you almost killed what Vicki and I have between us. . . ."

Yes, there were so many times when I couldn't be a wife to him, when I could barely stay alive.

Mark's eyes remain focused on his shoes.

My husband's voice returns to its normal calm: "Jenny's in heaven. Where do you think you're gonna go?"

Mark doesn't raise his eyes. "I'm in hell already . . . but I'm not afraid to die. Because there's nothing beyond the grave."

Greg almost smiles as something seems to occur to him. He asks Mark if he's ever thought of a way out — like provoking an inmate to stab him.

"I wouldn't wanna die like that."

No, not like Jenny, I think.

Mark shifts in his chair. Does he realize what he is saying? He raises his eyes and looks at both of us. "Greg, Vicki, I am so sorry for what I did . . . I loved Jenny too . . . more than I cared for any other girl." This time the marble eyes seem bright . . . with tears? He blinks a few times and turns away. *Is he finally realizing the enormity of what he did . . . what he was incapable of imagining before the crime . . . all of the fallout — not only to us, but to his own family, to himself?* "Mark, do you grieve for Jenny?" I suddenly ask.

Mark glances over his shoulder. He swallows hard and says in a constricted voice: "You don't cry in here."

Now it's Mark's turn to show us a picture — of his cell. It's very small, and he shares it with another inmate. What strikes me is the toilet, freestanding, next to the bed. No curtain, no privacy. With all the perks of prison, not one iota of personal dignity.

Is this picture another piece of Mark's manipulation — a way of exercising control over our emotions? So that we will eventually recommend parole for him? (I have learned that an inmate who has received a sentence of life without parole can solicit the governor every ten years to review his case and to commute his sentence to a specific number of years. If Mark were to do this, Greg and I would be informed, and our recommendation — either that his sentence be commuted or that he never be released — would carry great weight.)

Mark describes his day to us. It is all circumscribed. No freedom. On schedule he works out, showers, eats, goes to his metal shop, submits to searches. He sees his counselor once a month. He could study or have a real job in prison, but he chooses not to. A job would give him more phone privileges, but he says, "Who am I

going to call?" All the friends he had from high school who were
so supportive, who wrote to him, telephoned him, even visited
him in jail, are no longer interested in him. Nor are his parents;
they hardly ever come to see him.

It is almost as if he does not exist.

Four hours have passed. We shake hands, say good-bye, and
once more he says, "I'm sorry." Now I want to believe him, but
I'm still angry.

Driving back home in the car, Greg feels good — he has purged
himself — but even after all the venting I have done, I feel no
catharsis. I am even angry at myself for things I forgot to
mention — the threatening notes he sent Jenny, the times he
abused her, stalked her.

It will take time for my anger to subside . . . but the process has
already begun. *What is Mark's life?* I keep thinking, as I walk, as I ride
my bicycle in the crisp fall air. He is in exile. There are careers opening up, weddings taking place, babies being born, life events — but
not for him . . . any more than for Jenny. I feel the overwhelming
sense of the futility of his life . . . life in prison without parole. He
said he's dead; in a way he is. There was promise there once. He
might have been a successful auto mechanic or served his country.

I no longer see him as a monster. A creature to hate. He has been
stripped of most of his arrogance. In an ironic way, the greater his
suffering, the more inhuman the life he leads, the more human he
becomes to me. Perhaps to himself too.

From the letters he is writing to me, he seems to be gaining empathy:

> *After meeting with you and Greg, after taking classes here in prison
> to learn how the victim feels, I see what you have gone through. I
> never thought of that before — it was just me, me, me. That's what
> got me in here.*

And he has gained insight too:

> *I killed for control; I had to have control or I would lose control my-
> self. I realize now that I could have changed that need for control*

when I was on the streets. . . . I changed in here, it didn't even take me that long, now it's too late for me. . . .

His suffering, I now believe, has transformed him, made him truly remorseful, and I feel a gradual freeing from the ice of my bitterness. I seem to be on a path, leading somewhere. Surely not to forgiveness?

Six months after our meeting with Mark, I have a lucid dream — one in which I know I am dreaming:

Jenny meets me, she and I know she has been murdered eight years ago, but she looks beautiful and she is giving me this dream of reassurance that she's alive on another plane . . . truly a glorious gift. I hug her. She's warm and solid, natural and alive. She smells like a garden.

I ask her how it felt as it was happening — very painful? Was she terrified? She says, "Not as much as you think. I was mostly surprised." "Were you afraid of Mark? Do you hate him?" I ask her. She half-smiles and hesitates. "Well, no, not really." From her smile and her lack of anger, I feel that she no longer carries a grudge, that she is content with the "life" she is now leading, that she has forgiven him, or at least accepted what he has done as inevitable.

I awaken with the thought that Betty Brown, our mediator, prefers the word "acceptance" to "forgiveness."

I know now that I will never have the answer to the deeper *why* that goes beyond human understanding. But my bitterness — and hatred — are leaving me; the reconciliation session has had healing power. It has set Greg and me on a freeing journey. Why should we keep living our bitterness over and over? We can never forget what our daughter's murderer did, but we have accepted his remorse . . . spawned in prison though it may have been. And in a sense we have forgiven him.

Though I pity Mark Smith and pray for him, I believe he must stay in prison for the rest of his life and pay for the consequences of his actions. Jenny cannot ever come back; nor should he.

Recommended Reading

Betancourt, Marian. *What to Do When Love Turns Violent: A Practical Resource for Women in Abusive Relationships.* New York: HarperCollins, 1997.

Cohen-Sandler, Roni, and Michelle Silver. *"I'm Not Mad, I Just Hate You!" A New Understanding of Mother–Daughter Conflict. Surviving and Thriving During Your Daughter's Teenage Years.* New York: Viking, 1999.

de Becker, Gavin. *The Gift of Fear: Survival Signals That Protect Us from Violence.* New York: Little, Brown and Company, 1997.

———. *Protecting the Gift: Keeping Children and Teenagers Safe (and Parents Sane).* New York: Dial Press, 1999.

Dutton, Donald G. *The Abusive Personality.* New York: Guilford Press, 1998.

Dutton, Donald G., and Susan K. Golant. *The Batterer: A Psychological Profile.* New York: Basic Books, 1995.

Eagle, Carol J., and Carol Colman. *All That She Can Be: Helping Your Daughter Achieve Her Full Potential and Maintain Her Self-Esteem During the Critical Years of Adolescence.* New York: Simon & Schuster, 1993.

Estrich, Susan. *Sex and Power.* New York: Riverhead Books, 2000.

Garbarino, James. *Lost Boys: Why Our Sons Turn Violent and How We Can Save Them.* New York: Free Press, 2000.

Kindlon, Daniel J., and Michael Thompson. *Raising Cain: Protecting the Emotional Life of Boys.* New York: Ballantine Books, 1999.

Levy, Barrie (Editor). *Dating Violence: Young Women in Danger.* Seattle: Seal Press, 1998.

Levy, Barrie. *In Love and in Danger: A Teen's Guide to Breaking Free of Abusive Relationships.* Seattle: Seal Press, 1998.

Levy, Barrie, and Patricia Occhiuzzo Giggans. *What Parents Need to Know About Dating Violence.* Seattle: Seal Press, 1995.

McShane, Claudette. *Warning: Dating May Be Hazardous to Your Health!* Racine, WI: Mother Courage Press, 1989.

Meyer, Stephanie H., and John Meyer (Compilers). *Teen Ink: Our Voices, Our Visions.* Deerfield Beach, FL: Health Communications, 2000.

Nelson, Noelle. *Dangerous Relationships: How to Stop Domestic Violence Before It Stops You.* New York: Insight Books/Plenum, 1997.

Pipher, Mary. *Reviving Ophelia: Saving the Selves of Adolescent Girls.* New York: Ballantine Books, 1995.

Pollack, William S. *Real Boys: Rescuing Our Sons from the Myths of Boyhood.* New York: Random House, 1998.

Rue, Nancy N. *Everything You Need to Know About Abusive Relationships.* New York: Rosen, 1998.

Shandler, Sara. *Ophelia Speaks: Adolescent Girls Write About Their Search for Self.* New York: HarperPerennial, 1999.

Wiseman, Rosalind. *Defending Ourselves: A Guide to Prevention, Self-Defense and Recovery from Rape.* New York: Noonday Press, 1994.

Wiseman, Rosalind. *Queen Bees and Wannabes: Helping Your Daughter Survive Cliques, Gossip, Boyfriends, and Other Realities of Adolescence.* New York: Crown, 2002.

Help-Giving Resources

National Coalition Against Domestic Violence
1532 16th Street NW
Washington, D.C. 20036
202-745-1211
Hot line: 1-800-799-SAFE (7233) (24 hours)
www.ncadv.org

For referrals for state domestic violence coalitions, shelters, and therapists specializing in counseling those in abusive relationships.

National Organization for Victim Assistance (NOVA)
1730 Park Row NW
Washington, D.C. 20010
202-232-6682
Hot line: 1-800-TRY-NOVA (879-6682) (24 hours)
www.try-nova.org
Cheryl@try-nova.org
Marlene@try-nova.org

Provides crime victims with information and referrals to crisis counseling and case advocacy services near their homes through directories that list ten thousand programs. Also serves as the primary counselor and advocate for many victims.

National Center for Victims of Crime
2111 Wilson Boulevard, Suite 300
Arlington, VA 22201
703-276-2880
Infolink program: 1-800-FYI-CALL (394-2255)
www.ncvc.org

Provides information on the closest, most appropriate local services for victims of crime, as well as access to an array of critical services, including crisis intervention, research information, assistance with the criminal justice process, and counseling and support groups.

Nassau County Coalition Against Domestic Violence on Long Island (New York State)
Dating violence hot line: 516-542-0404 (24 hours, 7 days)
Rape/Sexual assault hot line: 516-222-2298

Teenline
PO Box 53277
Oklahoma City, OK 73152-3277
405-522-3835
1-800-522-TEEN (8336)

For teens across the nation seeking advice from other teens and counselors who have been trained by professionals in the field of dating violence.

Break the Cycle
PO Box 64996
Los Angeles, CA 90064
310-286-3366
1-888-988-TEEN (8336)
www.break-the-cycle.org

Provides free education, legal advice, and representation for young people,
ages twelve to twenty-two, who are in abusive relationships in California
and gives free advice to their parents.

The Family Violence Prevention Fund
383 Rhode Island Street, Suite 304
San Francisco, CA 94103-5133
1-800-313-1310; 415-252-8900
www.fvpf.org

Provides advice for teens in abusive relationships — as well as for their parents and friends.

Legal Advocates for Abused Women
1027 South Vandeventer Avenue, 6th Floor
St. Louis, MO 63110
1-800-527-1460
www.laawstl.org

Gives nationwide lawyer referrals.

WAVE: Women Against Violence Europe
43-1-548 27 20
www.wave-network.org
office@wave-network.org

For counseling centers; women's "refuges," or shelters; hot lines / help lines;
and prevention and training focusing on violence in intimate
relationships — provided through a network of European women's non-
governmental organizations.

Education Programs and Curricula
Available to Schools

The Empower Programs
1312 8th Street NW
Washington, D.C. 20001
202-882-2800
www.empowerprograms.com

Empower offers *Owning Up*, an award-winning violence prevention curriculum for boys and girls in middle school and high school.

Expect Respect Classroom Presentation Manual and/or Support Group
Curriculum Manual for Preventing Teenage Dating Violence and
Promoting Healthy Relationships
SafePlace
PO Box 19454
Austin, TX 78760
512-267-7233
www.austin-safeplace.org

The Expect Respect curriculum is formulated to help middle and high school teens recognize dating abuse, to give them support, and to teach them skills for developing healthy relationships.

In Touch with Teens: A Relationship Violence Prevention Curriculum for
Youth Ages Twelve to Nineteen
Los Angeles Commission on Assaults Against Women (LACAAW)
605 West Olympic Boulevard, Suite 400
Los Angeles, CA 90015
213-955-9090
www.lacaaw.org

An innovative curriculum that teaches youths ages twelve to nineteen how to build violence-free relationships. Selected by the United States Department of Health and Human Services as one of five model programs for the nation.

NCJW Teenage Dating Violence Program
National Council of Jewish Women, Essex County Section
513 West Mount Pleasant Avenue
Livingston, NJ 07039
973-740-0588

A complete curriculum and teacher's training guide for use in nonsectarian high schools.

Reaching and Teaching Teens to Stop Violence
Nebraska Domestic Violence Sexual Assault Coalition
825 M Street, Suite 404
Lincoln, NE 68508
402-476-6256
www.ndvsac.org

A curriculum developed by one of the state coalitions serving on the National Teen Dating Violence Advisory Committee of the National Coalition Against Domestic Violence.

Teen Dating Violence Resource Manual
The National Coalition Against Domestic Violence
PO Box 18749
Denver, CO 80218
303-839-1852
www.ncadv.org

Includes lists of fifty state coalitions and thirty-five curricula from programs throughout the nation, as well as several dozen videos, along with suggested strategies for getting programs into schools.

INDEX

Blake, Meredith, 111–12, 144, 146, 147, 159, 164, 201
blame, 23, 80–81
Blinder, Martin, 183
boundaries, 59
"boy code," 83
boys who abuse, 76–90
 addiction to violence and, 85–86
 alcohol / substance abuse and, 87
 blame and, 80–81
 categories of, 86–87
 chaos and, 81–82
 "conduct disorder" and, 89–90
 cultural expectations and, 83–85
 DNA and, 89
 early childhood influences, 78
 emotional awareness and, 82–83
 factors that produce, 89
 fear of intimacy and, 82
 jealousy and, 77–78
 models of aggression and, 78–79
 neurological damage and, 87
 nurturing and, 81, 83, 90
 possessiveness and, 77–78
 shame and, 79–80, 89
 violence as a choice, 77
 See also children who abuse, parents and their; girls who abuse
Break the Cycle, 112, 144, 201, 248–49
Broome, Dan, 123–32, 133, 165, 186
Broome, Gwyn, 96, 109, 123–32, 133, 134, 186
Broome, Kristy, 62–66, 123–32, 133, 134, 165–66, 185–86, 201, 227, 230
Brown, Betty, 238–39, 241, 242
Buel, Jacey
 on boys who abuse, 78, 81–82, 84, 86–87
 on prevention, 236
 on witnessing abuse, 211
Buel, Sarah
 on alcohol, 99
 on breaking away safely, 165
 on confronting abuse, 136–37, 143–44, 145–46, 147, 149–50
 on deception of victims, 65
 on dress code, 232
 on focus on dating, 101
 on girls who abuse, 224, 226
 on intervention, 113, 116
 on parents of abusive boys, 220
 on restraining orders, 157, 158
 on school programs, 149–50, 236

 on sexually active girls, 32
 on witnessing abuse, 208

Campbell, Jacqueline, 170–71
caretakers, 62–66
Centers for Disease Control and Prevention, 16, 170
children who abuse, parents and their, 213–26
 change for abusers, 221
 courts and, 216–18
 denial and, 219
 emotional reactions and, 219–20
 healthy relationships and, 221–22
 intervention and, 219–20
 stopping violent behavior, 222–24
 warning signs for, 219
 See also boys who abuse; girls who abuse
Coalition Against Domestic Violence, 45, 170
code words, 139–40, 141
coercion, 25, 31, 32, 59
cognitive restructuring, 188
cohabitation, 49
Coleman, Jennifer, 104–5, 154, 159–60
college, dating violence in, 166
communication
 confronting violence and, 136–38
 importance of, 100, 106
 intervention, 112–13, 115, 117
 for prevention, 227, 229–30, 233
 strategizing and, 120–21, 131
 See also learning about the relationship
community, 236–37
"compulsively masculine," 10
"conduct disorder," 89–90
confronting violence, 133–50
 balance for parents in, 135
 communication and, 136–38
 "fine line" approach to, 134–35
 getting professional attention and, 141–44
 laissez-faire approach to, 135
 legal options for, 145–46
 primary aggressors and, 146–47
 resources for, 144–45, 148–50
 safety planning and, 138–41
 unintended consequences and, 135
 zero tolerance approach to, 133–34
 See also intervention; restraining orders
corporal punishment, 228
counseling. See therapy / counseling
creativity, 192–95
criminal justice system, 160, 198–99

ABOUT THE AUTHORS

VICKI CROMPTON became an advocate for teen dating violence education and prevention after her daughter Jenny was murdered by a boyfriend in 1986. Since her daughter's death, Crompton has given more than two thousand workshops and presentations across the country and has spoken for criminal justice organizations and federal prosecutors. As a consultant to the Office of Violence Against Women in the U.S. Department of Justice, she has worked to strengthen antibattering and antistalking laws nationwide. She lives in Davenport, Iowa.

ELLEN ZELDA KESSNER'S articles have appeared in national magazines and newspapers. She has coauthored and coproduced several historical plays that depict famous women's lives and have been performed at schools, libraries, and women's organizations in the New York metropolitan area. She lives in Valley Stream, New York.